A Listening Heart

Sacred Teachings

on the

Beatitudes

To Susanse,
God loves you
1 Jn 4:8
Josephine

Josephine Matranga

Scripture References are from the *Saint Joseph Edition of The New American Bible*, copyright ©1970 by the Confraternity of Christian Doctrine, Washington, D.C.

Quotations of the Blessed Virgin Mary were excerpted from messages given to Reverend Father Stefano Gobbi, taken from the book: *To the Priests, Our Lady's Beloved Sons*, ©2009.

St. Padre Pio quotations were taken from *Padre Pio's Spiritual Direction for Every Day* from the English translation copyright ©2011, St. Anthony Messenger Press.

St. Clare of Assisi's words were excerpted from *Clare, A Light in the Garden* by Murray Bodo ©1992.

St. John Neumann's prayer was condensed from a meditation printed in the Magnificat magazine, March 2018.

An excerpt of St. Catherine of Siena's letter to a friend was taken from *Catherine of Siena, A Biography* by Anne B. Baldwin. Copyright ©1987 by Our Sunday Visitor Publishing Division.

St. Bernard of Clairvaux's prayer was condensed from a meditation printed in the Magnificat magazine, August 2018

Quotation from St. Faustina Kowalska was taken from *Diary of Saint Maria Faustina Kowalska*. Original Polish Diary copyright ©1981 Congregation of Sisters of Our Lady of Mercy.

Quotation from Saint Thomas Aquinas was excerpted from an article in the Magnificat magazine, April 2018

Quotation from Saint John Bosco excerpted from an article in the Magnificat magazine, January 2018

Quotation from Saint Alphonsus Liguori taken from the Magnificat magazine, August 2018

Quotation from St. Augustine of Hippo was taken from the Catechism of the Catholic Church copyright ©1994.

Cover Image purchased from 123RF.

A Listening Heart, Sacred Teachings on the Beatitudes
copyright ©2019 by Josephine Matranga

DEDICATION

This book is dedicated
to the honor and glory of
Almighty God of the Universe,
for it is the work of His Hands,
from the beginning to the end.
May all glory be His!

SPECIAL THANKS TO

Barbara Graham
for editing and prayerful support
in preparing the book for publication.

TABLE OF CONTENTS

PROLOGUE

A Listening Heart is fruit of studying the Bible according to the Head to the Heart Bible Series written and taught by Angie Lake at Women's Christian Fellowship. For eighteen years, I have followed this method of meditation, listening in silence before the Lord, and writing whatever He deigns to reveal to my heart.

When I understood that the Lord was guiding me to write a book on the Beatitudes, I rolled up my sleeves and began to write. Immediately, I hit a brick wall. I had nothing to say! That is when I lost my peace, grew tense and insomnia set in! I had forgotten the first rule: wait for confirmation from the Lord. What God commands, God supplies. Only then will the work be easily and swiftly accomplished—no sweat! So, I prayed and waited for further guidance.

A few weeks later, I received this consoling message: *"My child, I am here always to help you. I have asked you to write this book. What I ask, I provide. Begin this way: pray the Holy Spirit Prayer, then sit quietly and listen to what I say. Yes, I will dictate to you what I want written. It will be a holy book to inspire others to take on the attitudes of the Beatitudes. Remember, I am asking you to write this book, so I will supply what you need."*

What a relief! The pressure was off! The Holy Spirit was going to tell me what to write! This was going to be His book! All I had to do was sit still and listen. How easy is that? I was going to be a pencil in His hands just like Saint Theresa said!

And so, we began. I followed the agenda that had been laid out for me: I prayed, listened and wrote. One day He said, *"Every word I speak is important. Do not change my words unless it clarifies my intent and makes it easier to read. I want everyone to know me better because it is for their salvation that I speak to you, so they may read and learn how severely I suffered to save them, to atone for their sins, so they may enjoy eternal life with me in Paradise."*

On another day, the Lord said, *"Insert these personal messages to you so they will clearly understand that the other messages are addressed to them. They are my personal word to the readers of the book. I hope they will take my words to heart. I only write to comfort and guide them because I love them infinitely!"*

Finally, after nine months of dictation, He said, *"We are finished with the book on the Beatitudes. Get busy now with editing my messages. I will open doors so you will know how to proceed with the printing, the front cover, and other details. Tomorrow we will begin a new project. You will never be bored in my service."*

Dear Reader, beginning with the Introduction, you will be reading the words of God addressed to you personally. This entire study of the Beatitudes is centered on your life, your attitudes, your struggle to change and to learn who you are and where you are going. This book is for your transformation so you may cherish yourself as the special, unique child of God whom He loves dearly!

May you have a listening heart to hear what God speaks to you every day, that you may fall in love with this good God like I did. As a result of working on this book, I have found within myself a force of love for God that was never there before! Today, my heart cries out: "Abba! Abba Father! Keep me in the palm of your hand! Make me holy as You are holy!"

Introduction

Speak, Lord, your servant is listening.

I began to teach the Beatitudes to encourage and motivate my disciples to change their attitudes, for the spiritual battle is in the mind: as a man thinks, so he is (Proverbs 23:7). With the attitude of the Beatitudes, man gains a way of life that leads to the reward of heaven, to live in paradise where there is no more crying and sadness, only joy.

This is why I came proclaiming the gospel of God: *"This is the time of fulfillment. The kingdom of God is at hand. Repent and believe in the Gospel"* (Mark 1:15). I came so my people will be free to live in the light of my love and my protection. I defeated Satan on the Cross, and if you believe, my life will be in you to conquer the evil spirits who darken the minds and hearts of mankind.

Repent and believe in my love for you. I came to set prisoners free. Walk in the light from above. I will come again to judge my people. Choose to be among the faithful, the trusting, obedient to my teachings. Begin with the Beatitudes. Change your lives and live in my light.

4/27/18

Without You, Lord, I can do nothing.

The Beatitudes are ways to change your life-style. They are my ways that a disciple who loves Me and who wants to obey Me will conform to in like manner. I am the Light of the World (John 8:12), and I call my disciples to spread my light wherever they are. I have plans for the life of every individual in the world. Because I am everywhere in the world, I know all things. If I should desire, I could create a whole new world. The time will come when there will be new heavens and a new earth, as it is written (2 Peter 3:13).

My disciples must groom themselves with the attitudes of the Beatitudes. Then they will know my will and fulfill my word. They will bring my word to the nations. And my light will subdue the darkness once and for all.

My joy is this: that my people will be with Me, for Me, and gather with Me. I need and want them to fight the good fight, as my servant Paul said (1 Timothy 6:12). I want them to think as I think. They will if they repent their own way that leads them away from Me and choose to follow my way. Then they will live in the light of day, rejoicing in my love and power to create, save, and judge the world. Tell my children to come to Me with their burdens and cares, for I am always there to carry the burden for them (Matthew 11:30).

5/6/18

Sing your song in me, Lord, that I may sing your praises.

Today we start anew. I have much to teach you. Do as I say and you will sing one day in my Kingdom where there is joy and laughter, and each day is one of consummate bliss with the Angels and Saints at your side. There is only light there and everlasting peace.

Those who learn the attitudes of the Beatitudes will sing and dance with joy, for they are divine attitudes: I never change (Malachi 3:6); I am Love (1 John 4:8); I am Truth (John 14:6); I am Just (Deuteronomy 32:4); I am merciful, meek, and a

4

peacemaker. These are my attitudes toward all my people—those who are with Me and those who are against Me.

In order to change your minds and hearts, you must receive and accept my grace. You must open your hearts, trust my words, accept my plan for your life, and learn to know my dreams for you. If you surrender to my love, I will crown you with jewels beyond compare; I will rejoice over you (Jeremiah 32:41). Yes, I will place garlands of flowers and pearls on your head and you will live in Paradise with Me forever.

Remember who **Jesus** is for you: **J**oy of my life, **E**cstasy of my spirit, **S**ong in my heart, **U**nion with God, **S**avior of my soul.

5/12/18

Transform me, Lord, by your powerful word.

Today is a day of renewal. The times are dark and dreary, devoid of light. No one can find their way home to my Kingdom. My disciples must be the light in the world (Matthew 5:14). They must move out into the darkness and bring my light and love to a starving nation. But first they must be filled with light themselves. They must be poor in spirit, mourn their sins, be meek, merciful, hunger for righteousness, become peacemakers. When they are transformed, then they can become warriors like Saint Paul who endured all types of persecutions (2 Corinthians 11:23-29). Make him your model.

"How do we do this?" you ask. Yes, ask (Matthew 7:7)! I will not refuse my grace to anyone who asks, trusting in my love for them and my presence with them. They must have faith in Me before I can work in them (John 14:1). Faith opens the door to my grace and light. With their acceptance, I will gladly pour my light into their darkened minds. They must seek Me and want my help. I will not force myself on anyone, except those little ones who are unable to comprehend my love for them.

Yes, there it is again: Love, the motivating element in the salvation of all my people. They must love Me with all their hearts (Mark 12:30), and then I can move quickly and powerfully in them. I would pour out my grace into their minds and hearts, but they must welcome Me. Otherwise my grace falls on stones, withers and dies (Matthew 13:5).

"Let my children live!" is the cry of my heart. Let them live in my light. Help them to see the truth of my love. Pray for them. Fast for them. Tell them the truth. This must happen before they can change their attitudes into the Beatitudes.

5/14/18

I trust in You, Lord, set me free.

The Beatitudes are signposts on the road leading to heaven. They are road maps to follow that will take you safely home. Heaven is a place of rest, peace and joy. My light shines eternally; no more darkness or doubting that you are following my will. My will inspires you to act justly. My will is for all people to be with Me in heavenly joy. This is why I taught the Beatitudes: to train my disciples in right thinking, that they should take on the mind of Christ to guide them on the perilous journey (1 Corinthians 2:16).

There are many pitfalls in the present life. There are land mines wherever you walk. You need to be able to see the safe way to travel, and I have shown the Way (John 14:6). I was rich but became poor. I mourned and suffered for the sins of my people. I was merciful and healed the blind, the sick, the lame (Luke 7:22). I was meek before my detractors. I hungered and thirsted to do my Father's will (John 4:34). I made peace between my Father and his people. I suffered the utmost persecution to save my people, and I will to the end of this lifetime.

This present age will end in glory, but much must be done. Minds and hearts must change. I came to bring light into the world (John 8:12). I came to help my people find the way to eternal life. If they do as I say, they will find Me. I live in love. If you change your attitudes, you will find life and live peaceful, well-ordered lives. Follow my way of the Beatitudes. They are the stars in the sky lighting up the darkness in men's hearts.

I have given you the necessary grace to fulfill my will and to purify your hearts. I already did it on the Cross of Calvary. I opened the temple of my body to pour out my blood over all mankind. You have been washed clean and purified by my shed blood on the cross. My Passion purified your hearts. Freely I give to all who come to Me for mercy and forgiveness. My heart is open to everyone. Live in my love. Taste and see that I am good (Psalm 34:8). My love is for you, my people. Trust Me. I love you.

5/18/18

Redeem me, Lord, and make all my paths straight.

My child, I have much to say about the Beatitudes.

- They are my attitudes.
- They are road signs on the journey.
- They teach/train my disciples to be like Me.
- I instituted the Sacraments as physical signs; the Beatitudes are mental and emotional traits.
- The Beatitudes give light into the recesses of the mind.
- They instruct my people in proper behavior.
- My Beatitudes give life to the simple.
- In following my Son, one gains his true self.
- The old man gives way to the new.
- New ways open the mind to new ways of thinking.
- With new thoughts, one takes on a new behavior.
- What before seemed impossible, now becomes possible.
- New horizons appear to the mind.
- The Beatitudes are beacons of light in the darkness.
- Who takes the road of the Beatitudes finds Life.
- The Truth is molded on man's conscience and right decisions are made.
- The Beatitudes are holy.
- They form the character according to God's will.
- My people find peace, contentment, and courage in struggles, and strength to carry on.
- They know the ever-present love of their Creator.
- They persevere for they trust in God's faithfulness.
- They know that redemption is at hand for their Redeemer lives.

5/23/18

Your commands, Lord, give me life.

Let us begin today with an instruction on servanthood. To be a faithful servant and to deserve a just wage (Jeremiah 22:13), the servant must have the correct mindset. He knows he is hired for a specific purpose. This requires a mental adjustment: "I need to obey my employer and fulfill his demands and expectations and not mine." In other words, he bends his will to that of his employer.

For instance, take a housemaid, her employer wants her house cleaned thoroughly, everything swept clean. She does not want her home damaged or her floors left soiled. So likewise, I have asked my people to care for My world. I want it cared for. I expect my servants to be diligent and faithful to my requests, my commands.

I have called my people to know, love and serve Me—not for my sake, but for theirs. John the Baptist got it right: I can change stones into children in more ways than one (Luke 3:8). I command that they love Me with all their heart, mind, soul and strength (Mark 12:30), because I am their only good. It is good for themselves to love Me because this is the Way (John 14:6) to be open to receiving my love in return. The more they love Me, the more love they receive from Me and it begins to overflow on to those around them.

Learn and grow. Trust and obey. I am God and there is no other (Deuteronomy 5:6). You are my servants. I have given each one work to do in my Kingdom. Let Me train you. Be open to my Spirit whom I send to sanctify you, to prepare you for the joy of eternal life. Do you see why I want a change in attitude? Know who I am and you will know who you are in Me. This is imperative for your survival. I want you in my Kingdom. Be wise. Choose wisely. I have given you a free will which I will never deny.

6/7/18

I will follow You, Lord, show me the way.

I am the Beatitudes. They illustrate the attitudes of my heart, my character, and my demeanor. They present the characteristics of holiness, gentility, good manners, and good attitudes. These are the hallmarks of a good and faithful servant of the Lord. They represent divine qualities that all my children must emulate, for I made them for greatness—not mediocrity. I am their Father, their Creator, and they must become holy as I am holy (Matthew 5:48). "Chip off the old block," as they say.

Not only that, but I came down to earth to teach my children how to gain Heaven so they could be set free to follow Me, to hear my voice, and so I could take them out of this sphere and into the next. This is the meaning of life eternal: lasting peace and contentment. Yes, it is possible to be content in the earthly life, except for the constant temptations of the flesh and the devil. I came to show and to be the Way to Heaven (John 14:6). Who believes and follows Me will have eternal happiness; whoever does not will have eternal damnation.

O my people, choose life! Choose joy and obedience. Choose to be faithful to my teachings. Love yourself and your neighbor (Mark 12:31). Be good to yourself by loving, knowing, and serving Me, your God, your only good. I came down from Heaven to lead the way out of prison, out of darkness, out of temptations and sin. Yes, sin exists in disobedience to my laws. Where sin exists, there is punishment—not reward.

O my people, I came so you might live. Why does a father procreate a child? To give it life and joy—not death and misery! Likewise, I willed you into existence, so you could know and share in my blessings and eternal joy with Me in Paradise. Love Me as I love you. Seek my way, not yours. Walk into my light and leave the darkness of sin. I am waiting for you with open arms.

6/9/18

Command me, Lord. I will obey.

This is what I want to say about the Beatitudes today. They are the foundation of holiness for all my people. Everyone I have created has a role to play. This was my plan from the beginning. Many fell astray rebelling against my will. They either refused to obey because of pride or they were deceived by Satan. In the end, they lost their souls.

At first, I sent a great deluge upon them (Genesis 7:6). Then I struck them with many different languages (Genesis 11:7). My people were outcasts, lost with no one to lead them. I had to do something to help them. My plan from the beginning was to dwell in the hearts of my people. So, we decided if atonement for sin was made by my Son, we could send the Holy Spirit to each individual who was baptized and consecrated to us. The plan was made and fulfilled (John 19:30).

Now all that remains is for my people to follow my plan. I would give them every grace and power to do so. I even established the Kingdom on earth to administer the treasure of my love: Baptism, Confirmation, Reconciliation, Eucharist, Matrimony, Holy Orders and Anointing of the Sick. All this to prepare my people to enjoy the delights of Paradise that was lost to them by sin. What more can I do? My Son's blood atones their sins, redeeming their souls (Galatians 3:13). My Spirit lives in them lighting their path, and my love secures their safety. I will not force myself into their hearts. They must welcome Me. I knock, but they must open (Revelation 3:20).

O my people, invite Me into your hearts. I only want your good. What can you give Me that I have not already given to you? I ask, plead for your obedience. It is the sure way to holiness so we can be together. No one can see God and live (Exodus 33:20), but when you are holy as I am holy (Matthew 5:48), you will live and see the Beatific Vision, wherein lies all the treasures of the Garden of Eden.

Come, open your hearts and receive.

7/5/18

Teach me, Lord, so I might gain wisdom.

Anyone who is willing and able will learn to trust Me and obey Me. Once they have learned to follow in my footsteps and made the Beatitudes their own, they will be like shining stars in my Kingdom. It is then that the secrets of the Kingdom will be made known to them. All the light and love from my heart will fill theirs. They will see the world with a deeper understanding. They will know the truth and the truth will set them free to think new thoughts and feel new feelings (John 8:32). They will see and understand my movement in their life and in the life of others. They will see my action in governing the world. They will see miracles where others see nothing.

They are now ready to do great things for Me and I will use them, teach them, guide them, fill them with grace and power. The important thing is that they will listen to Me. They will sit in silence and hear Me speak, differentiating between my voice and the voice of evil. They will know and understand my will for each day and fulfill it.

Yes, do not look at what others do, especially those who do not know Me personally, who do not follow and obey Me, who do not love and serve Me. For I am the Creator of the universe (Isaiah 40:28). My power is beyond understanding, to know Me is unthinkable. Just know the love and grace I pour into your heart. That is proof of my power over you and my power to move men, to change stony hearts and rigid minds, and to change and control world events.

Do not fear the unknown forces in the world. In the end, all will be made clear to the obedient, listening, loyal heart. My will stands forever. I am immutable (Hebrews 6:17-18), unchanging, merciful to those who love Me and just to all others. Learn the Beatitudes. They will lead you home.

Blessed Virgin Mary on the Beatitudes

"Contemplate me at the moment when I present the Child Jesus in the temple of Jerusalem. He is so small, delicate and fragile; it is only forty days since He was born. I carry Him in my arms; with love I press Him to my heart; enraptured, I contemplate his eyes which gaze at me and enfold me in his divine light. Thus, I myself come to be carried by Him upon the way of the Beatitudes."

Chapter One

First Beatitude
"Blessed are the poor in spirit,
for theirs is the kingdom of heaven."
Matthew 5:3

4/28/18

Teach me who You are, Lord, and who I am in You.

The poor in spirit are those who long for Me, for those who desire to be with Me alone. The poor in spirit are those who hunger for my word, to be with Me in heaven, to be obedient to my word, to be open to hearing Me speak and who desire to obey every command. The poor in spirit are those who cherish my word, study my word, speak my word. They long to be alone with Me in the silence, to consume Me in Eucharist, to teach my words to others. They shall know happiness in the next life. This is my promise to the poor in spirit that the reign of God will be theirs.

What does it mean to reign with God, you ask? To reign with God is to be rich in my Spirit. The Holy Spirit will overshadow you and you will know the Truth and be filled with his light, his love. Your soul will be consumed by his love, your mind transformed and you will rejoice to be united in mind and heart with your Savior. Your life will be transformed and renewed. My Word has promised you abundant life to live in peace, love and joy (John 10:10). Your heart will be content with what you have. Strife is replaced with my peace.

O my people, choose life not death. Respect life. Promote life. Cherish your own self, for you are made in my image

14

(Genesis 1:27). I have chosen you for life in my Kingdom. Reign with Me and for Me. I am always with you.

4/29/18

I call with all my heart, Lord, hear me.

My love is a refuge for the poor in spirit. It is a shelter of grace for the downhearted. I provide for every man, woman and child. Ahh, how I love the children! Let them come to Me. I will place them on my knee and teach them how to follow Me. They will see what I see. They will understand what I understand. They will be as little children bouncing on their Father's knee. *"Suffer the little children to come to Me"* (Matthew 19:14). Tell them of my love for them. They must be told of my love, that I sent my own beloved Son Jesus away from Me to earthy chaos and to suffer at the hands of hateful men. He obeyed valorously, giving the example of how I want my children to obey.

I am always willing to comfort my children and guide them to victory over their enemies. I am always there as a bulwark to comfort and console them. They will only find rest in Me. I am their Creator (Isaiah 54:5), and know what they need. They suffer damage to their souls when they disobey Me whom they need. They draw away from the light when they need Me the most. They are deceived and lured away by the empty promises of wealth, beauty, pleasure. Beauty is a crown of sorrow luring many into sinful pleasures. Wealth can never satisfy the heart that hungers for their God. They must choose Me or Satan.

Choose wisely, my children. Seek my will and live in the light of my love. Hold fast to the teachings of the Roman

Catholic Church. It is the Church founded by my Son on earth. It is a sanctuary for the lost, a home for the poor, a school for the ignorant, a refuge for the needy.

5/26/18

Give me life, Lord, by your decrees.

These are my words for today: Poverty brings wealth. The impoverished spirit becomes gold. This is my power at work in a soul that is emptied of fear, selfishness, personal pride— all the capital sins of lust, hate, anger, sloth, gluttony—a gluttony for material things. What I want and ask of my disciples is to desire my love, and to be eager to do my will; and even though they do not understand fully what my will is, they will try their best to obey. They know the Ten Commandments and know they must obey the law of love: *"Thou shall love the Lord thy God with all thy mind, soul, spirit and strength, and love thy neighbor as thyself"* (Mark 12:30).

I do not leave them alone (John 14:18). I am always near. I speak to open hearts when they listen. I have ways man has not yet discovered. The Truth may be known by all. He came for all. He died for all. He will never abandon anyone, even those far from Me. My love is unending.

I ask my disciples to pray for those who do not pray. Prayer opens hearts to my grace. Prayer gives Me permission to work in souls who know Me not. Prayer is a force for good. It can tear down walls of resistance. Prayer is a force that tumbles down walls of ignorance, hate and pride.

This is a subject on which we will speak at another time. I can teach volumes on the capital sin of pride, the downfall of many. *"Pride comes before disaster"* (Proverbs 16:18). Even the poor commit the sin of pride. It is not an exclusive sin or attitude.

5/27/18

I trust in You, Lord, for all my needs.

Let us begin today speaking on the subject of poverty. It is the first Beatitude for many reasons. One of which is because I came in the poverty of a stable with lowly animals, dirt on the ground and little shelter from the night wind in the desert. I chose poverty as a rule to follow because my Father chose a humble handmaid to give Me a human body. My earthly parents were poor and humble people. Secondly, I chose to leave my glorious Father in Heaven and to lower myself to become man. This was my Father's will and We (Holy Spirit) agreed in this plan of salvation for the human race. Thirdly, I came in poverty to show the world its great need for the riches of the spiritual life. The contrast between heaven and earth is stark. The spiritual life is far greater than earthly life.

I chose poverty to give an example of how to achieve the treasure of my Father's grace—only in grace and with grace does one gain the wealth of Heaven, my Kingdom. Yes, I came to bring my Kingdom down to earth, and you have witnessed the marvels of Kingdom-living. You see lives transformed. I came that they might learn my ways that lead to Paradise. I showed the way by laying down my life to become man, by gathering disciples to hand down my Sacraments, the flowers of Heaven, by suffering the Passion, Death and Resurrection as proof of my love, to pay the debt to my Father for offences against his rights as Creator of

Heaven and Earth and of all who dwell therein; and lastly, to save my people from the fires of hell.

You see how poverty leads to wealth?

6/5/18

Help me, Lord, to understand your will.

Let us begin today speaking on the subject of poverty. I have said much already but it is important to understand our relationship to each other. I am God, you are my offspring. I am your Creator, you are my creation. I determined your sex. Your parents cooperated with my power to generate life and you came into being. Had I not wanted you in my world, your parents would have not been fruitful. Their union of love bore fruit because I willed it. I willed you into being; I breathed life into your soul (Genesis 2:7).

Now I did not leave you alone in your parent's care. I provided for you. I gave you eyes to see, a nose to smell, a brain with which you retain knowledge, perceive and compute mathematical functions, philosophize, make decisions. I gave you a sense of touch to distinguish between hardness and softness, cold and heat. The fingertips can calibrate embossed literature on tablets. I provided everything for your wellbeing. You were a child unable to fend for yourself.

But I never left you alone. I nurtured you, educated you, disciplined you (Hosea 11:3). I was proud of you when you took your first steps, spoke your first word, graduated from elementary to high school. Let us not forget your first Holy Communion. This gave Me much joy. It was the first time I could tangibly come into you. I rested in your beating heart and virginal soul. You were so close to Me then. It was a precious moment. And you grew to adulthood just as I had planned.

What has this to do with poverty? Where would you have been had I not willed your existence? A human being can only exist in Me; without Me, it cannot. It is lifeless. It is a no-thing. Without Me it has nothing: no vision, no purpose—it is poor, impoverished.

Know and understand your need of Me.

6/15/18

Your love, Lord, enriches my soul.

Today we speak of poverty of spirit. This pertains to one who does not know who she is or to whom she belongs. Poverty of hope is to not know who you are in the scheme of things. Poverty of faith is to not know where you are going. Poverty of love is to not know who is guiding you or where you are going. In other words, poverty of spirit means to be deprived of love, knowledge, wisdom and understanding.

Yes, all these virtues are found in the Holy Spirit who is received originally in the Sacrament of Baptism and re-affirmed in Confirmation. The Holy Spirit comes to the aid of those who repent of wrong doing—for example, disobeying my commandments; and to those who desire to know the truth and hunger for wisdom and knowledge. Then and only then is one ready to be converted.

Then the Holy Spirit baptizes the soul in his fire. The soul is transformed by the love of Christ who died for that soul, and the living waters of the Holy Spirit bring it to new life.

19

The Truth infills the soul and sets it free from the burden of sin, one at a time, slowly and carefully so as not to damage the weakened, oppressed, and wounded soul; to lift it into the light of grace that cleanses the soul of sin, purifies the heart, frees the mind to think new thoughts, and to find a new direction in life (2 Corinthians 5:17).

The soul is then on a new path of solid ground, a firm foundation, and from there grows new faith, richness of hope and charity and a new, replenished spirit to conduct its activities in the light of Christ. This opens the door to a world of joy, of walking in the Spirit, taking on a new way of thinking with the mind of Christ (1 Corinthians 2:16), and bringing every thought captive to the reign of Christ the King (2 Corinthians 10:5).

So, you see how poverty of spirit turns into riches? I have traced out a path to follow. It leads to happiness and obedience and glory.

6/24/18

Put light, Lord, into the darkness of my mind.

Today our subject is pride. Pride is the worst of sins because it puts self before God. There is no one greater than God. I am the First and the Last (Revelation 22:13). I am the Creator (Isaiah 40:28), the Origin of all things. I left nothing undone when I created "existence." I am the Father of all that is seen and unseen. I speak and life begins. I created mankind for a purpose: to help Me rule the world, to inhabit the earth (Genesis 1:28), to obey my least command and to give an example of my greatness.

Because I love what I create, and because I put myself into every living being, I speak and they respond. Yet, sin, rebellion, disobedience entered the world. Because I made everything with intelligence, beauty and love, pride entered the hearts of mankind. They thought they were just as powerful as Me. Because I gave them a free will, they thought they could live without Me. They knew I loved them, wanted their love in return, so they turned that knowledge into rebellion against Me. My kindness and generosity turned their hearts against Me. They chose to disobey.

Pride kills. It destroys long-standing relationships. Pride interferes with my plan of salvation, for I created my people's hearts with a need for my love. I want them for myself. I respect them, love them, want their love in return but they refuse. Pride is stubborn, destructive. Instead of being a power for good, it does evil; instead of helping, it hinders. There is nothing of value in pride. It sickens man's heart, robbing him of peace, love and joy. This is totally contrary to my will for his good, for his prosperity and peace of mind and soul.

I demand man's obedience because it is necessary to maintain the bond between us. I place my Spirit, a portion of myself in everything—animate and inanimate—because it is required to maintain life. They cannot live without Me. I am the source of Life (John 1:3). I breathe air into the lungs. I command and the world responds. Man cannot survive if I withhold my Spirit from them. They will whither away in darkness without my light. They will be consumed by evil if my power does not protect them. Man cannot exist without my love. His heart dries up, devoid of love's comfort and companionship. I alone sustain the heart and soul of man.

Where does air in the lungs originate? From Me! Where do thoughts come from? I speak to the mind of man and he thinks! I created every cell in the life-blood coursing through the body. Who else could have created the wonders of human flesh? Who else could have created the ear, a sophisticated wonder? No! Without Me, man dies, returns to dust from which I created him. No! Without my love, man's heart turns cold, hard, hateful. No! Without my grace, man sins, and sin kills (Romans 6:23). The root of sin is pride, and pride kills. It destroys the link between man and Me, the only source of life and love.

Man needs Me. I made him with that need. There is a Fatherly bond between Me and my creation. Pride ruptures that bond and this is not my will. Man chooses either life or death (Deuteronomy 30:19). Pride interferes with the soundness of his mind and he cannot choose correctly. In fact, he has already chosen himself instead of Me. It will not work. That is what I have been trying to prove.

7/2/18

Teach me, Lord, to obey your commands.

This is what I say today on the Beatitude of poverty. Use what I give you each day. Do not worry about tomorrow (Matthew 6:34). This is what I instructed the Israelites to do on their journey: Collect the manna just for the day's meals and I will provide more for the next day (Exodus 16:4). So, to you I say: Do not store up wealth for the thief to steal from you (Matthew 6:19). Use your riches for the day's needs. I will provide for tomorrow.

Poverty entails more than a lack of money. Some suffer poverty of love, some of friendship, some of faith, hope and love. Some have no joy or peace of soul and mind. These are the riches one garners from knowledge of my love and my providence. They have not because they will not. They will not trust, pray, obey. They choose to hate, lie, steal. How can they have peace when they strive for the wrong things in life?

Their real treasure is stored within themselves (2 Corinthians 4:7). I have planted my seed in every man, woman and child born to man. They must water that seed and it will grow. But some lack knowledge, some lack a sense of rightness, some are lazy, weak, some procrastinate. I say: Do not put off for tomorrow what you can do today (Proverbs 3:28). Tomorrow may not come. Yes, you know all these things. It has been said before but it bears repeating, for many do not understand at first. Repetition is a good teaching tool.

So, let us summarize the facts of true poverty. Poverty is a lack of knowledge, wisdom and understanding from whence come all the true treasures of spirituality. This is poverty of spirit. What is the remedy? *"Ask and it will be given to you; seek and you will find; knock and the door will be opened to you"* (Matthew 7:7). It is that simple. They receive not because they ask not.

Let Me tell you a secret. I am a loving, merciful Father to my children. If they will walk in my light, I will provide abundantly all the grace they need to prosper, to do good works, to love and be loved. If they will obey Me, doors will open and more grace will be poured into their hearts. I am willing to do my part. Will you do yours? What is your part, you ask? *"You shall love the Lord your God with all your heart, with all your soul, with all your mind and with all your strength; and love your neighbor as yourself"* (Mark 12:30).

Oh, you say it is too hard to do? Nothing is impossible for those who love Me. Try it. Put your toe in the water of my love and it will wash you and cleanse your spirit. You will know then the truth of what I can do for you, in you, and with you.

Come, enjoy the fruits in my vineyard. Refresh yourselves at the streams of living water (John 4:10).

8/11/18

Fill me, Lord, and use me.

Today I want to tell you about the mystery of the Trinity—Father, Son and Spirit. We live in and through and with each other. I, the Father, live in my Son and that makes the love we have for each other doubled; and then, our love overflows into the Holy Spirit who in turn, returns our love multiplied by three. It is simple but unexplainable and mysterious.

When one reaches the higher levels of holiness, it is easier to grasp because in that state of holiness, one is freed from the darkness of sin and can then see the Light of my Son the Christ, the Anointed One (Luke 4:18), who shed his blood for all my creation. We communicate to each other all that We see and hear and We decide what is good for the world, what is best for my creation, what We should do next. We are the governing Trinity. Our word is final. I created the Angels to do my bidding, to patrol the seven continents of the world,

24

to take my messages to the chosen ones as Gabriel did to Mary (Luke 1:26).

You know well the Christmas Story, how my will was carried out that my Son should be born in poverty to show the world the beauty of poverty. It is a noble virtue. From the poor little cave arose the splendor of the Catholic Church in which the Holy Spirit of my Son reigns and guides my people to the Promised Land of milk and honey where my Son and I together with the Holy Spirit await the arrival of our children.

Heed well the teachings of the Catholic Church for the Holy Trinity will be found in its midst. Just as my Son was found in the cave by the three Wise Men (Matthew 2:10), so too, will you find him in the Vicar of my Catholic Church.

In poverty, one finds the richness of my Word taught, lived and spread about the land. It is the "yellow brick road" leading to Heaven. Take the way of poverty. It is the royal road to my Heart.

9/22/18

Give me eyes to see You, Lord, in the poor.

To all my disciples, I give this grace to love Me in the poor. No one was as poor as I made myself, although I was rich sitting by my Father's side in Heaven. I ruled the universe, but I chose to make myself poor by taking on human flesh. This was my Father's plan to restore his people, and I agreed willingly to do my part. You see, it is because of my Father's love that I put my Spirit within all things, animate and inanimate.

Yes, my Father so loved the world that he gave his only Son, so you would not perish (John 3:16). I am speaking personally to you who are reading my words. I did not count the cost to save you. I made myself poor purposely so you might be rich. I am speaking of your soul's eternal life. It is richly provided for in Paradise (John 14:3).

On earth, there shall be groaning, travailing, suffering, sadness, wars, hate; but lift up your eyes to see the beauty of the earth: the sun to rule the day, the moon and stars to light the night, the wonders of technology and medicines to cure sickness. Yet all these wonders are nothing without my love. I make the world turn. I keep it in place by the law of gravity. I make the rich. I make the poor. All—everything is in my hands. If I did not breathe air into your lungs, you would expire. I am in you, keeping you alive.

Do you believe Me? I exist in you and call you to be mine (Isaiah 43:1), my own special creation, dear to my heart. And because I live in you, my Father is loving Me in you. Do you understand our plan? I live in you and you exist because my Father and I live in you. My Father and I are one (John 17:21) and we make you one with us. It is simple but complicated. It calls for a response of faith. Faith opens eyes to truth and understanding, wisdom and knowledge. With faith in the heart, I can work miracles.

But for today's lesson, I want to open your eyes to understand the reason why I came not as a wealthy man but as a poor one. I chose a simple, humble maiden to be my Mother who was betrothed to an ordinary carpenter. This was my plan to prove that I can more easily be found in poverty than in wealth. The more a soul is poor, the more I exist there. In poverty, one only desires food to feed his hunger. He is content with one pair of pants and a coat to warm his body. He does not waste his time on superficial dreaming. The overarching demand is to stay alive. I am found in the poor because they cannot help themselves. On the other hand, with the soul that is well fed, he is concerned only with accumulating wealth. He does not concern himself with the welfare of others. His heart is divided.

In my eyes, all are poor and in need of my love, my protection, my guidance. You see Me in the poor because I alone am providing for them. I alone equate myself with them. When you are poor: you see with my eyes, you feel with my hands, you comfort with my arms. I live in the poor as I live in everyone.

Help the poor, you help Me. Love the poor, you love Me (Matthew 25:40). Dress the poor, you dress Me. Make yourself poor in my eyes and you will see my face. Deprive yourself of wealth and you will see my treasures. Hang on to your faith in Me, in my love for you, and you will see the unseen. Love yourself and you love Me, for I am in you. I am in everyone. I am everywhere. Look and you will see my face in the poor.

10/6/18

Pierce me through and through, Lord, until I become like You.

Yes, I am in your thoughts and in your heart. Trouble yourself not about material wealth, take on the Beatitude of poverty of spirit, for then the Kingdom of Heaven will be given to you. Do you not still believe that I am all you need? In Me, can be found all the riches necessary for life, happiness and peace. Do not let Satan rob you of your faith. Trust in Me to provide your daily bread. You have been walking with Me and I have taken you to this juncture in the road to salvation. It looks scary but do not fear for I am at your side always, and I will never leave you.

This is what is important at this time. I must build you up to complete dependence on your Father in Heaven. Nothing must separate us—not even a hint of fear. In love there is no fear for love conquers all fear (1 John 4:18).

Yes, keep the attitude of gratitude for all the grace you have received thus far. Look back on your life to see how far we have traveled together. Have I ever deserted you? Have I not provided for you through the years? Yes, you are my special possession. I love you. No matter what happens, I am always with you.

In poverty, your eyes are opened to the truth. In poverty, you depend more and more on Me to provide for you. In poverty, your perspective changes. You see that you can no longer depend on wealth. Your crutch has been taken away. You sense a great loss: the carpet has been pulled out from under your feet. You stagger but you will not fall because your inner strength has been fortified by the grace you have stored up from all your prayers, good works, frequent Holy Communions. I will never let you down. You have trusted in Me. You have obeyed Me.

Now I am taking you to a new place that will require complete trust in my love. Yes, I know that you know that I know what is best for you. My plan is going forward for your complete transformation. Take my hand and follow Me.

10/20/18

Let me adore You, Lord, with humility and gratitude.

Yes, this is a result of poverty of spirit. When one gives up everything, has no use for things of this world, and no longer seeks pleasures, riches, fame, then the heart is empty and eager to receive what only I can give—love, divine love, merciful love, unconditional love.

Poverty leads to riches. The soul's one desire is to be close to her God, to live in his light, to eat of his flesh and drink of his blood, to listen to his voice and obey his commands, to please her God in little ways. She exists to do his will. Whatever happens to her, she is confident that I have allowed it in order to strengthen her faith, or that something good will come from all the bad she sees in the world (Romans 8:28).

The Teacher appears when the disciple is ready. Her soul is ripe for harvesting. My vineyard is rich with lush, juicy grapes, and I can make quality wine from the holiness that I see in her soul. By deeds of mercy, she glorifies Me; by acts of kindness, she pleases my heart; and she sings praises to the God who loves her, who protects her and keeps her close to his heart. There is no fear in one who owns nothing, because she knows that in Me she has everything!

So, my children, to adore Me with humility is to know your poverty—that you are nothing without Me, that you can do nothing without my grace. Then when you ask in prayer, specifically the Lord's Prayer, I will grant you your daily bread—all your needs will be provided—and you will give thanks humbly and with a grateful heart because you know beyond a shadow of a doubt that I am your loving, caring, generous and merciful Father who showers down heavenly graces to flood your heart and soul with a peace that is beyond compare.

11/22/18

Speak to me, Lord, about the poor in spirit.

This is one of my favorite subjects because great things are accomplished by those who devote themselves to poverty. First off, I led a life bereft of luxury. I had no home to call my own. I traveled up and down Jerusalem without a place to rest my head (Luke 5:58). As I have already stated: I was born in poverty, lived in poverty, died in poverty—yet I am the richest of all because everything and everyone belongs to Me. I created gold, gave it value, and thus, it is the standard for financial transactions. Men seek the wrong kind of gold. They kill for it. They ruin innocent lives for their lust for it. A good thing has been used for evil.

Another reason I chose poverty: the one who lives in the state of poverty, depends not on himself or herself. They depend on Me. They place all their needs in my hands, trusting in my love, in my word, in my power to provide for them. This posture requires great faith, and great faith can not only move mountains (Mark 11:23), it calls upon my sovereignty, my providence, my power and my paternal desire to care for my needy children.

All who hope in Me are granted life, liberty and happiness. Their joy is based on a solid rock of faith in their God, knowing full well that I will keep my promise to shine on them, in them and through them. They know beyond a shadow of a doubt that I will never disappoint them or forsake them. They relate to Me in glorious fashion. I am their God and they are my people (Jeremiah 32:38). They know their history of how I took them out of darkness and brought them into the light of my love. And in my love, I set them free from bondage to sin. Chains that bound their spirit have been broken and they are free to live in peace with serene hearts and joyful thoughts. They are free from worries, anxieties, fears and doubts. They know that they know I am for them, with them and in them. They can ask what they will and I will grant it—only for their good. They also know that when their prayer is not answered, it is because I have something better in mind for them. They know that I will only grant desires of the heart that will lead them safely home to Me. They trust in my will for it is perfect for them.

This is what I mean about true poverty. It is freedom to trust my love, knowing my love provides all they need to live fully in the light, peace and joy of my Son through the Holy Spirit in this world and into the next.

11/28/18

Strengthen me, Lord, in my weakness.

Today I will speak to you about courage. This is a valuable tool to carry on the upward journey to holiness. Courage is a virtue granted from God, the Son, in order to fulfill the plan I have arranged for you. One must be strong in faith, hope and love in order to bear fruit in the vineyard of the world. The fruit of these virtues is the ability and strength to stand your ground against the onslaughts of the evil one. (He can't stand to be called evil because he thinks he is justified in his rebellion against my rule.)

But back to our subject of courage. Satan is powerless in the face of courage. He runs away when you stand firm, disbelieving his lies. My Son knows how to handle him. Satan tried to tempt Jesus in the desert, but my Son calmly rejected him by using my words in Scripture: *"Man does not live on bread alone but by the word of God"* (Luke 4:4). My word is so powerful it turns Satan back on his heel, so to speak.

What has this to do with courage? Everything! When one knows my word, and stands on my word, knowing beyond a shadow of a doubt that I back my word, what is there to fear? Nothing! They know the truth that no one and nothing is more powerful than the God who loves them! They know that I love them enough to be crucified for them, so why would I not defend them? When one has faith and knowledge of who I am, they have courage to face down the enemy. They become fearless warriors because I have their back and they can trust Me.

So, you see, firm faith leads to concrete courage, and this leads to victory in the battle against evil, sin, sickness—my love heals sickness of body, mind and heart. Just have courage to persevere through the daily trials with hope in my word, that I promise will never fail you. My word is my bond. This is the Lord who speaks!

11/29/18

I am needy, Lord, enrich me with your Spirit.

Yes, I will pour out my Spirit upon the world, and all will long to see my face. I will renew the world and all its inhabitants. You doubt that I can do it? Do you not yet believe in my almighty power to change the hearts of men? If I could change you, why not others? Oh, you say, "I wanted to be saved! I hated my life and my ignorance! I wanted to be wise and happy."

Yes, that is the proper condition of mind and heart where I am allowed to enter and begin the work of transforming the soul. But, you see, as that happened to you, it can also happen to everyone else in the world. My power is not confined to a few hungry souls, but it is unleashed to all. I need to open your mind to think beyond its limitations. This is my work in the soul. Remember, nothing is impossible for Me (Luke 1:37).

You feel that you are still in the dark? Well, that's a good place to be, for there you are safe from unhealthy thoughts. Your imagination is constrained and unable to process what the world expects of you. Only I can reach into the dark night of the soul and flood it with my light. In this way, I achieve the change of mind and heart proper to this state of development. I alone can draw the soul into contemplating the mysteries of my heart. I alone have power to enrich the soul with gifts of light, wisdom and understanding. I can and I will change the hearts of men.

Yes, I write straight with crooked lines. You do not understand? Let Me enlighten you. My will is to save all my children (1 Timothy 2:3). Sometimes, I cannot take them straight into contemplation, so I use twists and turns as they journey; but they eventually find the straight, narrow road to my heart (Matthew 7:14) where I am waiting to receive them. Do you understand? No? Let us try another example: say you have a preference for music. I lure you into the desert (dark night of the soul) by quelling the desire; I take it away from you. Suddenly, all desires are gone. You just drift along. But down in your psyche, I am at work with my grace, the Holy Spirit, and I am working my power to change, remold your psyche—the hidden part of your consciousness. I am planting new desires there that will draw you back from wrong thoughts and desires and put you on the right road that will take you to the next level of spirituality.

Earlier, you were thinking that what was written in the Book of Revelation were the things Saint John the Evangelist saw while in the state of contemplation. You are correct. Everything written in the Bible is for your information, to help you on your upward journey to holiness.

Enough for today. Read the Bible and learn of my love and power. You will be amazed by what you read.

11/30/18

May all my deeds, Lord, be done for your glory.

Today we will continue with the subject of the poor in spirit. They are the ones who are lukewarm in their faith. They are the ones who give up when the going gets tough. They lack substance in their knowledge and understanding of who I am for them. Yes, my people perish for lack of knowledge (Hosea 4:6). They have not heard or understood that I died on the cross for them, that I love them enough to leave my throne in Heaven, lower myself to be born a man, suffer a life of poverty, be scorned by the religious leaders of Israel, condemned to death and crucified all for their sake! How sad it is that my people suffer for lack of understanding. What to do?

The Good News must be told to the ends of the earth. Every ear must hear what I gladly did for them. How can a man have faith if he has not heard (Romans 10: 14, 17)? How great are those who spread the news; and greater still are those who accept the gift of faith.

There is an acrostic for **Faith**: **F**ather **A**dored **I**n **T**he **H**eavens—and Heaven begins with faith here and now on earth in your everyday life. Where I am, there is Heaven because I am Spirit, and my Spirit is everywhere. You cannot escape it. I am the air you breathe, the light in your eyes, the beat of your heart. I am the Way to Heaven and future glory; I am the Truth of salvation and redemption; and I am the Life that sustains all life on earth, in Heaven and everywhere (John 14:6)!

You cannot escape from my love. It is everywhere and so close you can reach out and grasp it. It's as close as a prayer. People have not because they ask not—or they ask wrongly, for things that will harm them or damage their soul or squelch their tender faith.

Pray, my little ones. Pray for those who cannot or will not pray for themselves. Intercede for the blind, young and old.

This is how to glorify Me with your life of **Prayers**: **P**atience, **R**osary, **A**doration, **Y**earn for Me, **E**vangelize, **R**ecreation, **S**ervice.

12/3/18

My heart is ready, Lord, to receive all You have for me.

And I have much to give you: my whole self, that is why I died on the cross for you. First, to free you from slavery to sin, but also, to send the Holy Spirit to you in the Baptism of water and of fire (Matthew 3:11). Without being clothed with the Holy Spirt, you are unprotected in the world of darkness and sin. You must be fortified with my sanctifying grace which is to say, the Holy Spirit.

Yes, as John the Baptist said, *"He (Jesus) must increase as I decrease"* (John 3:30). In and with the Holy Spirit alive and working in and through you, I will increase my presence; and hence, my power within you. You will know my will and obey it. You will be convinced of my love for you, and nothing will deter you from obeying Me. I will be your Master and you will be my servant. I promise you that you will rejoice in my power over you.

Suddenly, you will sense peace come over you like a cleansing shower, washing away unhealthy thoughts and false beliefs like unworthiness. In Me, you are worthy. With Me, you can overcome evil in your heart. With Me, you can move mountains of doubts, and bad habits will be changed like day and night. You will become a new creation with new faith in God the Father; you will have firm hope in Me, God the Son; and you will fall in love with my Mother through the Holy Spirit (2 Corinthians 5:17).

I have so many gifts to impart to you, so many that it is necessary to free yourself from unnecessary burdens to make room for the new ones. Yes, my yoke is easy and my burden light. Come to Me, you who are weary, and I will give you rest (Matthew 12:28). You will know a peace you never knew before.

Oh, if only my people would turn to Me and obey my Word, I could shower them and wash them in the living waters of the Holy Spirit and we would be one in heart, one in mind; and the unity between us would work miracles of healing, conversion of souls, and the transformation of hearts and lives.

Blessed Virgin Mary on the First Beatitude

Blessed are the poor in spirit. The Lord, omnipotent and omniscient God, is totally present, reduced to nothingness as it were, under the appearance of this, my little Son. He is born amidst great poverty, in a cave; He is placed in a manger; He spends his first days of life in a poor and bare dwelling place. And now I am bringing Him to the temple of the Lord, supported by my most chaste spouse, Joseph, and we offer for his ransom two little doves which is the established price for poor people."

St. Padre Pio on the First Beatitude

"When failures occur because of flawed motives on your part, there is no need to be surprised. On the one hand, hate the offense that it gives to God; on the other hand, have a joyful humility, because then you are seeing and understanding your spiritual poverty."

St. Clare of Assisi on the Virtue of Poverty

"O blessed poverty which brings eternal riches to those who love and embrace it! O holy poverty—to those who possess and desire you, God promises the Kingdom of Heaven and without doubt eternal glory and a most happy and blessed life. O poverty dear to God, our Lord Jesus Christ, who made heaven and earth and rules them all, who spoke the word and the world was made—it was He who bent down to embrace poverty. He said the foxes have their dens and the birds of the air their nests, but the Son of Man—that is Christ himself—does not have whereupon to lay his head but bowing his head He gave up his spirit."

Chapter Two

Second Beatitude
"Blessed are those who mourn,
for they shall be comforted."
Matthew 5:4

5/3/18

I grieve, Lord, for sinning against You.

I want to speak today on the Beatitude of mourning your sins. I have much to say about this second Beatitude.

One must be in the right frame of mind before their God. Without grief over their sins, they do not acknowledge their dependency on my power to forgive them and my willingness to do so. They must mourn their sins to ascertain their need for Me. They cannot obey the Ten Commandments without my grace. They cannot make themselves holy without my help. They must know and recognize the damage one small sin works on their soul. Multiply that with a mortal sin and the soul is marred beyond description and recognition. I can no longer live in a soul so dark for it is bereft of the light of love.

Love needs light to grow. Love needs joy and peace to exist. Love needs trust to increase. I cannot exist or work my grace in a soul that is not open to Me. Yes, I will not force my grace on those who do not seek Me or want Me.

I have much work to do in the world. My children are dying for lack of knowledge (Hosea 4:6) and understanding. You ask for ways to understand how to be open to my grace? Pray. Humble yourself. Know who you are: dust—from dust I created man (Genesis 2:7), and to dust he shall return.

How can dust compare to Godliness? To laying down my life for love of you?

My children, please, your Father is asking you: learn what sin is, what damage it does to your soul, mourn the sins that have scarred your beautiful souls that I created so carefully—you are wonderfully made—made for greatness and glory (Psalm 139:14).

Oh, how it pains Me to see so many of my children running to destruction. They turn away from Me, their only source of Life, their only good and hope for mercy. Child, tell my children that I love them. I want them with Me, not against Me. Make my plea for their love.

4/30/18

You are faithful, Lord, forever.

Love soothes all passions. Love conquers all fears. Love is the antidote for loneliness, and a comfort in sorrow. My love is a healing potion for all the wounds of the heart. Only my love suffices for grief and sadness.

My people must learn to give Me all their pain, their troubles, their burdens and I will carry them on my shoulders. That is why I am called the Good Shepherd (John 10:11). I carried all the sins of humanity on the Cross of my crucifixion, and sin was defeated once and for all by the power of my Resurrection. Satan's power was destroyed, and my reign established forever. Divine, sacrificial love is triumphant!

The pathway to my love and mercy began with the Cross. There are many types of crosses to bear in the world: cross of sorrow and regret, cross of illness, both emotional and physical. Grief in the heart is an illness that only love can cure. Yet the greatest illness is unrepented sin for it destroys peace, love and joy; it blocks the access to my grace and mercy. The darkness of sin obscures the light of my love. Mourn for the loss of my love.

"Set me as a seal on your heart, as a seal on your arm. Be swift, my lover, like a gazelle or a young stag on the mountains of spices" (Song of Songs 8:6, 14).

6/29/18

Have mercy, Lord. I am a sinner.

That is the attitude of the second Beatitude: recognizing and admitting the state of the soul before its God. I know everything about my children's souls. All are sinners before their God. Only one was created Immaculate, my Mother, the Virgin Mary. All others are stained with the sins of their parents. Examine the characteristics of your parents, and you will see yourself. We imitate what we see as children, and we think this is normal behavior. Woe to those who mislead others. They will mourn their sins greatly (Matthew 18:6).

Examine yourselves. Know what you do and say. Compare it to the standard of my Commandments. Do you love God, neighbor and self? Learn to know Me. I am kind and gentle, meek of heart, mild-mannered, forgiving and merciful. Grieve where you have failed to be like Me. Pray for the grace of repentance and sorrow for your sins. Not just to be right with Me, but because sin robs your peace away. Sin begets more sin, and if you do not mourn for them, they will rob your salvation away!

Another thing about committing sin: the bad example it gives to others. Sin is ugly. Look at all the people who hate today—the protesters, the murderers. Are they not at war in themselves? They are consumed by the evil of sin. Yes, mourn your sins. They kill the soul and torture the heart.

Listen to my words: repent and be converted (Mark 1:15) and you shall be comforted. Confess your need of my mercy and forgiveness and you shall receive peace in your soul. If not for yourself, you who are parents, do it for the love of your children. Take Jesus as your model. He loved you so much, he chose to lay down his life for you. Can you not do the same for your own?

6/30/18

Justify me, Lord. I believe in You.

Today we will speak about those who mourn the loss of loved ones. They grieve and believe they are alone, and yet they are never alone, for I am with them grieving in them. I am a very compassionate God. You see how people who are kind, suffer when they see suffering? That is my compassion working in them.

Then there are those who mourn the loss of love, say in a divorce situation. This is a loss of personal self-esteem. They feel diminished in the eyes of the world. They feel they have lost esteem in my eyes. But I suffer with them. I feel their pain. Are they not flesh of my flesh (Genesis 2:23)? What they feel, I feel. They are hurt, so I am hurt in them. Do you not see that I mourn more than anyone? I exist in my children. I sense their pain. No one can suffer more than I do! Multiply my pain by the millions. Yet, my sacrifice on the cross satisfied and redeemed all the suffering in the world. There can be no suffering that I have not already atoned for. I paid the price of man's sin once and for all (Galatians 3:13).

No one who mourns shall not be comforted. They will know my love and sense my peace. Their grief shall be wrapped in grace and returned to them purified like gold refined in fire. These are my words you are reading, and my words never return to Me without accomplishing my will (Isaiah 55:11). *"Blessed are those who mourn for they shall be comforted"* (Matthew 5:4), in the knowledge that I suffered before them; I am suffering now in them, and I will always suffer with them. They are never alone. Their grief gains a great reward.

7/7/18

Show me the light, Lord, so I may walk in safety.

What have I taught you thus far? Grieve because sin against Me hurts your soul. Mortal sin separates you from my love, care, and guidance. The soul is lost in a wind-storm and cannot find its way to safety. Lack of love for neighbor hurts the soul because I exist in every creature: man, woman, child, and all animals. I exist everywhere—in everything that lives and breathes. Otherwise, they could not exist. Where I am there is life. Without Me is death. Unless I breathe into your lungs, you could not aspirate. Without my light, all life, human and animal, cannot see. They walk in darkness.

To love Me, it is necessary to love your neighbor. This is the law of love I gave my disciples. Why? Because love covers a multitude of sins (1 Peter 4:8). I am Love (1 John 4:8). I increase in the loving heart. I rejoice in my people's love. Where there is love, there is faith and hope. Hope for a lifetime of loving Me, the only Good (Luke 18:19) for the world. I exist in the hopeful and trustful heart; and in that soul, I pour my light and grace. Slowly the wheel of faith turns, and my light transforms the soul so it resembles its Maker.

Another reason why loving Me and those around you is important because love grants peace. Multiply love in the soul and peace is multiplied. Peace leads to contentment in the heart and love increases. Love begets peace and peace begets love. It is a win-win situation.

How does one receive more love, you might ask? Pray and I will answer. Obey and I will grant more and more love to you. It will spill over and nothing will stop it from flowing back to Me. I will return it to you purified and you will love with my sacred love and the lives of those around you will be healed and transformed. They in turn will pray and love more and the wheel turns faster and faster until many more are touched by my sacred love and they become contented and peaceful, and love and peace gradually fill the earth.

You see? Peace and love can work miracles. The earth would be filled with joy. Is this not Heaven on earth? All is possible for one who loves God, neighbor and self (Mark 12:28). This is important. It is necessary to love yourself, to cherish yourself. I have wonderfully made you (Psalm 139:14), poured my grace into your soul, labored to teach and enlighten you, disciplined you so you might know my will and obey it. I have shown you the way to my heart and filled you with love. Would I ever stop now? No, never!

While there is life, there is hope of complete salvation.

8/9/18

I am yours, Lord. Use me.

Today we speak on the subject of sorrow or mourning for sins, the second Beatitude. It takes a generous spirit to express sorrow and regret for willfully committing sins. First of all, one must know and understand how sin offends Me, your God and Father.

Picture yourself on my knee. I am holding you safely in my arms. I care for you, shelter, feed and clothe you. I provide all you need and give you a beautiful world to spread out your wings and enjoy the fruits of my labor. Instead of loving Me, you push Me away and refuse to accept all the wonderful things I have provided for your life and happiness. Instead of being grateful, you choose not to accept my gifts and turn away from Me. Instead of living the life I gave you, no—you refuse: "I want to do it my way!" What grief this gives Me who loves you so much. Do you see and understand how sin hurts Me? I who created you am rejected and maligned. I do not ask anything of my creatures. I provide everything for them. I am the source of their existence. They need Me.

You see why I am described as merciful, compassionate, long-suffering? I wait patiently for my children to mature in wisdom, knowledge and understanding until they come to grieve the loss of all the good I have done for them and the loss of all the love, joy and peace I have ready to give them. I wait patiently for them to come to their senses and return to their Father. Yes, I am the Father who rejoices at his son's return in the story of the Prodigal Son who grieves his sins, his mistakes and bad choices (Luke 15:11). I am the merciful Father who eagerly forgives his repentant children.

44

O my people, grieve the loss of my love when you choose to walk away from my Light. Love is not lost forever. It is always waiting for you, calling you to return. *"Arise, my beloved, my beautiful one, and come! For see, the winter is past, the rains are over and gone"* (Song of Songs 2:10-11). Come, I am waiting with open arms.

8/19/18

Remain in me, Lord, so I may live.

Today let us speak of mourning sins in the heart and soul. There is a difference. Sins of the heart are when we fail to love self and others. Sins of the soul are offences against your God. These are more serious because I am your lifeline. I breathe life into your soul and you live and breathe, walk and talk, move and listen. Is it not in your soul that you listen for my voice and wait for my guidance? Yes, I remain in you as long as you love, honor, and obey Me.

The difference is that once a soul shrivels up with hate, it has stepped out of my sphere of grace. It has chosen to reject my power in them and because I do not force my grace upon them, they no longer receive my light, my protection, my comfort. Yes, fear for them. Pray for them.

Although it is true that I exist in all things, they have chosen to reject my grace. They refuse my love. Again, I will not force my grace upon anyone. They must accept it. You ask how does one accept my lifesaving grace? It is received through prayer. *"Ask and you shall receive"* (Matthew. 7:7). One who does not pray does not receive. I hear every prayer (1 John 5:14) and I never forget a prayer. My people forget Me, but I never forget nor reject one solitary soul who turns to Me asking for my help. Remember Me? I am the merciful Father of the Prodigal Son (Luke 15:11). I rejoice when my children come back to Me seeking forgiveness, mourning and repenting for their sins.

We will speak another day on the subject of sins of the heart. I have much to teach you about myself, my love and my mercy.

8/20/18

Open my eyes, Lord, that I may see.

Today we begin where we left off yesterday. *"Blessed are those who mourn for their sins, for they shall be comforted"* (Matthew 5:4). We speak of sins of the heart: sins against self, others and all my living creatures—human and animal. To sin against self leads to sin against others. Without compassion for one's self, it is impossible to have compassion on others—that is why they say, "Charity begins at home."

Why would one sin against oneself? Possibly, they compare themselves to others and see they fall short. Maybe their pride tells them they are inferior to others, and they believe it. Maybe they set too high of a standard and when they fail, they become discouraged and depressed. Consequently, they lose their peace. What is the antidote? Prayer, submission and acceptance. They must realize that no one is perfect—all are sinners and fall short of the mark (Romans 3:23).

This is why I sent my Son to pay the price for their sins. The debt was paid and the way opened for the Holy Spirit to begin the work of restoration. By the Blood of the Cross, all humanity is renewed in the Spirit of my Son. Those who hate can now love. The Truth was made known and set all captives free (John 8:32)—free to become the loving, kind, merciful people I planned them to be.

On the other hand, the door was opened to freedom of choice—the choice to accept or reject their salvation. Many choose wrongly. They choose not to believe, not to love, not to accept the road set out before them. They look for happiness in all the wrong places, so to speak. They forget that charity begins at home within one's heart and soul. Instead of victory, they accept defeat because they fail to love and cherish the unique, special life I planned for them.

O my people, mourn the loss of opportunities to love yourself. Repair the damage lack of love has caused you. Change your lifestyle, your expectations, simplify your needs and wants. Lead a prayerful lifestyle, and all the graces of Heaven will be at your disposal. You will know such happiness and peace that you have never before known.

I promise you—you will be consoled. Let love motivate your life, your thoughts, your dreams. Pray as you have never prayed before. Prayer unlocks many doors—doors of resistance, of self-knowledge, of wisdom and charity to self and others. Be not hardhearted. Relax and transform your heart. You will know joy as you've never before known.

8/29/18

Shine your light, Lord, into the darkness of my soul.

Today our subject is on mourning. Those who mourn shall be comforted. Mourning is my way of releasing pent-up emotion over the loss of happiness. I created man to live in the contentment of Heaven, but man disobeyed my command and so lost the only true source of joy available to him. I am the source of life and all that is good. I am the Light of the World (John 8:12), and to lose Me is to lose all that is good in life.

Yes, I grieve when my children walk away from the Light. I grieve because they choose to live in darkness which leads to death. I am speaking here of eternal damnation, an eternity of fire and suffering. Why, oh why, do my children choose wrongly? I grieve for the loss of all those children of mine who are sent to Hell! Oh, why do they not choose to obey Me?

Yes, I know the pain of losing the life of a child. Did not my Son lose His life on the Cross? I, too, am a grieving parent. I feel the terrible loss but multiply that by the millions of my lost children who lose the joy of eternal Paradise!

Yes, I mourn when my children suffer, yet I have the power to save them if only they would turn to Me. I make good come from bad. You ask, "Why do I allow bad things to happen? Why do I not constrain evil?" Remember, I do not go back on my word. I give every man, woman and child the freedom to choose—either to obey and follow Me into Heaven or obey and follow Satan into Hell. Those are the choices before you: Life, Death, Heaven, Hell.

Remember another thing: I am the God of mercy (2 Samuel 24:14). Now, in this lifetime, seek my mercy. How? Pray and obey. My mercy is available to all who ask. Do not delay!

9/1/108

In my weakness Lord, strengthen me.

Today we begin with the mournful state of the soul that is without faith in her loving God. This is a soul that is alone in the woods susceptible to darkness, danger, and struggling to survive all alone. This is a soul afflicted with disease, injuries from without and within.

Let me tell you a story about a lost child in a world of darkness. She is filled with fear, doubts, hungry for knowledge and understanding. Loneliness overwhelms her natural desire for happiness. Her days are filled with sadness, hungering for peace in her life for she is totally alone, lost, hopeless and depressed. This is the state of a mournful soul who has lost her way.

Then one day, she begins to pray, and I am able to touch her heart and bring my Light into the darkness of her mind, and slowly she finds her way to discovering the love, peace and joy I was waiting to give her; and she is comforted.

The key is prayer—the prayer of the heart, the prayer of trust in Me, the Savior of the world. If only all my people would turn to Me and the world would be a better place. Instead of hate, love would reign.

Now let Me speak about affliction—the afflictions of the body. Most times they are avoidable but because my children indulge their appetites for rich, fatty foods, their health deteriorates. I made their precious bodies to function perfectly given the right nutrients. Most often, because of laziness or lack of time, because they are focused on making money or pursuing pleasures, they rush to fast food places. Greed destroys their health. Sin is the bottom line of much affliction. There are other sins that also damage the health of the body.

O my children, mourn your sins. Grieve your losses. Take comfort in knowing I can convert your mournful state if you allow Me to bring you back to Me. How? All you have to do is pray and obey, and I will do it.

9/9/18

Put your Spirit in me, Lord, that I may be healed.

Today we speak on the second Beatitude: *"Blessed are those who mourn for they shall be comforted"* (Matthew 5:4). We will address the issue of affliction of the body. Many suffer physically—loss of vision, hearing impairment, cancer, lung/breathing problems. All these can be healed either by medication, surgery or by prayer.

Faith heals. Trust in my Word also heals. I have given my disciples power to lay hands on the sick and they will be healed (Mark 16:18) in my name, the Name above all names (Philippians 2:9). Many of my disciples do not believe in my power to work through them so they do not even pray for healing. What a waste of grace! The obvious reason is they don't love Me enough and they lack faith in my love; otherwise they would practice this power more and more and my afflicted children would be healed. In this, they would be comforted.

Do you know that you are temples of the Holy Spirit (1 Corinthians 3:16)? Do you not believe that the Holy Spirit is alive in you? Guiding you? If you do believe, why do you not practice your faith? Read the last chapter of Saint Mark's Gospel where I send my disciples forth into the world, commanding them to heal the blind, cure the sick (Mark 16:18). What do I have to do to convince you? Must I die on the Cross again?

O my people, take up and read my Book (Bible). Learn to know Me and understand how much I love you and do for you. Won't you try to trust Me, your Heavenly Father? Once you have known my love, you will want more of my love, and I will give it to you. Yes, ask. To ask means to pray. To pray means to obey. To obey means to receive. And what do you receive? My grace, and grace is my Spirit. You receive the consolation of my Holy Spirit who comes to you in the form of peace, love and joy; and you are comforted in your afflictions whether they be physical, intellectual, or spiritual.

Remember: I never abandon you (John 14:18). I am always here for you. I am as close as a whisper.

9/20/18

I grieve, Lord, for all my sins.

Let Me tell you a story about the negative effects of sin. It not only offends my justice, but it damages your soul. It leaves a mark, an indelible mark on your soul, and it takes many years of reparation to remove it. That is why the Church appends years of indulgences to prayers, devotions, novenas, and the like.

Yet I have mercy on my children for I know they know not what they do (Luke 23:34). The reason I established my Kingdom on earth was to help my children find their way home. My Church is a refuge, a source of grace. The Church is a home away from Home. It is the way to my heart where you find repose.

I formed my Church upon the twelve Apostles because I knew the needs of my people. There you find instruction, receive the Sacraments of life-giving grace to help you walk away from your sins, to amend your lives, to become new creations that hear my voice and obey my will.

Today our lesson is on grieving your sins for then you will be comforted. I promise you will. When you leave behind you the burden of sin with all its heartaches and miseries, you will walk toward the light of grace. Then you will know the truth and the truth will set you free (John 8:32).

You have heard the call of my voice and followed Me. Now the real work of transformation begins. You have tasted the sweetness of my mercy and hunger for more. You shall be satisfied. The more you grieve your sins, the stronger you desire the goodness of the Lord, of my love. You run to Church where you find peace and comfort—it's Home; and you relish my presence in the Tabernacle. My nearness brings tears to your eyes and you are comforted.

Yes, mourn for love's lost time but rejoice that I am always with you, caressing your soul, touching your heart with the nearness of my Spirit.

9/23/18

Live in me, Lord, that I may live in You.

Today I want to speak to you about the second Beatitude: *"Blessed are those who mourn for they shall be comforted"* (Matthew 5:4). It is good to cry for my help, for I alone am the

Healer of your soul (Jeremiah 30:17). Who else can give mercy and forgiveness for sins committed against the justice of God? No one! I am the Redeemer (Isaiah 59:20) of the sins of the world. There is no one greater than your God. I am the Victor over sin and I wash away the stain of sin from your intimate soul that is only visible to Me. I am the ultimate source of grace, and my Holy Spirit dispenses grace to the open and willing spirit who eagerly, trustfully prays and hopes for pardon of its sins.

Yes, my Mother assists all who ask for her help. I placed my life in her hands, so you can trust her with yours. You shall not fear when you do because I have willed her to be a Mother to you (John 19:26-27). And does not a mother care for her children? Does she not rescue them? Kiss their wounded knees when they are hurt? So, will my Mother, if you ask her. Another thing I want you to know about her is this: she is the Mediatrix of all my graces. She is the Treasurer, so to speak.

My Mother is the chief source of my comfort and consolation. You can rely on my word. Make her your friend. You will be grateful to Me for this advice. How to make her your friend? You already know the answer! Pray her Rosary. It is a powerful source of grace because, as you know, you are thinking of Me as you recite the prayers. When you pray the Rosary, you become my Mother's children and then, watch out! She will not only comfort you, but she'll help you to come closer to Me, her Son and her God.

Don't even try to understand how my grace works in a soul. It is a mystery until the time is right and all will be revealed to you. Then the dawn from on high will overshadow you (Luke 1:78), and you will see with new eyes, and understanding will flood your soul like rays of sunlight, and you will be lifted up to the seventh Heaven where my angels gather around Me to sing my praises.

For now, stay on the path of the Beatitudes—lament your sins, rid yourself of all anger and resentments. Trust that I am in you, that I am guiding you because I love you, because I am a loving God and Father to all my children. They are precious to Me. I want them with Me and loyal to Me. It hurts a parent to discipline his child but it is necessary for their well-being. I, too, am a loving disciplinarian. If I did not love you, would I not want you to be all you can be?

Yes, believe in my love for you. I am here always to protect, guide, and to teach you wisdom so you can one day enjoy eternal rest with Me in Paradise where there is no more crying, sickness and death.

9/26/18

Lead me, Lord, and I will follow.

Today we shall speak on the subject of mourning sin in the heart. These are the sins buried deep in the psyche that will be revealed, removed and redeemed by the conviction of faith—the belief in the redemption of all sin by the shedding of my blood on the Cross of Salvation.

In your mind, buried in your psyche, are hidden wounds, incorrect thoughts, resentments and anger that fester and erupt physically in your behavior and also, manifest themselves in your speech. Your entire demeanor and personality are affected by these culprits. We must search them out, bring them into the open, expose them to the light of my grace. Then, knowing the truth of these hindrances and releasing them, you will be set free. Knowing the truth leads to healing, freedom from chains that have bound you and distorted your thoughts, robbed you of the knowledge of who you truly are.

How does one achieve this grace? Yes, to trust in my love for you, knowing that I created you to be happy and through prayer. Pray at all times. There is a prayer specifically asking me to heal the subconscious mind—seek it in the Bible and pray it constantly (Psalm 19:13). Another way to seek healing through prayer is to pray with others. Remember your scripture in Matthew 18:19-20? *"Again, I say to you, if two of you agree on earth about anything for which they are to pray, it shall be granted to them by my heavenly Father. For where two or three are gathered together in my name, there am I in the midst of them."*

There are many ways to uncover who you really are in Me: seek counsel from your Pastor who is well-trained in psychology, join a charismatic prayer group or a contemplative group, or by working among the poor, just to name a few.

Just know and keep foremost in your mind that I am always with you, and I will lead you where to go and what to do. If you ask first, obey promptly and follow in my footsteps, I will lead you to places you've never seen before. There are wonders yet to be seen. Rejoice in my love for you. Feel my love around you. Does it not warm your heart? Do you not sense my presence within you? I am near, whispering in your ear. I never leave you alone. Come, take my hand and I will take you with Me where I am.

11/2/18

I am in awe of your greatness, Lord. You are magnificent!

Let us begin with knowledge of my power to create what I think. I create from nothing. I simply see in the eye of my heart and it is made. I saw the perfect woman in whose holy womb my Son Jesus would be conceived, and she was created: The Blessed Virgin Mary.

Everything I think into existence is beautiful: the trees, flowers, stars that twinkle in the night, the myriads of animal life, and finally, the creation of man and woman who were created perfectly, and in my image (Genesis 1:27). Yes, I designed the human body and breathed my Spirit into it, and it began to live, breathe, move, and think apart from Me. I designed human flesh and blood because it pleased Me to do so. I rejoiced in the work of my hands, and I took pleasure in their company.

But they rebelled against Me; they refused to serve and to obey my command that would have kept them from knowing and experiencing evil (Genesis 3:1-6). Thus, evil came into the world. Their hearts would never again be carefree. They would know the evil of sickness, anger, jealousy, hate, greed—the list goes on.

Imagine for a moment, my frustration: I gave them life and everything they could possibly want, their needs were provided for and they had a place in Paradise by my side forever—no mortgage, rent free. Incredibly, they refused my gifts, my plans for their welfare, not for woe (Jeremiah 29:11-12). What would you have done with such rebellious children? Yes, I sent them away to struggle on their own, to find food and shelter, and to bear children in pain (Genesis 3:16).

Hence, mankind lost their freedom. They made a bad choice. They left Me, but I never left them. I gave them their own Angel to guard them (Matthew 18:10) and to report back to Me. So, I always kept an eye on them. They were never abandoned. I was just a prayer away!

Blessed Virgin Mary on the Second Beatitude

"Blessed are the afflicted. When my Child is given back to me by the priest and placed in my arms, the aged Simeon, enlightened by the Spirit of the Lord, reveals to my soul that his plan is, above all, one of a great suffering: 'Behold, He is here for the fall and rising of many in Israel, a sign of contradiction, that the thoughts of many hearts may be revealed. And for you also, a sword shall pierce your soul' (Lk 2:34-35). As Mother, I am thus associated with Him on the road of affliction."

St. Padre Pio on the Second Beatitude

"When Jesus appeared to me, I was horrified to see two tears streaming down his face. He said, 'Do not think that my agony lasted for three hours. No, I will be in agony until the end of the world on behalf of the souls that have been most blessed by me. How badly they respond to my love! What pains me most is that they add disrespect and unbelief to their indifference.' Jesus is right to complain about our ingratitude!"

St. John Neumann on the Second Beatitude

"My Lord Jesus, behold me defiled by sin. Again, I have stained the holy garment of grace in my soul that your blood has cleansed so often. O Father of mercy, hear my prayer.

Give me a true spirit of penance that through the humble supplication of a contrite heart I may again receive pardon.

Alas, Jesus my God and Savior, I dare not raise my eyes to you. How can I who have so often violated my past resolves presume to ask pardon again? Behold me prostrate before you, O my God. My sinfulness weighs me down.

Cast not off your wretched child or I shall be forever lost. From my heart I grieve for having offended you. O Jesus, grant me a true spirit of penance. My Jesus, have mercy on me."

Chapter Three

Third Beatitude
"Blessed are the meek, for they shall inherit the earth."
Matthew 5:5

5/1/18

Change my heart, Lord. Make it like yours.

St Catherine of Siena is a prime example of the third Beatitude—meekness with might. Many consider a meek person to be a weak person, but far from it. Meekness requires strength of heart. My Son demonstrated meekness all his life. He was the Son of God yet called himself the Son of Man. Jesus did not throw his weight around. He never forced anyone to follow him. He always invited. He could have answered his interrogators but chose to be silent: this takes strength of character.

Meekness is power that Satan cannot endure, that he cannot stand against. A meek person knows who he or she is and stands firm in times of trial, temptation—even in death. The likes of which no man has seen was performed by my Son on the Cross. He had the power to destroy those who condemned and crucified him; instead, he practiced the courage and strength of meekness. He knew who he was and no one could take that away from him.

Meekness is to turn the cheek when insulted or demeaned. Meekness is to stand your ground when intimidated. Recently a child of mine, who is a public figure, demonstrated meekness the night she was excoriated. She could have responded in anger and hate but chose not to sin, instead she stood firm knowing who she is. She cherished herself and so must you.

Take for your standard the virtue of meekness. Lift it up like a banner of who you are in Christ's family. Be imitators of him who stood firm on the Cross of iniquity.

5/16/18

Cast out from my heart, Lord, the darkness of sin.

Today we talk about forgiving one's neighbor. This falls into the Beatitude of meekness. If one wishes to be meek, they cannot be proud and haughty; they must strive for humility. To be meek and gentle of heart, one must not harbor resentment—the opposite of forgiveness and letting go. If you are gentle, comprehending yourself as a sinner, then it follows that you will forgive your neighbor for the same frailty/fault found in yourself. So, to gain the kingdom of Heaven, one must be meek and firm at the same time. One must know that he or she is loved by God, been rescued from spiritual death by Jesus the Christ, and is indwelled by the Holy Spirit (1 Corinthians 6:19-20).

Yes, all the world and its occupants dwell in Me, the one true God, Creator of the universe. I am the driving force. My word commands the seas and rivers to flow. I speak and the clouds move to wherever I send them. My will is achieved by my own power. I command and the sun bows to my will. See the birds and animals bowing to their king, even the chipmunks. I enjoy hearing their joyful chatterings.

I am a gentle, loving, merciful God who knows all things, sees all things, senses all things of the soul and heart of every creature. If I have forgiven all the sins of mankind, surely you can forgive your neighbor. If not, if you struggle with this, seek my power deep in your heart. Ask and grace shall be given to you (Matthew 7:7). One must desire to obey my will and my commands because they mean life for the soul. Do good and be good to yourself. Then you will love your neighbor as yourself.

To sum up: to be meek, one must be strong in virtue, for faith brings hope, and hope brings love, and love produces strength, courage, and well-being that results in meekness. Nothing disturbs meekness. It stands firm, undaunted and inherits the Kingdom.

5/20/18

You are my life, Lord. Mold me in your image.

Today we will speak about gentleness. This is a virtue connected to meekness. One must be gentle when confronted with anger/hate. *"They know not what they do"* (Luke 23:34), I spoke from the Cross. They really do not understand the evil strength of the devil. He is a powerful adversary for those who do not follow Me. Without my grace, they are impotent against the evil one's temptations. They have not the strength to stand firm.

This is where gentleness comes into play. A gentle spirit is not provoked to respond rashly. A gentle spirit remains calm in the face of opposition. It takes stock of options available in the moment. Oftentimes, there is not time to think before responding. The gentle spirit calculates calmly, reflectively, and then proceeds to respond. In other words, gentleness is akin to humbleness where one knows who they are and reacts in the proper way. My grace is sufficient for humility. There is a peace beyond understanding in the heart of a gentle person.

Gentleness is also a tool of discernment. If a heart is agitated, it cannot contemplate calmly. It is too distressed. Hence, the saying, "Count to ten." Restore tranquility to your heart. This is a perfect time for the Serenity Prayer: "Lord God, grant me the serenity to accept the things I cannot change; courage to change the things I can; and the wisdom to know the difference." You cannot change others; you can only change yourself. Only through the grace of God, is this possible.

Stay in my light, and gentleness will be your guide, your barometer. Yes, it keeps your blood pressure under control. There are many good reasons to develop the virtue of gentleness. It leads one to peace, contentment, and meekness of mind and heart. *"Blessed are the meek for they shall inherit the earth"* (Matthew 5:5).

5/29/18

Here I am, Lord. I come to do your will.

Pride is the capital sin that causes the most havoc in the soul of man. We will speak now about the opposite virtue of humility. This virtue is best illustrated by the Blessed Mother. It is one of her many virtues. She knows who she is in Me, her Creator.

Pride overcame Satan and he would not repent which is a destructive feature of pride. They think they are right when in fact they have chosen wrongly. They believe their way is the best and only way to think and act. They are close-minded, impervious to other ways.

This is why I call myself the Way and the Truth and the Life (John 14:6). My Way leads to Truth and Truth leads to Life. I know the best way to holiness. By virtue of my omniscience, I know all and see all. This is why I ask my people to trust Me, to learn my ways and to obey Me. I know best. Pride blinds man's vision. It darkens man's mind; consequently, he cannot decide aright.

How does one rebuke pride? How does one become humble? In three ways, first: ask for knowledge of your Creator's will. "Father, what is your will in this decision I must make?" Second, seek knowledge of who I am for you. "Jesus, why did you die for me? What can I do for you?" Third, knock at my heart through prayer. "Holy Spirit, pour your light into my mind and heart so I may see the right path to follow. Teach me the way to proceed rightly. Give me what I need to die to myself and to live for you."

If you pray in this way, little by little, the mountain of pride will crumble at your feet, and you will walk in freedom with peace in your heart and a song on your lips forever praising the God who loves you.

6/6/18

Flood my heart with light, Lord, so I may see the right path.

I am your Master. I am your King. Every loyal subject bows before its King and Ruler, obeying his every command. This is the attitude my disciples must have to win the prize of glory. And what a great victory it is.

Consider what Christ Jesus did to enter his life of glory. He lowered himself as King of Heaven to become man. Jesus ate and slept on the ground, traveled up and down on foot, picked the lowly of society as his companions, healed the sick and cured the blind without recompense. He loved his disciples, groomed them as leaders of his Kingdom on earth, the Church, and gave his life so they could be filled with his Holy Spirit after he arose from the dead.

Christ's attitude was one of meekness, mercy, unselfishness, humility and obedience. He proved his love by his actions. He shed his blood for his people. He was not a king who sits on a throne and selfishly lives on the sweat of his subjects. He dwells with them. He simulates them to himself. He laughs in them, suffers in them, endures their crosses, even allows himself to be mocked, abused and degraded. All this for love and compassion because he knows his people are helpless without him. He knows what they are made of—he created them.

Think of this: of all the inhabitants on the face of the earth, Christ chose you, my reader. You are created and loved by God who bled and died so he might live in you to bring you out of the darkness into the true light so you might live in him and with him. All he asks for is your love in return. Is it so hard to love a King who gave up his throne so he might share his riches with you?

Be smart, dear ones. Know who he is. Learn what he wants. Bow down before your kind, gentle, humble, loving King and Master and let him save your soul.

8/8/18

Fill me, Lord, and make me whole.

Today we will speak about the meek who will inherit the earth. What does it mean to inherit the earth? I created the earth. Everything grows from the earth. I placed minerals, ore and oil and water in the ground for man to explore, cultivate, and to reap good produce. The land is fertile, rich. When man plants seed in the ground, they grow and multiply; and thus, man is fed and enriched by his land.

On another hand, I created man from the dust of the earth and breathed my Spirit into him and he lived and prospered (Genesis 1:27). So, man once fed and nourished from the work of his hands thrives, grows, matures. So, the meek thrive wherever they are planted and inherit all the riches the land provides. You do not understand?

One who is meek trusts in his Creator to provide for all his needs. He knows that whatever happens to him is his Creator's will and he accepts it. He knows that if he trusts, endures, does not lose faith or hope that all will be given to him. All his needs shall be fulfilled. He will want for nothing; he is that sure of his Creator's love and power. The meek are indomitable, undaunted, fearless. What can mere man do to him when God is his Protector (Romans 8:31)?

So, blessed are the meek for all things will come to him—all virtues: faith, hope and love. He will wait patiently just like the farmer who plants his seeds and waits for them to sprout and grow. He gives the seeds of his soul what it needs to grow in virtue: prayer, good deeds, love to God and neighbor. Slowly, through the grace of God, his soul is cleansed of sin and he is set free to think new thoughts and feel new feelings and becomes My new creation (2 Corinthians 5:17) fit to win the battle of life courageously knowing that his God is by his side. He is never alone.

The meek inherit the earth and much more besides. The Kingdom of God is at hand surrounding him, protecting him, providing for him. He is never again alone or apprehensive. He knows I will never forsake him, that I treasure his love and obedience, and I will reward him greatly in this life and in the next. He will be with Me always.

Meekness is power—strength—courage—victorious!

8/25/18

Give me courage, Lord, to follow your footsteps.

Let us speak today about meekness and truth, decency and modesty. These are important characteristics that all my disciples practice. It takes much love and grace to be meekly strong in these virtues. I say meek because it takes self-control to rein in our tempers, anger, judgments and criticisms. We want to lash out at injustice and cruelty. There are times when our just anger must be acted upon. Take the example when my Son overturned the money-changers' tables in the temple of Jerusalem. His Father's name was being desecrated, and He took action to right the wrong (Mark 12:15). But I expect my followers to use good judgment, kindness, to be meek with courage and strength, to patiently pray and ask for my grace to work in trying situations.

Meekness involves stages of growth in truth, decency and modesty. For instance, take a nobleman of great distinction—can he not exert power over lesser men? Yes, but with meekness, he knows that without Me, he is nothing; so, he reins in his 'rights', does not act with force, and submits to my Holy Will. Knowing the truth sets him free (John 8:32).

Now take decency and modesty—the meek, humble servant knows I am God who loves him and has given him all that he needs and more besides. He is happy and contented to be in his Master's service, so he treats everyone kindly, fairly—yes, decently honoring them as the beloved children of God; and they are modest in that they know they are nothing without my grace; without my permission, they would be lost, helpless, incapable to survive the evil in the world. They modestly, yet gratefully accept their position in the scheme of things—not kicking against the goad, biblically speaking. They hold modest, decent opinions of themselves as well as others. This is truly a meek disciple and he will inherit the earth!

8/26/18

Come, Lord, my heart belongs to You.

The subject for today is meekness. What shall I say? Is it kindness? No. Is it wisdom? Maybe. Is it love? Partially. It is the attitude of sameness: I am no better than others, but I am just as good; I am what I am in God—no more but no less (1 Corinthians 15:10).

Meekness is the third Beatitude with the reward of inheriting the earth. Someone who is confident and sure of who she/he is in Me, wins the approval of others. Without this appealing behavior, one is overlooked as insignificant, lacking promise of success in the eyes of the world.

A meek person stands firm in his beliefs, is sure of where he is going, pushes always forward to reach his goals; and he is undaunted by setbacks—be they health issues or loss of his good name, or jealousy of others, or loss of friendships. No one deters him when he knows he is right and no one hurts his loved ones. A meek person defends and protects his family, home and country. Meekness is not weakness; on the contrary, meekness takes courage and strength to turn the other cheek, to stand your ground, to push forward on your journey.

Would that all my people would have this blessed attitude. It takes faith in Me, trust in my love, surety of my power, conviction of my will, knowledge of who I am—the God above all gods who loves deeply and whose word can be trusted completely. No harm shall come to those who stand firmly on my promises.

So, my beloved people, rejoice in my love for you. Make merry the way to my heart. Take courage. All I have is yours for the asking. Do you not enjoy pleasing your children? Why would I be different? Trust and see the goodness that surrounds you. The sun brightens the day, the moon and stars light the night, air and rain nourish the earth to make fruit and vegetables grow. Is not my Divine Providence enough for you?

Be satisfied with my love, my designs on your life. I have placed my Spirit within you. I will never leave you. Stay close to my heart where it is safe. Do not wander away alone from my safe haven. Stay with Me so I can keep my arms around you. Do not step foot into the enemy's camp. He will mercilessly devour you and rob you of your inheritance.

How do you stay close to Me? Yes, it is simple: stay meek, humble, trust in my love, and pray constantly. I will show the way.

8/30/18

Thank You, Lord, for being here.

Today let us talk on the subject of meekness. It takes courage to walk the walk of meekness. It means putting self aside, to step back and let someone else take the glory or win the prize, whatever the case may be. It takes great love for neighbor to root for his victory, his acclaim. Meekness means to die to self, to give up your own aspirations and work toward the success of a friend, or spouse, or one's own children. Meekness means to step out of your own hopes and dreams and devote your attention to the hopes and dreams of others. It means to be unselfish, undemanding. It means to have compassion for others, to be loyal and generous with your time and affection to whoever it may be.

Let Me tell you a story. There was once a girl who lost both her mother and father. It was during the Second World War. They were Jewish people interred in a concentration camp. They suffered terribly but because they loved their daughter, they gave her their daily ration of food. You see, they wanted her to survive and tell their story to the world. And she did. Those parents were meek, loving and unselfish. Their sacrifice gave life to their daughter. This is the work of meekness in a soul.

Wonders are worked by a meek soul. It is an appealing virtue. The opposite attitude is one of pride. Everyone has seen pride at work in the world. Look at the 'me' generation, all the sex abuse, and worst of all: abortion. Parents are so concerned for themselves, they kill their own flesh and blood. So, you see, a meek person accepts life and all its responsibilities. The meek inherit the earth—meaning they unselfishly, humbly submit to my rule over them. The others revolt, hate, murder. What road do you choose?

O my people, choose life, choose whatever happens to you. Remember my Son's story: He meekly accepted crucifixion and reaped the reward of Resurrection—He was victorious over death. He abolished death once for all. Every man, woman and child were freed from slavery to sin. Because of His act of meekness, light came into the world and Satan was defeated.

O my people, live in the light. Listen to my Son's words. Obey His teachings. You will find peace and happiness.

9/10/18

Mold me, Lord. I want to become like You.

I will because this is my desire for all my children. This is why I taught the Beatitudes. They are steps on the ladder that my disciples take on the upward journey to my heart. They, the Beatitudes, lead to sanctification of the soul, cleanse the heart of the vestiges of sin, and transform sinners into saints. This is my will and hope for all my beloved children, for they are precious to Me. Having said that, let us continue on our study of achieving holiness.

"Blessed are the meek, for they shall inherit the earth" (Matthew 5:5). When I gave my Sermon on the Mount, as Matthew recorded in his Gospel, I was speaking to my beloved Hebrew people, the children of Abraham, Isaac and Jacob. Yes, you heard someone extolling the virtues of my chosen people. I love them very much but when I came to them preaching the Good News of the Kingdom, they rejected Me who chose them in the first place. Nevertheless,

a remnant heard my voice, heeded the call to conversion, and followed Me. These are those to whom I preached the Beatitudes. They listened and were healed. My words touched their heart and penetrated their souls, and they became my disciples.

This is my hope for this book. I am dictating this teaching on the Beatitudes to a willing, receptive servant who meekly and willingly listens to my words and records them. This is the attitude I want everyone to take as their own. To be meek is to listen to my words, take them to heart; if necessary, write them down, study them, let them move deeply into your psyche, and you will find a treasure of grace that will fill your life with peace, love and joy and you will be renewed—molded into my image. Then the lamb will befriend the lion (Isaiah 11:6), hate will be swallowed up by love, brothers will cherish their brothers, and there will be peace in the hearts of mankind, and the face of the earth will be renewed.

O my people, listen to Me, the Creator of the moon and stars. If you heed my words, I will come to you once again and take you with Me into the new heavens and new earth (Revelation 21:1). Listen to my voice that comes to you as a whisper deep in your heart. You must listen quietly or you will miss your visitation. Humility and meekness opens the heart in welcome to its Savior and Lord.

9/13/18

I love You, Lord, with all my heart.

Today we will speak on the third Beatitude: *"Blessed are the meek of heart, for they shall inherit the earth"* (Matthew 5:5).

It takes meekness to sit still and listen to your God. Meekness is a treasure of love and grace, for meekness leads to sanctity.

The meek, gentle heart is filled with compassion for others; it senses the needs of others; it can read hearts and instinctively responds in mercy when they see suffering or injury done to others. Yes, caregivers, nurses, doctors are good examples of meek souls with merciful hearts. They have learned to put aside their own cares for the care of others.

Let Me give you an example. There was a kind, old doctor in a little town who drove in his car in the middle of the night to deliver a baby. Even though he was exhausted, he did not dwell on his need for rest, but with a heart filled with the joy of ushering a new life into the world, he fulfilled his work. This humble, selfless doctor delivered Thomas Alva Edison on that dark, dreary night, bringing into the world one of the greatest inventors. Thomas Edison ushered light into the world—just as my Son did.

So, you see how meekness can provide light in others' lives? This is one of the eight Beatitudes that works greatness in the soul, for it banishes the darkness, the destructive forces of the sin of pride. Pride kills the soul, destroys any hope of peace in the soul of man and in the world.

Listen to your heart. Is it peaceful or angry? Is it calm or restless? Many suffer heart attacks, even die because they are robbed of their gift of peace by the sin of pride. Be aware, my people, of how you think. You are as you think (Proverbs 23:7). Practice the virtues of kindness, gentleness with yourself and others. Rely not on your own understanding (Proverbs 3:5). Seek my will in all you do. My

Holy Spirit will guide you to peace and meekness of soul, mind and heart.

So, you see, the Beatitude of meekness gives life—extended life.

9/14/18

Open my eyes, Lord, to see your face.

I will, for this is what I want for all my people. This is why I came down to earth, took on human flesh, grew in wisdom and stature (Luke 2:52), united myself with my Father in prayer (Luke 6:12), proclaimed and established my Kingdom on earth, died on the Cross to pay the debt owed to God, my Father and yours.

This I did for the purpose of your sanctification. My blood cleansed you from sin. My Resurrection released the power of the Holy Spirit who comes to you in the waters of Baptism, Confirmation and through Holy Communion, and all the rest of the Sacraments that I invested in the Catholic Church. There are multiple ways to gain grace.

Do you see the process of sanctification? I give, you receive. It is my work to provide the means, to make grace plentiful and available, but you must accept it, receive it into your heart, mind, soul and spirit. I will open your eyes as I did long ago to the blind man in the Gospel (Matthew 20:29), and I will continue to give sight to many, especially to those who are blinded by hatred. Their vision is distorted by sin in their hearts. They see but don't see, for they are focused on the subject of their hate.

To see my face, my light, and all the love I would lavish on them, they must seek to humble themselves before Me, the God who holds their life in my hands. When they turn to Me, repent their sins, seek my will, and change their ways, I will open their eyes to see my face. For this to happen, they must resolve to put sin behind them, to walk in my light, to obey my commandments. These are the first steps to holiness. But do you see how the Beatitude of meekness plays into this?

Tomorrow, we will continue speaking about the process of sanctification

9/15/18

Tell me what to do, Lord, and I will do it.

That is what meekness is all about—putting aside your own will to do mine. Meekness is to seek my will over yours because you know that I know best. Yes, I want you to be precise in your words, writings, conversations, and in all your affairs. I have given you a well-trained mind (Isaiah 50:4) to know and understand why I created you: to know, love and serve Me, and to enjoy eternal life in Heaven with Me.

And one of the ways is by way of the Beatitudes. Know them and you will know Me, and in knowing Me, you will come to know thyself. So, you see why it is important to adapt the Beatitudes into your life? They will lead you straight into my heart where you will find a treasure of love, peace and joy. Take on the attitudes of the Beatitudes and you will become like Me. Then all things will work for the good (Romans 8:28).

Those who are meek in demeanor are strong in virtue, and virtue molds behavior, and then one is on the road leading to sanctity. Meekness is sister to holiness. Putting thyself aside when others are needy: this is meekness because it takes self-control, a merciful heart and a compassionate spirit to lay down one's life for another. Yes, in doing so, you imitate my Son Jesus, the Christ, and there is no one more holy and perfect.

Your upward journey requires taking on the mind of Christ—to imitate Him, to obey Him, to listen to Him, to spend time with Him like a friend. Think of ways to be with Him. He is very accessible. Just whisper my name and I'll be there. Then one day, I will take you by the hand and take you where I am, where you belong, safe in the shelter of my wings (Psalm 91:4). There you will find all that you've hoped for.

O my people, put yourselves in my hands, and I will lead you to places you've never known or even imagined. I will lift your spirit and you will see the glory of the Lord. Trust my Spirit to guide you, heal you, mold you and to fill your heart with my love, courage and strength.

Holiness is just one more step on the journey leading you home.

10/11/18

Incline my heart, Lord, according to your holy will.

Today I will speak to you about self-control, an attribute of meekness, and one of the fruits of the Holy Spirit. This is a quality ingrained in the soul of Saint Catherine of Siena. This virtue helped her to cope with forces in her life that were against everything she understood that was good and kind. She fought against evil forces: anything and everything that she knew was not my will for her and her world.

Self-control is needed when faced with the voices of opposition. The tendency is to respond in anger to defend the right. But in drawing on anger to rectify the wrong, causes you to lose your peace, become confused, and confusion leads to muddled thinking. In that situation or state of mind, rational thinking has disappeared.

Instead, if you maintain an attitude of self-control, the blood pressure lowers and consequently, the mind is cleared and rational thinking comes into play. From then on, peace is restored in the mind and heart and my grace and wisdom are released, ready to solve the problem or change the pre-determined course of action. Yes, you are free to think new thoughts and take new actions, to find a better solution.

In short, self-control leads to sound reasoning and right behavior. In this, you give your Father in Heaven glory and honor and my heart expands with delight in my child's wisdom, so much so that I shower you with special graces. For when you show a little faith, hope and love, I give you more.

Self-control commands the day. It opens doors that are closed, builds up trust in my power to change the hearts of your opponents. Self-control is a matter of restraining unruly passions that cloud the mind, that tend to lead one into sin.

Seek my power over weakness. In Me, you are strong (Philippians 4:13).

10/16/18

Instruct my heart, Lord, to fear your name.

Today our subject is meekness of heart, soul and spirit. There is a difference. Let Me explain: meekness of heart consists in total abandonment to my will. Meekness of soul is to submit to my instructions, and meekness of spirit means to move with the Holy Spirit.

Yes, the first condition honors God, the Father; the second is to live together with Me, God the Son; and as already mentioned, your spirit is captivated and dedicated to the workings of the Holy Spirit. In other words, you are completely infused with your Triune God. You have one mind, one heart, one soul—you are totally Mine. You move and live in obedience to my will. You rejoice in my power over you. You look for ways to please Me. Like Saint Teresa of Calcutta said, "Let us do something beautiful for God."

In this stage, the soul earns merit by living in the light of Christ. The soul longs for her Redeemer; she has lost any fear or hesitation to follow my plans for her salvation. She trusts my words to her and obeys willingly, joyfully, for she knows who I am and the power I have over her, and in the world around her. She has seen with her own eyes the transformation my grace has worked in her soul and in others around her, and even in the world. She is amazed, grateful, and relieved to let go and let God.

In this stage of abandonment, I can move the soul easily. The soul is open to inspiration and guidance. I send my holy angels to protect her and take her where she should go. My angels watch over her lest she dash her foot against a stone (Psalm 91:12). My angels keep watch over her in the night whispering to her soul the words of love I have for her. Yes, this is why the Angel Prayer is said before retiring for the night.

> Angel of God, my guardian dear,
> to whom God's love commits thee here.
> Ever this day be at my side
> to light and guard, to rule and guide.
> If I should die before I wake,
> I pray the Lord my soul to take.

Remember what you were taught: I have assigned an angel to each one of my children (Matthew 18:10). They love and protect you, and report your progress to Me.

My power is infinite, immeasurable, incomprehensible. It can scrutinize the inner depths of your being. Yes, I count every hair on your head (Luke 12:7). Trust that I keep you in the palm of my hand (Isaiah 49:16). Trust my desire to save you, to teach you, to elevate you to sainthood. You should be holy as I am holy (Matthew 5:48). Remember the formula for **Trust**: **T**otal **R**eliance **U**pon **S**piritual **T**ruth.

And the truth is that I love you so much that I died for you!

10/17/18

You are my hope and strength, Lord. May I never despair.

Today let us talk about what it takes to be meek of heart. Of course, it begins with a solid working relationship with my Son, the Lord Jesus Christ. You must journey with him on a daily basis. How can you know the heart of a friend if you don't converse with him or spend time with him? So, it is with Jesus. Talk to him. Tell him your concerns and your desires and dreams.

Dreams can reveal aspects of your nature that you never suspected. Record your dreams, pray over them. The people who appear in your dreams are significant for your healing. Something about them is true for you. It may be a fault in them or on the other hand, it may be a good quality that you also have. Pray, also, for the revelation of the dream so you may understand its meaning. There are many roads of healing available to you.

Now I will address despair. It means to be hopeless, to give up hope. I am the Hope of the World (Matthew 12:21)! If you walk with Me daily, holding my hand securely, if you have faith in my love and power over you, despair will never knock at your door! I promise.

Those who are meek and humble of heart are courageous, hopeful, faithful, and trust their God's Word! I will never abandon you or leave you orphaned (John 14:18). I am a God of my Word.

Walk in my footsteps; they will take you places you've never before traveled. You will see wonders never before experienced. Life is a beautiful thing when journeyed with your King. And I am the suffering King who gave up his throne just to be your Savior.

Would I ever leave you when I have invested myself in you? No, never will I leave you alone, deserted, storm-tossed, lost. My heart cries out for your safety. You must believe my promises in the Bible. They are written there just for you, for your salvation, for your hope and strength so you might not despair.

Take up and read! Your eyes will be opened to the Truth. Your heart will be changed forever. You will see my power working in your soul, transforming you into something so beautiful that you will be amazed at my power—the power of grace, holy grace, the gift of my heart. Faith grows slowly, just as my Son said in the Gospel of Luke. The kingdom grows as yeast in the dough (Matthew 13:33); slowly and surely it takes root in your heart. As you water it with prayer, your faith grows. One day, you will be amazed, grateful, and you will return my love to Me with all your heart—ready to do my will.

10/19/18

Take my heart, Lord, and make it like yours.

Today's lesson will be on the humble heart. It is my desire that all my children shall come to Me for I am meek and gentle of heart (Matthew 11:29). Medical experts have discovered the connection between anxiety, stress, mental anguish and cardiac arrest. As a man thinks, so he is. If you are agitated, you have lost your peace and your blood pressure rises.

I created man to be kind, gentle and loving—not angry and hateful. Murderous thoughts lead to heart attacks. This is not my will, I created man's heart to be peaceful, relaxed and as one with mine. The heart and spirit of a man needs to rest in his Creator—trusting Me at all times to guide and protect him under my wings (Psalm 91:4).

It is up to the individual to seek to know his Creator's plan for his life and follow it. There are some who do and they lead tranquil lives. Many do not know who they are; they do not know who I am for them, and they struggle unassisted by my grace.

There are two choices open to mankind: Are you with Me or against Me? As I have said, the choice is yours because I have endowed every human being with a free will. I do everything in my power to entice them, but they must choose and ask to have a relationship with Me which I would gladly grant to them for I love my people; I want them with Me, not against Me.

So, give Me your hearts. Trust Me to mold them in my image. I could make you little 'gods' like unto your Heavenly Father who dotes on you, who looks on you with tender love and mercy. I have a big heart with which to envelope all my little ones and hold them close to Me. I take them into my arms and smother them with my love. If they come to Me, I would raise them up to Sainthood and they will be my closest friends. They will see my Face and rejoice all their days.

Yes, in Heaven there are no nights. The Light of Christ shines forever.

10/31/18

Remain with me, Lord, lest I perish.

Today's lesson is on openness to my will and humility. These virtues make it easy for Me to have my way in your heart. I ask this willingness of heart from all my children. In essence, they are telling Me, "Have your way in my heart, Lord, lest I perish. I need you more and more, Lord Jesus, to mold my inner self the way you want me to be. I rejoice in your reign over my life and my soul, for I know that you only want good for me. You want me to live forever with you in a state of holiness. And I want this, too, my Lord and my God. Please have your perfect way in my heart. Mold me into your image. I gladly accept all you have for me. I cherish your grace and mercy and holy will."

When my children speak that way to Me, I pour out an avalanche of grace into their hearts. I take over their will, and they obey Me. This is the ultimate form of humility when they trust Me with their very life.

My hope and plan, the desire of my heart is that all my people would abandon themselves into my hands! Then I would quickly restore my Kingdom in their hearts. The enemy would be vanquished; there would be peace on earth and good will among all men. I would return and walk among you; there would be joy and laughter and abundance of rich food and good wine to warm the hearts of men.

Ah, how beautiful is peace in the world! This is what I desire first and foremost, that my children would love Me with all their heart, soul and strength, and their neighbor as themselves (Mark 12:30). This would hasten my return. Yet, sadly, it is not so. Men choose to hate and slander good men; they hunger for power over their fellow man, seeking riches that they will never enjoy because their hearts are bereft of peace. They know not what they do—tragically. This is why I devised a way to save my blind, willful, stubborn, hard-hearted people.

Yes, I am a merciful, compassionate God who cares for his children. I already laid down my life and shed my blood to save them. Now I need to do it again and again in my disciples who open their hearts to my grace, and who will humble themselves to serve Me in whatever way I ask. Will you say, "Yes, Lord, I come to do your will."? Or will you make an excuse to refuse my invitation (Luke 14:18)?

Now you are asking, "What is it, Lord, that you want from me? Am I able to do it?" Yes, I never ask more from you that I am more than capable of giving to you. I supply whatever you need for every service you perform (Philippians 4:19). Never fear that I will not be there to hold you up; I will! I make it possible for you to succeed. I prosper the work of your hands. (Psalm 90:17). Trust is what is needed—not doubt. Have faith in Me (John 14:1). I will do it in you. I never leave you (John 14:18).

9/18/18

Teach me, Lord, the way of perfection.

Today our lesson is on meekness, the third Beatitude. Let us review what I have previously said on this virtue. Yes, virtues need to be practiced until they become a habit. Meekness leads to trust and trust leads to sanctity. Meekness is the courage to turn the other cheek (Matthew 5:39), to stand firm on your convictions. Meekness develops mental and emotional strengths, but there is another side of meekness and humility I want to stress in today's lesson: holiness as a way of life.

To be holy requires a plan of action. Let Me give you an acrostic for **Action**: **A**doration; **C**ontrition; **T**rust; **I**mitation; **O**ne-minded; **N**ew behavior. Follow these steps daily and you will become holy, humble, perfect. Now let us take them step by step.

Adoration: This can be done all day long when you offer the day to Me, your loving Father, and think of Me now and then as you work and fulfill your daily duties. A better way, when time permits, come and visit Me in the tabernacle in Church; daily Mass is ideal.

Contrition: Yes, be sorry for the wrong you have done and confess your sins. It is good for your soul to release pent-up anger and resentments.

Trust: Trust, of course, is Total Reliance Under Stressful Trials. This comes easy to a truly meek person, for they are habitually patient when injured.

Imitation: A dedicated person imitates, follows his mentor's ways. So, I ask you, invite you to walk in the footsteps of my Son Jesus the Christ. Do not think it is impossible, remember that nothing is impossible with God (Luke 1:37). These are my words and I fulfill what I say. Here's where trust comes in. Just decide to follow and I will provide the grace needed. You alone can make up your mind who to imitate—the decision is yours. But, if you truly want to learn the way of perfection, you must sell all you have and follow Me (Luke 18:22).

One-minded: You must have one purpose in mind and do all you can to achieve your goal. Keep in mind, when you seek God with all your heart, all things will be granted to you. So, you see, be one-minded, single-hearted, focused on achieving holiness and I will do it for you. Just relax and see my power at work within you.

This takes us to your New Behavior. You have become a new creation (2 Corinthians 5:17) with an adoring, appreciative attitude toward your Father in Heaven who lavishes his grace upon you. You have confessed with a contrite heart and released all anger, resentment, hate—all those things that weigh you down. So, now the burden is removed and you

84

sense more peace. You have learned to lift up all your troubles to Me, knowing that I alone can make things right. You have learned not to rely on your own judgment but on mine.

At this point, you have a new, brighter, more relaxed air about yourself because in imitating Jesus, you have found inner strength, more courage, and less fear—hence, you are more confident and grateful for the life I have given you. Now you are more one-minded, determined and focused on your upward journey to holiness. You open your heart to receive all that I have for you because you know I am good, loving, kind, trustworthy and generous.

Now we have traveled the road of meekness leading to a new way of life which, in turn, leads to perfection. *"You must be perfect as my Father in Heaven is perfect"* (Matthew 5:48).

Blessed Virgin Mary on the Third Beatitude

"Blessed are the meek. Contemplate in this Child of mine the reflection of meekness and goodness. His hands are opened as a divine caress upon every human suffering; his eyes cause light to shine down upon every shadow of sin and evil; his feet are formed in order to journey along barren and insecure roads to seek out those far away, to find the straying, to help those in need, to heal the sick, to welcome back sinners, to give hope and salvation to all. His Heart beats with throbs of divine love to fashion the hearts of all in meekness and compassion."

St. Padre Pio on the Third Beatitude

"You need to keep yourself far away from three things. First, keep yourself from ever quarreling or being in strife with anybody. Second, keep yourself from vainglory or self-conceit. Third, never put your welfare ahead of that of others. These break the bond of love that should always unite Christians."

St. Catherine of Siena on the Third Beatitude

"Make two homes for thyself, my daughter," she wrote to Alessia Saracini, "one actual home in thy cell . . . and another spiritual home which thou art to carry with thee always—the cell of true self-knowledge where thou shalt find within thyself knowledge of the goodness of God."

The author goes on to say that "Catherine discovered the basic principles of contemplative prayer: the cell of self-knowledge. This cell is the starting place for all spiritual growth because within it the soul finds knowledge of God and knowledge of herself. Knowledge of God leads the soul to love God, to seek him, to obey him. Knowledge of self leads the soul to be humble, to know her own sin and to hate it. The soul who has knowledge of both herself and God can embark on the great spiritual journey, growing in imitation of God and in time becoming "one thing with God."

Chapter Four

Fourth Beatitude
"Blessed are those who hunger and thirst for righteousness, for they shall be satisfied."
Matthew 5:6

5/11/18

Lead me, Lord, to walk in your ways.

We will begin today with the attitude of hungering and thirsting for righteousness. This Beatitude was taught by my Son Jesus to explain what it means to hunger and thirst for my grace to uphold you in the midst of your problems, in times of testing, and to increase your knowledge of my will—not just for yourself, but also my will for the world.

The psychiatrists say, "Know thyself." I say, "Know your God and all will be made known to you." I am all that a soul needs to gain peace of mind, serenity amid chaos, and to achieve everlasting life with Me in Paradise. Yes, I promise eternal joy to those of my people who obey my commandments, are baptized into the life of Christ, and follow the leadings of the Holy Spirit.

One must know the Truth of the world, uncover the dictates of the New Covenant made by the death of Christ Jesus on a cruel Cross and know and hunger to be right with Me, the Creator of the world. To do this is to achieve salvation of the soul. Find the purpose of life in the study of my Word in the Bible and in the writings of the Saints, especially my Popes, the Vicars of Christ on earth. Seek to know the wonders of creation. In this you find yourself.

When one knows their need for Me, for my help and providential care and guidance, everything falls in place and the horizons of the heart and mind expand. Seek Me and you will find me tucked away in your heart.

Love surrounds you. Love exalts you. Love transforms you, and thus you become righteous.

5/25/18

I want what You want, Lord. Let it be.

Tell my people that I want them to love Me, to hunger and thirst for the righteousness my Son sacrificed his life to give them. My Son obeyed my will gladly, fully, and joyfully. He agreed with Me that this would be for the salvation of all the world. The three of us, Father, Son and Holy Spirit, agreed on this plan of action. Jesus would leave my side, be conceived by the power of the Holy Spirit, become man, shed his blood in atonement for all the transgressions of every man, woman, and child born throughout the ages.

Righteousness means to be made right with your God who created you. Righteousness includes repentance and reconciliation. Repentance is to mourn one's sins and to turn to God. Reconciliation is to be accepted by Me, forgiven for mistakes and willful disobedience, in order to live in my good graces.

Righteousness is a great gift freely given to those who hunger and thirst for it. This means to seek my will above your own, to die to yourself and follow in the footsteps of my Son Jesus. He is the Light of the World (John 8:12), the Way and Truth and Life (John 14:6). I might add, He is the Joy of the world.

To be righteous is to be joyful, contented, at peace with oneself, God, and the world. Seek to know the Truth—it is life for one's soul. It is a gift bought and given to you by the Blood of Christ. It is a gift to one who believes, asks, and seeks for it (Luke 11:9). I gladly offer it to the world.

6/2/18

Guard my steps, Lord. I trust in You.

Today we speak of those who hunger and thirst for righteousness. They shall be satisfied because they are seeking their God, their Creator who formed them in their mother's womb, who created them in my own image (Genesis 1:27). I gave them an eternal soul to live in my light, to know Me and love Me with all their heart, as I love them with all mine. My people are precious to Me. I created them to be my sons and daughters—a family. I put my Spirit into them with the breath of my mouth and they came to life. I nurtured them as a Father, held them to my cheek and taught them to walk (Hosea 11:3). Yes, every human being came from my desire, my will. I placed my Spirit in them to draw them close to Me. Just like the Parable of the Seed (Matthew 13:18), some responded fully to my call and produced good fruit to last for eternity. These shall be satisfied to be my children and hungry to do my will.

I grieve for my lost children who do not know Me nor love Me because they are deceived by wrong teaching or by the bad examples of bad parents. They make wrong judgments; hence they remain in the dark, dissatisfied with their lot in life. What to do? I sent my Son Jesus to save them (John 3:16). He redeemed them for Me. He gladly suffered and laid down his life so they might live.

What kind of love is this? It is divine, infinite love. Great enough to make up for all the sins committed and yet to be committed. It is everlasting love, freely given to those who hunger and thirst for it. I am a merciful Father, good and caring, providentially caring for my children, providing all the grace necessary for their salvation.

Bring your children before Me (Matthew 19:14) so I may bless them, touch their hearts, heal their wounds, correct their false beliefs that they, too, may know the goodness of their Creator and come to know the joy of heaven here on earth and in the next.

6/4/18

Open my ears, Lord. Help me to hear your voice.

Let us begin with the joy in my heart for what I have accomplished in the soul who prays, obeys, and listens to my word. I can do great things when my children are docile and obedient. It takes trust in their God to be open to hear my word. This is a grace I bestow on one who loves Me, who has yearned for righteousness to the fullest degree.

I am the source of all holiness. I shower down grace constantly, as steady as the sun stands in the sky. My grace is all one needs to achieve perfection. Think of Saint Rita de Cascia, a humble, obedient wife and mother who put aside a higher calling to a cloistered life in obedience to her parents' will, and who chose that her sons should die rather than lose their souls. Her trust was so great that she knew they were safe in Heaven with her God. Imitate her unconditional obedience, her willing obedience. And think of my Son's obedience and love for Me that he willingly suffered crucifixion. Yes, love is mind-changing. Love commands the heart to be brave, noble. Love eagerly seeks to fulfill God's will. Love does all things good, gentle, kind, unselfishly. Love for God creates Saints.

One more thing I have to say today: hunger for righteousness. You will find love and peace of mind, and your heart will be malleable in my will. I can do great things in an open, docile heart and spirit. My Spirit will mold a willing spirit into something great and wonderful that will give Me due honor and glory for all ages.

Think of the Saints before you. They were ordinary, everyday people who opened their hearts to welcome and receive my grace, light, love; but their obedience won them crowns of righteousness. To hunger and thirst for righteousness leads to Sainthood.

6/14/18

You are my strength, Lord, and my courage.

We begin today with the fourth Beatitude: *"Blessed are those who hunger and thirst for righteousness for they shall be satisfied"* (Matthew 5:6). To hunger is to thirst for something great and wonderful. Study Saint Bonaventure's book: *The Soul's Journey into God.* There he describes who I am for you. I am the only good in life (Luke 18:19). I am the all-knowing God who exists now, then, and forever. Everything is mine, so you belong to Me. Saint Augustine said it very well. "My soul is restless until it rests in you."

For eternal peace, long for your God who loves you. Hunger to be alone with Me. Thirst for knowledge of my will for you personally. I created you with special thought. It did not happen on a whim that you are what you are. I thought of you. I chose you to live at this time. It was not an accident that you are as tall as you are or as small. I determined and sculpted your features and made your soul in my image (Genesis 1:26). I place the desires in your heart (Psalm 37:4). I call you by name (Isaiah 43:1). You belong to Me. You are my own special possession, and I have plans to make you great (Jeremiah 29:11).

Hunger for my Word. Thirst to obey my will. It is spelled out for you in the commands I gave to Moses (Deuteronomy 5:6). Hunger and thirst for Me. I am God and place no god before Me (Deuteronomy 5:7). You know in your heart that I am only Good, and I died on the Cross to prove my love. You are my child. Come back to Me with all your heart (Hosea 6:1), and I will give you the graces of my heart. You will be contented to live in my light. Hunger and thirst to obey Me. Eagerly worship Me on the Lord's day.

Do not hate Me by hating your brother. What you do to my people, you do to Me (Matthew 25:40), your only good. In Me, you will find peace, love and joy. Your conscience will be free of evil thoughts that cause many ailments. Peace of mind leads to health. What you think determines how you feel. Think good thoughts, happy thoughts, holy thoughts, loving thoughts, and you will think like Me.

7/10/18

I am ready, Lord, to do your will.

Today our subject is the fourth Beatitude: *"Blessed are they who hunger and thirst for righteousness, for they will be satisfied"* (Matthew 5:6). Once a soul reaches this stage they have reached the status of purification from all their sins. Let us look back on what has taken place. They have been called, anointed, have repented and recognized their need for mercy. They know who they are in Christ Jesus. They know their need for their Father's love and they rejoice in their personal walk with God. They have come to know their spiritual poverty, the first Beatitude; and they hunger to know their Creator. They have mourned, regretted and reputed their past sins and have resolved to sin no more because they love their God intensely.

Next, they have submitted to my will for their lives; they have accepted what I ask them to do—not once, but always. In all things, they refer to my judgment. They seek my advice and do not move until they have prayed and sought my guidance. You see, they have already reached the fourth step: they are hungering to know my will and thirsting to hear my word. They trust I am always with them and for them. They trust my love is all they need, and they pray for more and more love to overwhelm their sinful self—more love to consume them until they are perfected in love and obedient to my commands. They long to be right in my sight, thirst to be right in my light, and hunger to hear my voice.

At this stage, my Spirit has found a docile heart to mold and inspire and use for my glory and purpose. In their meekness, I am powerful. They have heard my word and understand my will for them. The world has opened up to new, yet old realities. They discover new ways to serve Me, their one true God and Savior.

The day is brighter. Their hearts sing a song of love. Their spirit rejoices in God, their Savior and Lord. They rejoice and celebrate their fresh, renewed faith in my power. They know that they know they belong to Me and rest in this knowledge. They have grown to trust that I will never forsake them, that I will be with them and for them for eternity.

7/11/18

Love me, Lord, so I may love You more.

Those who seek Me always find Me. You know the parable of the lost coin (Luke 15:8). It was very valuable to the woman who lost it. She searched high and low for it and then rejoiced greatly when she found it. So, it is with Me. My children are precious to Me. I search and search for their love and obedience, and when they seek Me with all their heart, I rejoice and smother them with my love and graces galore.

So, it is with those who seek Me, their only treasure, their only good. I alone can fill that empty place in their hearts. They understand that I created them with a longing in their hearts to know Me, love Me, and serve Me. As I said, I am their only good; and to seek Me is to find Me (Matthew 7:7). To find Me is the greatest joy in human life. It is the search of a lifetime of peace, love and joy. Only I can satisfy the hungry heart. I alone can fulfill the dreams in their hearts. I have it in my power to fulfill every desire. I shape hearts and place desires in hungry hearts. All they must do is respond to that desire. How? With all the grace that I supply. When I touch a heart, I give it what it needs.

They must stop and consider what this means. After all, I do not want robots for disciples. I want hungry, thirsty, longing hearts to do my bidding. I want hearts that are kind and gentle and loving. I want them to want Me. Yes, I need them to love Me, how else can I satisfy them?

So, this is why the fourth Beatitude is an important one. When they hunger for my love, I rejoice just like the woman who found her lost coin. I am the Father of the Prodigal Son—the story my Son told his disciples (Luke 15:11). I celebrate in Heaven with all my Angels every time one of my children thirst for Me. It brings tears to my eyes and comfort and delight to my heart because I will move quickly to shape their minds and hearts according to my will. My plan can then go forward for their sanctification and ultimate union with Me, their Triune God.

8/21/18

Train my heart, Lord, to seek the light.

Today we speak about those who hunger and thirst to be right with Me, the Father of all goodness. When they come to Me, I fill them with my light and they are satisfied—they are filled to overflowing. Their joy brims over onto those around them.

Those who hunger for my grace walk in my light and crooked roads become straight. Life is beautiful, all they see is goodness. They understand that my way is the way of holiness. They thirst for knowledge of their God in Heaven. They seek to know my will and follow my laws impeccably. Nothing is too much or too difficult for them to do. They become pillars of strength and achieve victory over their sins. Why? Because they hunger for serenity in mind and heart and with others, and they seek to find ways to please

Me and to obey Me for they have learned that I am their only good (Luke 18:19).

Where I am there is mercy and kindness. In seeking my righteousness, they are seeking for the pearl of great price (Mt 13:46), and they expend all their energy to find it—and they will succeed because I will it. I am here for those who long for Me. My grace is sufficient for every man, woman and child (2 Corinthians 12:9). It is an endless fountain of life—the source of all that is good and they know it, for they have tasted the goodness of the Lord (Psalm 34:8). They know my love for them is real and holy and they hunger to find ways to satisfy their hungry hearts. They follow the Light and they never stop yearning for my justice.

Those who hunger and thirst for righteousness find the way of perfection. The goal is always before them, leading them on to victory over selfishness, pride, vanity—anything that hinders them or thwarts their desire to be perfect in the Father's eyes. No obstacle is too high in the search for their goal. They train as athletes to win the golden crown. Their hunger drives them to exert will-power and self-control to the utmost, knowing that in the end only by the power and will of God and his sanctifying grace do they achieve the prize of righteousness with their holy God.

Only Jesus Christ is the Victor over sin and death. Only in and with the Lord Jesus Christ, does one overcome all unrighteousness. Only through the grace of God does one see the Light on the path. Only with Jesus Christ does one become worthy to stand before God. Those who seek God, humble themselves before his greatness and wait for his perfect will to work its transforming power in their mind, heart and soul.

Only in God's hands does the world turn toward the Light. Only then—only in his time and grace.

8/23/18

Come, Lord Jesus, fill me with your light.

Today our subject is hungering for righteousness, the fourth attitude a disciple of mine shall develop in his ascent up the mountain. It takes much prayer, trust and hope to make the upward journey into holiness. It can be done. Many of the saints have achieved it. It does not take great intelligence or effort because I have given you the Holy Spirit of truth and wisdom to accompany you on the way. Trust is needed, determination and persistence. These are gained through prayer.

Prayers accomplish all things because I am a merciful God and enjoy pouring out sanctifying grace upon my people. The first letter in the word **Prayers** is P. This stands for **P**atience, one of the fruits of the Holy Spirit listed in Saint Paul's Letter to the Galatians (Galatians 5:22). The second letter is **R** which stands for **R**osary, the special prayer of my holy Mother who is my Masterpiece. She delights in teaching my children how to be good followers and devoted disciples. Her Rosary is a special means to gain wisdom and purity of heart. **A** is for **A**doration, another quality my Mother teaches her devotees. She leads all of them to Me, her Son. **Y**, the next letter, implies a condition of the heart which follows adoration. It is the **Y**earning, hungering and thirsting of the fourth Beatitude. Yearning to know, love and serve Me, your Triune God, your only one, true God who loves his children and desires only good for them. Did I not say to my prophet Jeremiah that my plan for your life is for

97

good not woe (Jeremiah 29:11)? How is it possible that where love exists there could exist anything other than goodness? Yes, I am only good to my people. Whatever I permit to happen is meant for their welfare, for their salvation. Always keep this in mind: my cruel death on the Cross was not good, but what we accomplished by it was very good. We accomplished salvation from sin and death for all my people—no exception!

But let us get back to the acrostic for the word Prayers. The next letter is **E** for **E**ffort. Any good thing is worth the effort. When you are too tired to pray, do it anyway. When busyness takes up your time, find a few moments to lift up your heart to your Lord and I will multiply the time. Trust Me. Try it. The next letter is **R** for **R**ecreation. Have you ever considered that I would enjoy relaxing and having fun with you? Am I not an emotional God? I cry over my people, over their pains and struggles. My Mother grieves for my lost children. Why would I not enjoy my children's achievements? I reward good, kind, loving behavior. I enjoy making my children happy. But let us go on. The last letter is **S** for **S**ervice. The hungry, thirsty heart looks for ways to serve her God in his people. It can be a simple prayer for a sinner's conversion, or something greater like sacrificing your time to help a neighbor. There are multiple ways of serving Me.

Just keep in mind that when you have this attitude of hungering for righteousness, I am there in you supplying all the grace you need. Am I not a generous God? All you have to do is pray!

8/24/18

Cleanse me, Lord, so I may obey You perfectly.

Today we speak about grace, my sanctifying grace—the grace needed to make the upward journey to holiness, and to satisfy and fortify those who hunger and thirst for holiness.

Grace is the gift for righteous living. So, how does one live in a state of grace? First of all, they must love Me, their Father in Heaven, so deeply that they would never offend Me again. Second, they will be determined to obey my life-giving commandments handed on to them by Moses, my servant (Deuteronomy 5:6). Third, they will admonish themselves carefully and gently which means they forgive themselves for their sinfulness, retire into themselves and offer up to Me the wounds caused by sinful behavior. Fourth, they amend their mistakes/sins against others— either through prayer or by confrontation. This must be done kindly and gently. It takes great courage to admit one's sins to another, especially to the injured party; but that's where my grace goes into action. It is called actual grace.

Actual grace strengthens and empowers the sinner to walk away from sin. It gives them courage to amend their mistakes. It gives them wisdom to change their lives, to put aside false beliefs. It gives them knowledge to know themselves and by knowing themselves, they come to know their need for a Savior. Grace is the deciding factor between victory and defeat. Without their Savior, they are lost, helpless.

They need my grace which is always available to them. You already know the many ways to receive grace. It's as easy as speaking: you just need to ask (Matthew 7:7), and my grace is yours—and for the keeping. I do not take back what I give.

On another note, my Son gifted you with salvation and it is always yours for the asking.

Trust is needed when we do not see with our eyes. You must see with the heart. That is why the hungry heart yearns for my grace. It thirsts to become whole and right with their Lord and Master. Nothing else satisfies them. They willingly, joyfully simplify their life-style. They begin to understand great Saints like Francis of Assisi who begged for the grace of poverty. It is the pearl of great price (Matthew 13:46). When one is poor, there are few 'things' to distract them from communing with their Master. Without 'things' cluttering up their lives, they are at peace with the world. In my eyes, they shine like stars in the sky.

Take this as your own perspective of life. Do not let yourself be burdened with worldly things. Lift your eyes up. Focus your attention on heavenly affairs. Know my will and do it. Remember to ask, seek and you shall be satisfied.

9/5/18

Fill my mind, Lord, with kindly thoughts.

Let us speak today about the fourth Beatitude: *"Blessed are those who hunger and thirst for righteousness, for they shall be satisfied"* (Matthew 5:6). In this attitude, the heart is longing to know the Truth, to be set free by the Truth, to think, act, feel like the Truth who is the second person in the Blessed Trinity, my Son Jesus the Christ. He is the way and the truth and the life (John 14:6). Without him living and abiding in your soul, you, my people, are lost.

He is your Savior, your righteousness. You can do nothing without his light in your eyes. You must see that he lives and breathes in you. You must taste and see his goodness in that you live and breathe by his holy will. He is your All in All (Colossians 3:11).

He, my Son Jesus, gave up his life so he could send the Holy Spirit to be with you (John 14:16-17), move in you, increase in you. Won't you welcome him in your heart? Will you see and believe that he lives in you? Won't you understand that he loves you personally? This was my plan from the beginning that you should be with Me forever.

The Psalmist says that he thirsts like parched land for running water (Psalm 42:2). You see, he knows how good I am. He knows the truth that he cannot live without Me. My grace must fill his heart with life, truth, wisdom, knowledge, light, or he will die.

The hungry heart longs for God and knows that I alone can make her righteous because she wants to see my face. She wants to be with Me and not against Me. She knows I am the pearl of great price (Matthew 13:46) and yearns to give glory to Me by how she lives.

So, what is needed to achieve this high calling of righteousness? It is my grace. And how does one obtain this amazing grace? Ask, seek, knock (Matthew 7:7); repent of sin and grieve for your sins, obey my commandments, live by my law of love, and all things will be added to you.

It is my work to mold you into the image of my Son. It is my work to redeem your sins, faults, mistakes. It is my work on the Cross that delivered you from the hands of all your enemies. And I am a relentless God. I never give up. I never tire pursuing and wooing my children. I have so much to give them. The world and all that's in it belong to Me. Am I not a generous God? Have I not been patient, waiting for my children to convert their hearts? To return to Me, their Father who would give them the world (Joel 2:12-13)?

O my people, humble yourselves before your God who made you. Listen to my words of consolation and truth. Change your mindsets. Learn the truth. I am always available with my grace. It is free for the taking. Take my love. I give it freely. Come to Me, my people, and find your place in my heart and you will find rest in your souls. Live in my light. Reject the darkness of ignorance of who I am for you.

It is your choice. Choose wisely. Your future eternal life is at stake.

9/7/18

Prune my heart, Lord, so I may bear good fruit.

I speak to you today as your Lord and Father. My word is of love and mercy, for I know the desire of your heart. It is to become holy as I am holy (Matthew 5:48). This is the true desire for a disciple's heart—to be one with Me, to love as I love, to imitate Jesus by following in His footsteps, to take on the mind of Christ (1 Corinthians 2:16), to humble yourself before God and man.

Your love has been tested and found wanting in one area—self-love. You still do not understand the depth of my love for my children—of which you are one. You belong to my heart. I created you for love. I had you in mind when I created the world. You are my special possession and I have devoted my life to you, choosing death to atone for your sins

102

so you will live eternally. Do you not yet understand the truth and depth of my love for you?

Let us pretend that you do. OK, look at yourself in a mirror. What do you see? Yes, you see your imperfections. Do you know what I see? I see a heart that loves and a spirit that longs to be perfect in my eyes. I see the desire to be right in your Master's eyes. That is the right disposition of a disciple's heart.

Grow in my love. Live in my light. Let the truth of my love set you free from self-doubt. Do not diminish who you are in Me. I have lifted you up, dusted you off, and placed you in my Kingdom. I have groomed you for sainthood. I have taught you to trust in my power—that nothing is impossible for Me (Luke 1:37).

So, my word to you today is to cherish the love, time, effort I have lavished upon you to make you 'right' with Me. I thank you for your willingness to obey Me, but now I ask you to value and cherish my work in your soul. I have borne fruit through you. Believe and don't doubt my power over you and in you.

Pray, ask and see my love in action.

9/17/18

Disperse the darkness, Lord, with your light.

Today, listen as I tell you secrets of my heart. Long have I waited for your turning to Me with your whole heart (Hosea 11:1-9), to trust Me completely, to depend on Me totally, to put your life in my hands, and to have my way in your heart and spirit. I have groomed your soul by the power of my love.

Would that all my children would open their hearts to my grace. I could work miracles in a docile, willing spirit. I would cleanse the soul of all vestiges of darkness and purify that soul with the fire of my love—a powerful love that would fill the heart with peace and rest from striving for material possessions. All that is needed is to be right with Me, the Father of all who provides for his docile, obedient, kind and loving children.

For Me to move and groom a soul into my image is to have a trusting spirit. To trust means not to fear for one's salvation. To trust means to believe the truth of my Son's Passion, Death and Resurrection. To trust, one needs knowledge of who I am, the love in which I created you, the power I have to move mountains, in the power I have to recreate the heart and soul of anyone and everyone who turns away from sin, and then I would take that soul/heart and purify it until it shines like gold.

Let Me tell you that the streets in Heaven are lined with gold from the hearts of my Saints. A Saint is nothing other than a soul who loves her God with all her heart, who obeys my Word, and lives to please her God by loving her neighbor whoever he may be. A Saint has no fear because she trusts my plan for her salvation whatever it may be. She believes in my love. She knows I live in her heart and will never abandon her. This is a level of sanctity in which my grace thrives and multiplies.

O my people, seek my righteousness, appropriate my grace that is sufficient for your journey through the snares of worldly enticements and the mine-fields of the enemy.

Remember, I am the Light of the World (John 8:12), whoever follows Me will not walk in the dark but will have the light of day. This is my word and promise to all who love and obey Me.

I am God and there is no other (Isaiah 45:5). Heed my words and be safe, my beloved children. Stay close to my heart. I love you.

9/24/18

Grant me the grace, Lord, to understand your way in me.

Today our topic is discerning my will so you may become righteous. This requires the attitude of the fourth Beatitude—hungering and thirsting to be right with Me, your God. You must want to know Me, love Me and serve Me above all else. You cannot desire wealth or what the world tells you what you should be. To be right with Me requires self-discipline, strength of character and a willingness to obey—not only my commandments, but whatever needs to be done to further your knowledge of Me. In other words: knowledge of my Word in the Bible.

The Bible was written by my followers under the inspiration of the Holy Spirit. It is your heavenly Father's book. In it you learn of my love, power, mercy and my ways and thoughts of your salvation. The Bible was written for you to come to know and understand your Father in Heaven who waits for you to want Me in your heart, to long for Me like the Psalmist says in Psalm 63: *"For you my flesh pines and my soul thirsts like the parched earth without water."* You will find Me when you long for Me. When you seek Me above all else, I will come to you and fill you with my Spirit of all wisdom, knowledge and understanding, and you will be satisfied.

Salvation is a two-way street: I call, you answer. I grant grace, you receive. I have already taught you how to approach my throne of grace to receive my help (Hebrews 4:16)—you come with love in your heart, and trust in your soul. Then you will be blessed with all I have to give you.

Let us sum up: I created you to know, love and serve Me and enjoy eternal life with Me, and you responded obediently, willingly, faithfully. It is a win-win salvation. This is my will for all. How many will accept my grace? How many will receive my gift of salvation? There are many distracting voices calling out to my children. It is not easy to hear my whisper in the clamor of worldly voices. Take heart. Take time to sort them out. Be patient and cunning as a serpent, but wise and gentle as a dove (Matthew 10:16). I am always calling out to my people. I never give up and I give many second-chances. I will be found by those who hunger for Me, and they shall be satisfied.

9/29/18

You are my God, Lord, teach me to do your will.

Today I will speak on the subject of hungering for righteousness because that is the beginning of wisdom. To desire is to receive: *"Take delight in the Lord, and he will grant you your heart's requests"* (Psalm 37:4). I place the desires in your heart. I want you to desire to be right in my eyes. I created you for myself, to enjoy being with Me. I love my people so dearly that I want them to be happy, and I am the only source of happiness for them.

You do not find happiness in the world of darkness with all its evil desires for wealth, power and fame. It is the wrong source. Its end is the destruction of goodness and right. You must seek the Kingdom of God (Matthew 6:33), of light, of goodness and mercy. I am the only hope for the world. I alone grant light, understanding, peace, contentment and fulfillment of love and joy. My purpose is to grant life in all its glory.

This is my will for you that you live out your time on earth in search of my eternal truth, to find the pearl of great wisdom (Matthew 13:45-46), to persevere on the journey with courage and strength of conviction that I am with you, guiding and protecting you from harm.

And what keeps you plodding down the road to victory? My Will! You have given Me your permission to mold you into my image, to train your mind according to my principles and morals, and you have decided to live your life in obedience and gratitude for the grace I give you. You have given Me an open mind and heart so I can fill your faculties with knowledge and love, wisdom and understanding. Had you not willingly desired to know, love and serve Me, I should have found some way to convince you to seek Me. Am I not all powerful? Infinite Wisdom? Yes, there are many roads leading to my heart and I make them all available to my beloved children.

Oh, if only my children would know and understand my way in their hearts! I would pour out torrents of grace to wash away every impurity and they would shine like pure gold. I value them so much that I made each one special and uniquely different from any other person in the world. You are, each one, originals with much value in my eyes. Turn to Me with all your heart and I will teach you my ways.

10/2/18

Fill my hungry heart, Lord, with your Holy Spirit.

Today I will teach you how to live in the world but not be of the world. I have created the world for my pleasure. I created man to fellowship with Me. For this purpose, my Son commissioned his Apostles to baptize in the name of the Father and of the Son and of the Holy Spirit (Matthew 28:18).

In Baptism, I give you a portion of my Spirit—as Paul says in a letter to one of his churches: it is a down payment on your inheritance (Ephesians 1:14). I, the Holy Spirit, exist in you, and I must increase daily to do the work of transformation in your soul. Allow Me access to your soul. Open your heart to my wisdom and grace. The more knowledge you have of my love and power, the more you will be open to receive my Spirit into your heart and the more you will act like Me and think like Me. You will be my disciples knowing my will and obeying my will. Then knowing the truth will set you free (John 8:32) from the world of darkness. The more you walk into the light, the more you will hunger to draw closer to Me, your only good. Without my light, you stumble and fall. At those moments, your faith diminishes and you leave my protective cover over you.

Run, my children, back into the light of my love. The world will destroy the beauty of your soul, rob you of your peace and you will become a victim of the enemy. He will torture and taunt you to lose faith in my love. Don't let him trick you. Stay close to my side. Reject and rebuke Satan in my name immediately, before he gets a firm grip on your soul and tears you away from my light! I died on the Cross for this reason—to free you, to defeat the enemy.

Do you know who is the most powerful human being that ever lived? My Mother Mary! She has more power over the enemy than you know. Didn't my Father say that she would stomp on his head (Genesis 3:15)? Yes, let Me teach you about my Mother. She is all holy, pure, innocent. My Father preserved her soul from all evil. Her soul is spotless. Do you know why she stayed on earth so many years after my Resurrection? It was so she could strengthen, comfort and protect my Apostles in the great work I gave them which was to spread my Kingdom on earth. She longed to be with Me, her Son, but humbly remained on earth for as long as I asked her. Her love for you, my people, is great, true and powerful. She is the ultimate Intercessor. How can I refuse my Mother anything when she is so good, kind, unselfish and loves my people so much?

So, this is how to remain in the world but not belong to the world: follow my Mother's example, stay close to the Church. Serve others. Comfort and console those who are sick. Never refuse someone in need. Learn to know my Father's will for you and obey it. Become a faithful prayer warrior to intercede for others' needs, and lastly, be devoted to my Mother and yours.

10/5/18

Shelter me, Lord, in the shadow of your wings.

Today our subject will be righteousness in the heart, body, soul and spirit—yes, totally. A man's heart cannot be divided and see God. To be right with Me, the heart must be filled with love, mercy, forgiveness. It will be a heart that only remembers the good that has been done to him. His soul will be filled with gratitude to his God for giving him life in the first place.

Mankind exists because I will it. I give life and breath to the soul of man and he lives and breathes and exists in the light of my love. It is not easy to comprehend, but it is the truth. I willed you into existence and you became a creature of my heart. Then I breathed a soul into your body, and that soul consists of a memory, intellect and a will to freely decide whether you will follow Me, the good; or the evil one who destroys. Becoming righteous is to decide, to discern what choice you will make. Choose Me and you will live. Choose Satan and you will die. And the memory contains all that you know about good and evil. The intellect tallies up the score: what is the best decision to make, the best choice; and the function of the will is to put the discerned choice into action.

Do you see that the trilogy of memory, will and intellect resemble the Blessed Trinity living and acting in you? Yes, you are made in my image (Genesis 1:26). I place holiness within you. I have given you a heart to know, love and serve Me. When your heart is in the right place, then you become righteous. What you do and say will always be kind, gentle, loving, merciful and forgiving because these are the traits of your Father. When you become righteous—that is, you

110

make good decisions, having discerned my will, you will live in peace. You will be content with what you have. You will see that there is no need for fear or worry because you have taken on the mind of Christ (1 Corinthians 2:16), your loving Savior. You have matured in the ways of your Father. Wisdom, knowledge, understanding, all the gifts and fruits of the Holy Spirit are at your command (Galatians 5:22).

I have sheltered you in all the storms of your life (Psalm 27:5). I have kept you in the shadow of my wings (Psalm 91:4), protecting and keeping you safe until my Spirit increased in your soul—until you could fully understand that you were created in love, saved by love, nurtured in love, and live fully in my love. You have become a "chip off the old block," as the saying goes.

Your Father and my Father shines his light upon you. Use the gifts you have inherited wisely. They are given to build up the Church (1 Corinthians 14:12). As I have invested myself in you out of love, do likewise; then you will truly be my disciple and you will know the truth and the truth will set you free (John 8:32).

10/15/18

I hunger for your word, Lord. Let it wash away my sins.

Today we will speak about righteousness. No one is good except the Father; so, from him comes righteousness, beauty and truth. No one can endure to the end without his grace and favor. Pray to be right in his sight. This makes all the difference between salvation and condemnation. That is why I came in the flesh to atone for man's sin against the righteousness of my Father. No one could follow the law.

Everyone sinned (Romans 3:23). No one could save himself. I alone, the beloved Son of the Father, could make compensation on man's behalf.

How can a sinful human being make reparation to the Omniscient God, the Creator of mankind? Only I, the Son of the Father, equal and one in him together with the Holy Spirit worked out your salvation. In this is man saved by the will of the Father, by the life of the Son, the Christ; and by the fulfillment of our plan of salvation through the Holy Spirit. This is my Word come in the flesh to save all mankind.

No one is exempt from my love. All are equal in my eyes (Romans 2:11). My Son's blood wiped the slate clean. My light shines like the sun in the sky. All are touched by it, guided by it. Lift up your head and see the light on the path that leads you home to my heart.

Let my Spirit infill you with power to leave your own understanding behind and seek to find my way into your heart and soul. I am knocking; open the door and I will dine with you (Revelation 3:20). I will fill you with my Spirit and you will become my new creation molded in my image and protected, covered in the blood of Christ (2 Corinthians 5:17).

You become 'little gods' for you are my off-springs—little Christians scurrying around for my favor. Your one desire is to please Me, to obey and serve Me, to become right with Me and to love Me with all your heart, mind and strength (Mark 12:30)!

Then, finally, I am able to work wonders in and through your willingness to be totally Mine—to be totally righteous in my eyes.

10/21/18

Your word, Lord, is food for my soul.

Yes, today I will elaborate on the fourth Beatitude: *"Blessed are they who hunger and thirst for righteousness, for they shall be satisfied"* (Matthew 5:6). I shall speak of my suffering for the sins of mankind.

As you know, the Triune God (Father, Son, Spirit) decided together that I would come in human flesh—and this is where my Mother cooperated with us. When she said yes to my Incarnation (Luke 1:38), your salvation was assured; the great plan for the salvation of all mankind went forward.

It was just as my Father said in the beginning: *"Let there be light"* (Genesis 1:3). That is why I am known as the *"Light of the World"* (John 8:12). I came in human form to bring knowledge of my Father's love and presence in every living organism. I brought the Light of the holy Sacraments of Baptism, Penance (Reconciliation) and Holy Eucharist to nourish my people on their daily journey—yes, I am Manna (Exodus 16:4) sent from Heaven to strengthen those who decide to believe in Me and follow Me. Those who do believe are called children of God (John 1:12). So, I was born to die. I willingly accepted my mission.

Let Me tell you something. I enjoyed picking my Apostles (Matthew 10:2). It was fun to be with them everyday as we journeyed from place to place. They were so excited when I spoke to the demons and they obeyed Me (Matthew 17:18). They saw my people being set free of their infirmities. They were amazed when I healed the blind man (Luke 18:35).

Yes, I loved them for who they were. They hungered to see Me perform these wonders—and their faith in Me grew.

113

They began to see who I was and who I could be for them. Slowly, the truth began to take root, and Peter declared it in his famous words: *"You are the Messiah, the Son of the living God"* (Matthew 16:16).

O how I loved him at that moment, and I knew he was chosen by my Father (Matthew 16:17) to lead the Church on earth. And yes, words matter. My words are like that two-edged sword described in the book of Hebrews (Hebrews 4:12).

My Word came to set man free.

10/22/18

Be with me, Lord, for I am in trouble.

Yes, I am with you, in you and for you. I will never leave you orphaned (John 14:18), without my light within you. For I came to set you free from lack of knowledge—yes, *"My people perish for lack of knowledge"* (Hosea 4:6). I came that you might have life—abundant life (John 10:10). I came to establish my Kingdom on earth and now I am present sacramentally in every tabernacle in every Catholic Church world-wide. I can always be found by the hungry and thirsty soul who searches for righteousness. I established my Church to spread the Good News (Mark 16:15) of my love for every man, woman and child.

Sadly, I grieve for every little, precious soul who never sees the light of day. They are destroyed in the very womb where they were meant to see my light and my love for them. This is an abomination in my sight! You grieve when your little ones are hurt or mistreated; cannot I, the Author of Life (Acts 3:15), grieve for the treacherous murders of my own? Yes, woe to those who spread this evil! They know not what

114

they do (Luke 23:34)! My mercy is running thin. My justice will demand retribution. If they repent, I will be merciful. If not, my Word will stand (Matthew 25:46).

Believe Me, my Son suffers for the loss of every soul who is lost, who refuses the salvation for which He gave his life. He says, *"Suffer the little children to come to Me for I will give them life"* (Matthew 19:14). Death is the work of the evil one (Romans 6:23); he delights in the death of my children. Do you still not understand the difference between good and evil, life and death?

If my children understood, if they were wise, they would choose Life, and I would satisfy their hungry hearts. I would run to rescue them from the clutches of Satan, and they would lead joyful, peaceful lives, contented in the Life-giving love I offer them.

O my people, rejoice in my Word. He came to set you free. So, be free. Set your feet on the road to happiness. Take the upward road to holiness. Turn away from death!

11/3/18

Shine your light upon me, Lord, and I shall be healed.

Yes, those who seek my Face are blessed, indeed. I pour out my favor upon them and they are changed forever—for the good always. My light burns away the darkness from their souls and they are healed of many afflictions—too many to mention. Suffice it to say, that the light brings forth a radical change in their hearts, and they seek my righteousness over them. And in faith and with faith, I can move mountains of doubts, fears, anxieties, and many sins of resentment, anger, unforgiveness—all these things hinder the light from penetrating into the psyche and they, as a consequence, remain in the dark. But all is not lost. There is always hope for cleansing away the negative effects of sin from the soul, freeing it to burn and hunger for righteousness. It becomes a flame burning in the heart that only the light of my love and goodness can quench.

Yes, seek to know Me with all your heart. Search for knowledge and it shall be granted to you. Fan the fire in your heart (2 Timothy 1:6), and I will pour out my grace upon you. I will be the light on your path, and you will not walk in darkness. I promise to guide you up the mountain of my love, and you will find treasure beyond compare.

My treasures are everlasting, uplifting and concrete that no one can take away from you. My treasures are virtues that mold your soul into my likeness and you are recreated, made new. The old passes away, and what was once in the dark is seen in the light (Luke 8:17). Does not the light make a diamond shine brighter? Same with the soul. My light shines forth from a soul cleansed from sin, and then the enlightened soul shines its light upon other souls. Light cannot be hidden. It is a force for good.

So, seek my light upon you by doing good to others. Be my light in your world and see it shine. Let it shine and you will be healed.

11/16/18

My heart thirsts for You, Lord, like the dry earth.

Listen closely today for I have much to tell you about the thirst that overwhelms the heart of one who desires only to do my will. This pleases Me, not for my own pleasure, but

116

because that person is on the right track to glory. It is glorious to be in love with one's God—Me! I am the King of the realm. I can bestow riches upon my faithful—those who hunger for my grace/Holy Spirit will reach great heights of glory and faith, hope and love. Their hearts will expand with love, their minds with wisdom, their souls with peace and their spirits will be joyful—they will dance with joy before their Lord (2 Samuel 6:14), and I will shower down many gifts upon them—more than they can imagine, for eye has not seen and ear has not heard what I have in store for them (1 Corinthians 2:9).

Let Me tell you a secret: my grace builds character and character produces good deeds, and good deeds earn great benefits, and these benefits will last for eternity. The way to my heart is through my Son Jesus the Christ. He is the way, the truth, and the life (John 14:6). Whoever believes in him lives forever. They will have faith that moves mountains (Mark 11:23). They will know Me and obey Me, and I will be with them always. When they love Me with all their heart, mind, soul and strength, I will nurture them as a father nurtures his own child. I will lift him up and foster him like one who raises an infant to his cheeks (Hosea 11:4).

Now let Me tell you a story. There was a man with two sons. Both loved and obeyed their father. But one envied his brother's carefree personality and wanted to be like him. I gave him his own special characteristics, but envy for his brother's gifts, blinded him to his own. Thus, envy became a stronghold over his heart and he could not love his brother. Envy turned into hate, hate to anger, and rage consumed his soul. What was to become of him? What could he do to calm his fury? Yes, he destroyed his brother's reputation and spread lies about his family. What would you do if he was your son? Let Me tell you: wait for the Lord. Rome was not built in a day. I must work in his heart, correct his thinking, nurture his spirit, open his mind to the truth, and reveal my love to him.

Now, you who read my book, you who thirst for my presence in your heart, you who seek my Face, are you willing to lay down your life for the envious son? Are you willing to take his sins on your shoulders? To bear his burden? This is the kind of heart that I look for in my disciples. They must live for the good of others. They must pray for the salvation of souls. Those who hunger for Me will do what I did. Did I not lay down my life so you could live? Did I not shed my blood to ransom you from your sins? Yes, if you hunger for Me, hunger for my people's souls. What you do to the least of my people, you do for Me (Matthew 25:40).

11/19/18

Rescue me, Lord. I need You.

Yes, I will. Would that all my people yearned to be right with Me. If only they would respond to my call and use the grace that is offered to them so freely; then they would have no desire to struggle and strive to be right in the eyes of the world. If they would cooperate with my grace, their hearts would be filled with peace, love, and the joy of a good conscience. Then they would make right decisions, and they would not be agents of evil against their brothers and sisters.

How do people change? Sadly, bad things must happen to them before they wake up and see their need of my help, and then they call out to Me to rescue them. And I will—but that's not the point! I do not desire that my children suffer.

I suffered for them. No one can suffer as I did, for I am God. My suffering suffices for all mankind.

There are times when I ask a child to share in my suffering as an intercessor for a brother or sister who may be in danger of losing their right to salvation. Yes, that is a new thought for you. Everyone has a right to be saved—every man, woman and child on the face of the earth has the right to know what my Son did for them. Yes, he suffered and died to ransom them from slavery to sin. He did it for every person on the face of the earth.

So, freedom is at hand. My grace is waiting for all who ask. But, if one does not know the truth, or does not understand the truth of Christ's sacrifice, or if they have not heard the good news of Jesus Christ, how can they ask for their share of my grace (Romans 10:14)? How can they understand what his death means for them?

Yes, Saint Teresa said it: I need your hands and your feet. I need your voice, dear Reader, to share what you know of my love and how my grace has worked a profound change in your heart, that you now know the truth of my love, protection, guidance and providence.

Let all the world know of my Love that it may transform angry hearts and free them from hate, unforgiveness, treasured resentments that keep them in the dark. They must think new thoughts and feel new feelings to be set free from the strongholds of Satan (2 Corinthians 5:17).

Let Me tell you a story. There once was a woman who did not know that I loved her. She thought she was unimportant, not worthy of respect or love. She so desperately needed love, approval and acceptance, that she did everything in her power to gain it. She became a people-pleaser. If she was

119

told to jump, she would ask, "How high?" One day, she got on her knees to pray, and that made all the difference! I came bounding to her rescue, transformed her mind with my truth, grace and love. Today, she is my new creation (2 Corinthians 5:17) and worships her King with peace in her heart. She is just one of my many disciples who pray for the conversion of sinners because she has seen the Truth with her own eyes. She knows that I am a loving, generous God, and that I want all my children by my side.

12/2/18

Direct my heart, Lord, to obey your every word.

Today we speak of righteousness. It is the call to every Christian to be right with Christ who is the epitome of holiness. *"Be perfect as my heavenly Father is perfect"* (Matthew 5:48).

I was speaking to my disciples one day, teaching them the mysteries of the Kingdom, when a young man addressed Me with this question: "How does one enter the Kingdom of Heaven?" As you have read in the Gospels: I told him to obey the commandments. But to justify himself, he said, "Yes, I obey them, but what more can I do?" So, I told him: *"There is still one thing left for you: sell all that you have and distribute it to the poor, and you will have a treasure in heaven. Then come, follow me"* (Luke 18:22). But he went away sad because he cared more for his possessions than he did for his immortal life. How sad! He missed his call to be perfect as his father is perfect (Matthew 5:48).

Every boy wants to be like his father. This is an innate desire. So, what stopped the young man from achieving the purpose of his life? Yes, he did not know what it was! I created every human being to know, love and serve Me in this life so they may enjoy eternal life with Me in Heaven. So, every man's purpose is to come to know Me and love Me with all his heart, and if he loves Me, he will obey Me—in obeying Me, I lead him right to Paradise forever!

It is crucial to put aside anything and everything that stops you from obeying Me, for I am the Light that guides you; I am the Way to your eternal resting place; I am the Truth who teaches you to discern good from bad; and I am your Life for I live in you, inspiring you to achieve greatness and to be all that you can be (John 14:6).

O my people, open your eyes to see Me; open your hearts to feel my presence alive and acting in you; open your minds to receive all the good I have planned for you; open your arms to hold all the sanctifying gifts I have for you.

O my children, love Me as I love you. Receive, accept and use my love so you may become a great Saint in this life and in the one to come. And it is coming. No one knows when, only the Father (Mark 13:32), but he will send Me again. Bank on it!

12/5/18

Lead me, Lord, along the road of righteousness.

Yes, I will. I want all my children to take my hand and walk with Me. I know the path upon which they will find salvation. What is salvation but freedom from all sin, darkness, ugliness—all things undesirable. That is why I place right desires in the heart (Psalm 37:4).

I know the path they need to follow because I have already traveled it. I am able to guide, protect and shelter you in all the storms and pitfalls you may encounter. Take my hand and walk safely by my side. Many refuse, either out of fear or stubbornness. They prefer to go it alone. How foolish to refuse my power and my might, my wisdom and grace which are freely given.

Why do I extend my hand to help my people, you might ask? You can say it is my nature to give a helping hand. But the truth is that I love my children passionately. I am not a half-hearted God. Nor do I ration my love, or bargain for it. I am all-loving. My love is unconditional except that you must follow the rules. I keep order in my Kingdom. Everyone must adhere to the law of love (Mark 12:30-31). I will not tolerate meanness, unkindness. Hate has no place in my Kingdom. Love is the rule and divine order.

Picture a stormy sea, waves crashing against a wall of rocks. This is the state of soul and mind of my people who do not follow divine order. They scurry around looking for freedom from their fears. Their lives are in disarray. What is missing? My peace, love and joy. This is the result of disobedience.

Why do you think I instituted the Ten Commandments? For myself? No! So, my people could live in safety from the hazards in life, from the threats of the principalities and dominions of the outer regions. Order must be enforced, otherwise the world would be in chaos. Yes, the Ten Commandments are road signs leading to peace and order among men. They must be obeyed for the safety of mankind.

Enough for today. Take your rest. Remember to pray for your enemies. The prayer of the righteous man prevails much (James 5:16).

12/8/18

You are faithful and true, Lord. Possess my heart forever.

Yes, cry with tears of joy that your name is written in the Lamb's book of life (Revelation 3:5). I have come to you many times throughout the years and touched you with my love. Your grief and loss of a mother's love and care prompted Me to console you. Search back into your history and you will find special moments where my grace was present. I am always present to you, for I live and move in a docile heart. I can have my way with you because you are obedient to my word.

Obedience opens locked doors in the mind and heart. Obedience means that you respect Me, honor Me, regard Me as most and foremost of importance in your life. You put Me first, and that's where I need to be so I can work wonders of healing, guidance and protection. Obedience places you under my wings where you are kept safe and treasured for the unique person I created you to be. I take very special care of those who love and obey Me. On those who rely on Me, I shower heavenly graces until their cup overflows (Psalm 23:5).

Know and keep in your mind that I watch over you. I am with you wherever you go, so there is nothing to fear. Perfect love casts out all fear (1 John 4:18). Let not fear rule over you. Let not fear prevent you from living your life to the fullest. There is no room for fear when one loves their God and trusts and believes that I love you back!

What troubles the soul who is so wrapped in fear? Discouragement is one reason. Doubts which come when there is lack of faith—insufficiency of self-confidence is another. They don't really believe that I live in them so they rely only on themselves.

O my children! Believe in Me. "Let go and let God." I promise to possess your hearts if you will only trust Me. Why did I suffer death, if not to prove my love?

Blessed Virgin Mary on the Fourth Beatitude

"Blessed are they who hunger and thirst for righteousness. The Rosary is the prayer which I myself came down from heaven to ask of you. By it you are able to lay bare the plots of my Adversary; you escape from many of his deceits; you defend yourselves from many dangers which he puts in your way; it preserves you from evil and brings you closer to me, because I am able to be truly your guide and your protection."

St. Padre Pio on the Fourth Beatitude

"One seeks God in the reading of sacred Scripture and holy, devout books. With meditation one finds God, with prayer one knocks at his heart, and with contemplation one enters into the great theater of divine beauty that was opened up precisely through reading, meditation, and prayer."

St. Bernard on the Fourth Beatitude

"I hope for nothing other than the bare necessities from you, for I trust your Word, on which I threw everything else away. *"Seek first the kingdom of God and his righteousness, and all these things shall be yours as well"* (Matthew 6:33). For the hapless beggar commits himself to you; you will be the helper of the fatherless. If rewards are promised me, it is through you I hope to obtain them; if a host encamps against me, if the world fumes, if the evil one rages, if the flesh itself lusts against the spirit, I will hope in you."

Chapter Five

Fifth Beatitude
"Blessed are the merciful, for they shall obtain mercy."
Matthew 5:7

5/5/18

Have mercy on me, Lord, in your kindness.

Let us begin today with the Beatitude of mercy. The merciful shall receive mercy. What does that mean? In my economy, the merciful are those who think less of themselves and more of the other. The merciful know they have received mercy from their God of Mercy. They know and have repented of their sins and I have forgiven them. The merciful have big hearts and are generous with their love and compassion. The merciful know their own poverty, have mourned their sins, repented and have received mercy in return. My heart is a merciful heart and I provide for those who are merciful; they shall be rewarded beyond their expectations.

I have made allowances for the weak in faith for I know what is lacking in their trust. I have special, tender care for those wayward children who are far from Me; I do not abandon them (John 14:18).

Tell my people to pray for mercy from their God and they shall receive mercy. Yes, *"Ask and you shall receive. Seek and ye shall find. Knock and the door will be opened"* (Matthew 7:7). I will never reject one who pleads for mercy. I am greater than anyone knows. I am Infinite (Isaiah 40:28). I repair the destruction caused by merciless hearts. I reconstruct damaged relationships. I rebuild demolished structures, be they physical or spiritual. I make known the unknown. I am the God of the universe and the unseen realities. Nothing is beyond my power to repair or to build up. I can design new languages and create light and a whole new world.

Man cannot conceive my power to create anew or restore the old.

6/12/18

Lead me, Lord, and I will follow.

Mercy is our subject for today. **M** is for **M**other, my Blessed Mother. She was filled with mercy from the start. It was mercy that prompted her heart to respond to my call so quickly, not hesitating out of fear for what it meant for her reputation. I had prepared her heart to accept my invitation to the highest form of grace.

Yes, there are distinct levels of grace: sanctifying grace, actual grace, divine grace, empowering grace, discerning grace, humble grace, and enduring grace; grace for the moment and grace for eternity. Hers was a singular grace to give her body, soul and spirit in service to her Father in Heaven. She said yes to my invitation and laid down her life to give Me life. The act will never be repeated. It was the most momentous moment in history with untold repercussions for the world.

E is for **E**cstasy at the moment of my birth. She was in such ecstasy to bring the perfect man-child, the Son of God Most High into the world, that she only felt joy—not the pain of delivery. Remember, she is sinless; only with sin does pain appear (Genesis 3:16). Then the **R** in the word mercy is, of course, the first letter in the word **R**osary which my Mother presented to Saint Dominic for the comfort and consolation of the world. **C** is for **C**hristian. Every human being is called to follow Christ. He is the Way and the Truth and the Life (John 14:6), that I gave to the world for its salvation and the redemption of all its sins; and **Y** stands for the Hebrew word for their God: **Y**ahweh.

So, you see, mercy begins with Mother giving Christ to the world through the will of God, the Father of all. Mercy dwells in the Holy Family of Jesus, the first place to find mercy. So, in your homes, let mercy be found. *"Blessed are the merciful for they shall obtain mercy"* (Matthew 5:7).

6/20/18

Have mercy on me, Lord, for I am a sinner.

The fifth Beatitude is important to emulate because I am very merciful. I am God and I know the sins of my people. In sin you were born, but I created you in love and in my image (Genesis 1:27), and I came to show you the way (John 14:6).

To be merciful is a high calling, but with my grace it can be done. All things are possible when a soul turns to its Master (Ephesians 6:9) and cries for help. This takes humility. So, to be merciful, one must be humble. Being humble destroys the towers of pride and selfishness. I know a woman who in her selfishness and greed plotted to destroy a man's life to please her husband. Her name is Jezebel (1 Kings 21). The Jezebel spirit affects and infects many to this day.

What does this have to do with mercy? Everything. One must accept what happens to the soul. This means to accept the will of others before one's own. This is merciful living: not to impose one's own desires over those of others, not to

128

plot or scheme to achieve one's own happiness at the cost of another's displeasure; instead, what is needed is a generous, kind spirit to graciously defer to the other's needs, putting aside one's own needs.

This is mercy in action: to think more highly of others, to make others happy and to think less of oneself. This takes a different mind-set, a change of attitude: God first, neighbor second, self third. Is this not the order of my great commandment (Mark 12:28)?

All I said and did while I lived on the earth had multiple reasons. Every word I speak has special import and effect. The ultimate purpose of my Passion, Death and Resurrection was to restore order on earth: every human being loving God, neighbor and self. Then the earth would be freed of corruption. Every man, woman and child would be set free. Peace would be rampant and mercy bountiful.

Let there be peace on earth. Let everyone extend mercy to their neighbor. Let love triumph. It is available to all for my Spirit floods the earth. Nothing can resist my power. Grace is sufficient for all (2 Corinthians 12:9). Let my love flow from one to the other. It will never run out. It will multiply and run over.

7/16/18

With your grace, Lord, I will win the race.

Today is a new day. We shall speak about the fifth Beatitude: *"Blessed are the merciful, for they shall receive mercy"* (Matthew 5:7).

When one is misunderstood, the tendency is to be hurt, saddened, and consequently feels mistreated and becomes depressed. These are the times when one must take heart and rejoice. Turn the table on the temptation to respond in anger, instead, put the hurt feelings aside and clear the air. In other words, be merciful, compassionate, understanding. The devil enjoys the devastation he causes. Do not give in to him. Fight him with all the tools I have given you. Rebuke him! Denounce him! Command him to leave in my name! I have given my disciples power over Satan. Don't give it back to him. Be merciful to yourself and the other party. Extend your heart in heartfelt mercy. Offer an olive branch and make peace.

Mercy is close to my heart. If you are my disciple, you will pattern your life according to mine (Luke 9:23). I am the all merciful God who gave up my life to reconcile my people to my Father. Can you not at least try a little bit to be merciful to those who misjudge you? Can you not forgive their misguided judgments against you? Of course, you can! I have provided all the grace you need to do so (2 Corinthians 12:9). Trust my presence in your heart. Trust my peace in your soul. I have guided, trained you in my ways and in my light, I have formed your conscience.

Come to Me when you are weary (Matthew 11:28) of carrying the cross of battling the evil one. I am the Victor. The battle was won on the Cross. Satan is defeated! Cast him out of your mind, body and spirit. Not only be merciful toward others, but also be merciful toward yourself. Mercy must be in the soul of my disciples, then it works its way out to others.

When one is poor in spirit, mourns her sins, is humble and meek, longs to be in right standing with Me, is merciful toward others and self, has achieved purity of heart, aims to be in peace with self and others; then they gladly suffer persecution, misunderstandings, false accusations, trials of all sorts. They rejoice in their sufferings. They praise their God for his greatness. All is right in the world because they love, honor, and obey their Master (John 13:13).

Then and only then will they see my great power at hand. They will live in the Kingdom of love, peace and joy. They will frolic in the sunshine with hearts lifted to receive my blessings. They will see goodness all the days of their lives (Psalm 23:6).

8/5/18

I am yours, Lord. Do with me what You will.

Listen and learn. Today we speak about mercy—having a merciful heart. As you, my Reader, have discovered, it must begin with you first so that when you are filled with mercy and compassion for yourself, then you can treat others mercifully. It becomes a natural habit to think and act mercifully.

Just like the other Beatitudes. When you discover how poor you are and mourn for your sins, you see the same condition in others and you react mercifully toward them. Without realizing it, you become a peace maker because of the mercy you extend to others. Mercy leads to peace.

On another point: let mercy begin at home. Be kind and merciful to your loved ones. This means to recognize their spiritual needs as well as their bodily needs, for man is spiritual with a God-given soul that will one day return to Me for my judgment on what they did with the life I gave them. No one avoids judgment—the judgment that my Son spoke about in the Gospel of Saint Matthew (Matthew 25:31). All souls will come before my judgment seat and based on the good and evil they committed, I will make my judgment, either heaven or hell.

Yes, there are four major choices you can make: life, death, heaven and hell. Will you live the life I plan for you that leads to Heaven, or will you live your life to end in the second death in hell? The choice is yours. May I suggest that you should be merciful to yourself and live a Beatific life; after all, I have given you my own Life, my own Truth, my own Way to follow (John 14:6). I have put my Spirit within you. I have given you all my amazing grace and power to make good choices.

Yes, mercy begins at home with yourself. Stop second-guessing yourself, comparing yourself to others. I have made you unique and special—in my own image (Genesis 1:26). What more can I do that I have not already done? Isn't the fact that I died for you enough? I must think you are pretty special that I would submit to being nailed to a Cross to save you from hell. I want you in Heaven with Me.

Come now, I have shown you the way. I have taught you my Beatitudes. They will lead you to Heaven. So, be merciful to yourself and other sinners. I am.

8/17/18

I trust You, Lord, for You are a merciful God.

Put this in the book: Mine is a merciful heart and I have pity on my lost children. Would you not go searching for your lost child (Luke 15:8)? Well, so do I. They are precious to Me. I am their Father, Mother, Everything! They belong to Me. My Son Jesus gave up his very life for my children because we love them (John 3:16).

No one knows how deep my love is and how much I grieve for my lost children. They are at the mercy of our enemy and suffer grievously, instead of basking in the sunlight of my love where they would find shelter from the storm (Isaiah 4:6), comfort in my loving arms; I would be a safe haven for them if only they would turn to Me. Like in the story of the Prodigal Son, I would set out a feast for them (Luke 15:11).

I take consolation in knowing I have many faithful children who seek my grace, and I always make it available to them. I rejoice in their love for their God, and I work wonders in their souls, always keeping in mind the sacrifice my Son made for them, atoning for their sins with the sacrifice of his Passion and Death. It was a cruel death at the hands of merciless men, but he knew this when we planned it long ago.

Today they still pierce his hands and feet and persecute him with their sins against mankind with their hateful lies and ugly threats. Where is the man who will stand against them? Where are the good men who will fight the good fight for honor and decency, and protect the innocent who are being slaughtered every day?

O my merciful heart bleeds for my little, helpless children in the wombs that have become death chambers! Is there no one with mercy in their heart? Must money, pleasure, and selfishness continue to destroy my people? My patience and tolerance are infinite, but my love and justice will prevail.

The day will come when I will not hold back my wrath, and man will run to the hills but they will not escape (Matthew 24:16).

The day will come when this world will no longer exist. My mercy demands justice. Take heed while the sun shines. Mend your ways. Obey my just and merciful rule and live in my love. Be holy as I am holy (Matthew 5:48).

8/18/18

Save me, Lord, and I will do your will.

These are my words for today: Blessed are the merciful for they shall receive mercy when I come again for the General Judgment. All the good deeds one has performed in love for Me, shall be rewarded; all the bad deeds shall be weighed in a balance. I will bear mercy on those who were merciful, but just with those who were not merciful to my people.

Mercy is a great virtue used to alleviate pain and suffering—not that one should appease the suffering selfishly, but to comfort them in it. Suffering has merit. Did my Son not suffer and much good come from it? Did not His Mother suffer to see her Son's flesh ripped and bleeding? Yes, suffering has great merit.

A lesson learned through suffering has a life-long impact on one's conscience. It remains in the memory. This is why I remember every pain my children suffer. I am All-knowing (Isaiah 46:9-10)—I never forget a mercy given. I never forget a prayer said (Isaiah 49:15). I know all things and I decide rightly.

This is what I say to those who are far from Me: Listen and obey my commands, they will lead you to safety. These are my words to those who are close to Me: Have hope in my mercy, obedience wins a great reward. To those who are lukewarm, I say: Decide once and for all who you will obey—will it be God or Satan? It is your choice, but remember, your soul is at stake.

My child, write these words: Hope and pray for my Divine Mercy to fall upon all the wicked that they may have a change of heart and return to their Heavenly Father and receive all the blessings I have in store for them so that after these few years of earthly strife, they may rest eternally in my loving embrace.

9/2/18

Fill my heart, Lord, with love for You.

Today we shall speak on the subject of mercy. Have a merciful outlook upon the misery in the world. Understand the events at work in the world at this time. There is turmoil, hate is rampant. War is breeding in the heart of man. These are the root causes of man's sins against man.

In the past, it has caused civil wars—brother killing brother, for you are all my children. Unless one understands that I am God, the Father Creator of all humankind (Ephesians 4:6), they cannot conceive the validity of the truth that all are brothers and sisters to each other. Mankind is the work of my hand, my desire, my love. I am the Father of all (Ephesians 4:6). Therefore, all are my children.

Did I not say to love one another as I have loved you (John 15:12)? Can you not stir up a measure of kindness to your sister or mercy to a brother? Stop thinking meagerly, selfishly. Open your minds and hearts to others. You will

135

find treasures you never knew existed. Each individual has his and her own gifts and talents. Everyone is special and unique. I have placed my infinite spirit in mankind (1 Corinthians 3:16) for the purpose of creating diversity among you. Every human being has his/her own personality so it is not boring to be in their company.

What has this to do with mercy? Everything. The merciful outlook is a frame of mind that is determined to explore the depths of the inner workings of the hearts of others. It is the decision to accept others as children of God made in my image (Genesis 1:26) and just as special and unique as oneself.

If man could only get out of himself, he would find 'gold' in his brothers and sisters. Gold miners dig deeply into the cave. So, must you. It can be done for I will it. Remember Me? I am God and Father of all. I make it possible in a willing heart. I can fill empty spaces with my wonder-working love. I entreat you. Let my grace work in your heart. What have you got to lose?

9/3/18

You alone, Lord, bring fulfillment.

Today we will continue on the subject of mercy. I have much to say on the subject because I am a merciful God. I know my creation and I know what they can and cannot do. I know their strengths and weaknesses. I know my children have a disadvantage—the inclination to sin. So, in my mercy, I sent my Son Jesus the Christ on the mission to save them, to pay the debt due for their sins. He atoned for all sin by the shedding of his blood. Is this not the highest form of mercy?

Then we sent the Holy Spirit to stay with each baptized soul (John 14:16-17) to enlighten and guide my children through the miry depths of sin and evil to reach the ultimate goal of Heaven to be in union with their Triune God. Is this not merciful?

Then the twelve chosen Apostles (Matthew 10:2) established my holy Church through which my children receive the seven Sacraments that are seven ways of bestowing mercy on my beloved, faithful and obedient children—especially those who yearn to love Me with their whole heart and soul. The gift of the holy Bible, my greatest book—again, inspired by the Holy Spirit, is a testament of my mercy for the good of my people.

O my people, my thoughts and my designs are always for your welfare (Jeremiah 29:11). I created you for happiness, to live with Me forever. I did not create you to die and to spend eternity in the fiery depths of hell. I am too merciful to willingly send my loved ones there.

Again, I know the hearts of my people. I know that sin is in them, tempting them to hate, to do evil. And this saddens my merciful heart. I sent my Son; I send my Spirit; the Blessed Virgin and all the Saints pray for you. What more can I do to prove my love? Accept my grace. Pray all day for the day draws nearer. My merciful heart calls out to you.

9/4/18

Keep me, Lord, in your light.

This morning we will discuss the issue of mercy, the fifth Beatitude. To be merciful, compassionate, kind, understanding, tolerant—these are all aspects of mercy. If I were not merciful, the world would have been destroyed a long time ago. I allowed world wars to happen in the hope that man would resolve their differences once and for all. But the heart of man is hard, hateful, and as a result, the innocent die for the sins of their leaders. Instead of seeking peace, men war against each other.

Let us speak of man's heart, his beliefs and what I can do in a willing spirit. There is hope for the world as you know it. Hearts can be changed overnight and lives transformed. My Light is powerful to the overcoming of all sin in man's heart. Peace can prevail in the world. It takes effort but with my grace all things are possible (Luke 1:37).

Let me tell you a story. There once was a powerful King of a small country. This King had many subjects who loved him and obeyed his commands. One day the King was approached by a beggar who asked for alms so he could buy bread to feed his family. Now the King wondered why one of his subjects needed to beg when food was plentiful in his kingdom. The man was blind and could not work his land. So, the King took a stone, gave it to the man saying, "Take this stone and build an altar on it. Tell your family to find other stones to add to it and see what happens." So, the blind man did what the King commanded. Lo and behold, one of his children found a precious pearl buried in the ground; and they rejoiced at their good fortune. The blind man and his family ate their fill and rejoiced in the wisdom of their King.

So, why did I tell you this story? The wise King knew that instead of giving the blind man what he asked for: a piece of bread, it was far more merciful to give him work to do so he could support himself and feed his family.

Now look for ways to help others help themselves—to make them less dependent on others to supply their needs. The blind man obeyed the King and found a treasure of grace.

I, your God, am the King. You are the blind man. Your work is to cultivate the land of your faith in my love and in my power by obeying my commandments. I will lead you to the treasure of eternal life in Paradise where you will live a rich, full and contented life.

Remember to take your blinders off your eyes and see my grace working in the world. Things may look black but the sun always brightens the day.

9/19/18

Lead me, Lord, in your justice.

Today we will speak about the fifth Beatitude. Be merciful as I am merciful. You received my mercy the day I came to you, opened your eyes and you saw the Truth. That was the day of your conversion, or metanoia, as they say in charismatic terms. It was the day you began to walk in the Spirit and your life was changed forever, and for the better, I must say.

Would that all my children would pray for the grace of conversion—I would gladly fill them with my Spirit and lead them in my justice. But for some, sadly, it takes a lifetime before they surrender to my will. What can we do to awaken my little ones to the truths of their faith? to turn their hearts toward their God? to see my light?

Yes, I can lift up great saints who will gladly follow Me, give their hearts and souls to Me, and become my prayer warriors.

Then I will pour out my power into these willing servants who will obey my every command, love my people with all their heart, and sacrifice their time and energy to spread the truth of my love for them, the truth of my Passion, Death and Resurrection. Then their eyes will be opened to the beauty and mercy of their God, and they will love Me, obey Me, and their lives will be changed forever.

This is the way of my justice. Is it not merciful to pray for your brothers and sisters to be converted and come to see the light of my love for them? This is true justice and mercy to help others gain wisdom of heart and knowledge and understanding of the work and presence of my Holy Spirit in their souls. Would that all my people would be intercessors and bring others into the light. Then I should pour out my light and justice upon the whole world and there would once again be peace on earth.

At the birth of my Son, the angels spread the Good News to the shepherds on the hillside (Luke 2:10). Today my angels would sing on mountain tops heralding the second coming of my Son into the world. For this reason, I am calling you and all my faithful witnesses to grow stronger in faith, hope and charity. Be merciful to the downhearted. Pray for the conversion of your brothers and sisters. Be my light in the present state of darkness in the world.

Rejoice always (Philippians 4:4). Joy attracts others to your cause. And what is your cause? To spread the joyful, merciful love God has for every soul on earth!

9/27/18

Have mercy, Lord, in your kindness.

Yes, today we shall speak about my mercy. I must be merciful, and I am merciful, for I understand the misery of sin; the destruction it does to the souls of my children. The greatest sign of my mercy is the Crucifix. There you see the broken body of my beautiful, good Son—the second Person of the Holy Trinity, God the Son and your Lord and Savior. How can you look at his suffering and not feel remorse for your sins against Him who laid down his life that you may live?

Some call Me the eleventh-hour God because my grace comes to save at the last moment. But I would have it another way, gladly. If only my children would turn to Me immediately when they are in peril—without hesitation; I would answer immediately with my love, mercy, light and compassion.

Nothing more can be said about my merciful heart that has not already been revealed in my Divine Mercy Movement. Pray the Chaplet for your needs. Pray it for your lost children and their needs. The prayer of an intercessory-heart is powerful, for one is praying out of love for a neighbor unselfishly. It is good and necessary to pray for one's own needs—yes, ask, pray always and I will hear, but I do not answer until the time is right.

Let Me tell you a secret. Time is in my hands. Have you not noticed those times when you find time to do all that you planned to do and there was time to spare? Yes, I prolonged the time for you—even gave you more time than you expected. That is my infinite power at work in your life and in your soul.

Another point I want to make is this: If you want to receive mercy, then be merciful in return. When you receive an answer to prayer, extend mercy to someone else. Your Father in Heaven sees your good deeds and shines his light upon you. The more you give, the more you receive.

I am a generous God. Did I not give you my Son? I gave you my very life, and I will never stop giving. There is no end to my mercy. Give it away and I will give you more.

Listen, my children. There is no other God but Me (Isaiah 45:5). Money, wealth, power cannot give you happiness. Do not seek these things. Just seek my power over you and I will give you wealth beyond measure. I guarantee it.

10/4/18

Take my hand, Lord, and walk with me into the night.

Yes, my child. I have much to tell you about the Beatitudes. They are traffic lights in the spiritual battle. You need my light to light up the dark night of the soul, especially the fifth Beatitude on mercy. You have reached out your hand to the God of Mercy. I have a forgiving, merciful heart and those who seek Me will find mercy for their sins against my laws.

Laws are given to guide you on the journey, and to protect you from harming yourself. They are good laws but my people find them difficult to obey for various reasons—be it laziness, selfishness, pride. These most often are the major obstacles they must overcome. But even there, they find my mercy in that I understand their weaknesses and faults. This is why my Son Jesus the Christ came to earth to lay down his life as a ransom for the sins of all mankind (1 Timothy 2:6). Is that not the epitome of mercy?

Yet, I will not spoil my children by looking the other way. As a loving parent, I must discipline them (Hebrews 12:6), awaken them to the dangers in store for them when they leave my protective cover over them. I am their shelter in the storms they encounter (Isaiah 25:4). When they call to Me for help, I respond in haste. I am their refuge (Jeremiah 16:19), a safe haven, the light on the path. I hear the cries of the poor (Psalm 34:16) and make a way for them to find Me.

All roads lead to Rome, so they say, but the road of mercy brings you right to my door. One who extends mercy to his neighbor, will receive mercy in return. Yes, study the spiritual and corporal works of mercy. Find one best suited to your nature and develop it into a virtue. I will give you what you need. Never fear of extending yourself; I will supply what is needed. I just need a willing heart and I will do the rest. As you give mercy, so shall you receive. Then all the light you need to flush out the darkness of your soul will be granted. Trust my Word.

(These are the works of mercy:

Corporal Works of Mercy	Spiritual Works of Mercy
Feed the hungry	Admonish the sinner
Give drink to the thirsty	Instruct the ignorant
Clothe the naked	Counsel the doubtful
Shelter the homeless	Comfort the sorrowful
Visit the sick	Bear wrongs patiently
Visit the imprisoned	Forgive all injuries
Bury the dead	Pray for the living and the dead)

11/9/18

I have sinned against You, Lord, please forgive me.

Yes, of course. I forgave you long ago on the Cross of my crucifixion (Luke 23:34). I gladly forgive a repentant soul. Does not your heart melt when your child asks forgiveness? Mine does as well, only more so because I forgive every sin ever committed and every sin to be committed. You do not understand? Let Me explain. Because I am Omniscient, time is not a factor. I know, I see, I understand everything and always. I am the First and the Last (Revelation 22:13). I am from the beginning to the end. Everything that happens, every word that is spoken, every good and bad deed performed, I foresee it before it happens. I am never surprised because I know all things. I decide when to reveal knowledge and to whom I will reveal it.

Think of Thomas A. Edison and the invention of the light bulb. That is my power unleashed to him. He learned step by step, slowly understanding came to him. I do not reveal more than my people can comprehend. I move slowly, and light comes gradually into the mind; an idea is born and with labor and ingenuity, as in Edison's case—light was captured and regulated. It could be turned on and off. I have many amazing ideas to distribute. One must be open or they will miss my visit.

So, yes, I can forgive and have forgiven and will always forgive a contrite heart (Psalm 51:3-21), for in asking for my mercy, they recognize who I am and their need of Me. They have taken the proper stance before their God, their only hope of salvation. Humility avails much in my Kingdom. Humility moves Me deeply. I love my people and only want good for them.

144

Yes, my prophet Jeremiah spoke it for Me. *"When you call me, when you go to pray to me, I will listen to you. When you look for me, you will find me. Yes, when you seek me with all your heart, you will find me with you, says the Lord, and I will change your lot"* (Jeremiah 29:12-14). I have so much in store to give. I need willing, open minds.

Oh, there is one sin that cannot be forgiven because in refusing my grace, mercy, forgiveness, the sinner blasphemes against the Third Person of the Blessed Trinity, the Holy Spirit (Matthew 12:31). They cannot be forgiven because they reject my Spirit in whom lies all my power to save them. They condemn themselves. I did not come to condemn, but to save (John 3:17), and in refusing the gift of the Holy Spirit, they condemn themselves to a life of darkness, misery and death. That I cannot forgive because they do not permit Me to save them.

Remember my gift of free will? I gave it because I do not want robots or puppets for children. I want free-thinkers, decision-makers, virile movers and shakers—people alive, full of Spirit, willing to discover the gifts I have for them, willing to pursue their dreams, like Edison who would not stop or give up—he never despaired. He stuck to it and was rewarded beyond his dreams.

This can happen to you, my Reader. Know that your sins are forgiven. Know that I am rooting for you; I am in your corner. Pray and ask for my help to overcome all obstacles in your life that hold you back from fully and completely surrendering yourself to the God who loves you completely!

Blessed Virgin Mary on the Fifth Beatitude

"Blessed are the merciful. See in the Child Jesus the Father's merciful love made man. In the fragile semblance of this Child, contemplate the victim who must be immolated for your salvation. It is He who brings into the world the merciful love of the Father. It is He, the merciful Love, who renews the hearts of all."

St. Padre Pio on the Fifth Beatitude

"You already know this Lover (Jesus) who never gets angry with whoever offends him. The One (Jesus) I carry in my heart is infinitely merciful. When I ask what I have done to merit so many consolations, he smiles and only asks for my love in return. If Jesus can make us so happy on earth, what will it be like in heaven?"

St. Faustina on the Fifth Beatitude

"At the very beginning of Holy Mass on the following day, I saw Jesus in all His unspeakable beauty. He said to me He desired that such a Congregation be founded as soon as possible, and you shall live in it together with your companions. My Spirit shall be the rule of your life. Your life is to be modeled on Mine, from the crib to My death on the Cross. Penetrate My mysteries, and you will know the abyss of My mercy towards creatures and My unfathomable goodness—and this you shall make known to the world. Through your prayers, you shall mediate between heaven and earth."

Chapter Six

Sixth Beatitude
"Blessed are the pure in heart, for they shall see God."
Matthew 5:8

5/21/18

Come with your light, Lord, and make my heart your own.

Now I shall speak about purity of heart, the sixth Beatitude. This one is special because I must grant the grace of holiness which I do so easily in a heart open to Me. Your part is to ask in prayer for this grace, and you shall receive (Matthew 7:7). I want my children to want Me. I am their only good. I will take a willing heart and mold it into mine.

So first comes the desire to be holy, to purify the heart of lusts for pleasure. Saint Paul iterates many sins and faults in his Epistles. Look them up. Study them (Galatians 5:19). These vices mar the beauty of the soul. Pray for the grace to empty your heart and mind of them.

Grace is granted according to the desire. I will not force purity of heart and holiness on anyone. Yet I offer my grace to a hungry heart. Hunger and thirst for holiness and you will be satisfied: the promise of the fourth Beatitude. You see how righteousness leads to purity of heart?

Welcome my Spirit into your heart. Seek my will in all your ways. Let Me purify your heart. Be willing to obey my Word-become-man. My Word is sacred and powerful. I exist in my Word. It is written in the Bible for you to read, study, meditate and contemplate. The Word is holy and powerful unto cleansing the heart of man.

So now, I have given you several ways to cleanse your heart: pray/ask and know my Word in the Bible. There are many ways to receive grace. My Son opened up the storehouse of my love by shedding his blood. That is how important it is to make your heart ready to receive the greatest of all virtues: my Divine Love.

5/22/18

Grant me the gift of faith, Lord, to move mountains.

Today we take up where we left off yesterday—purity of heart. Listen carefully, I have much to say on this subject. My people must have pure thoughts to have a pure heart. So, it begins with what and how one thinks. You see how important it is to think rightly? One must be taught to think aright for the mind controls the feelings. If you think good thoughts, you will feel good about yourself.

Do you see why I taught my disciples the Beatitudes? You must take on these attitudes to have a heart that is pure. A heart full of joy and love keeps a person healthy and in peace. So, study the Beatitudes. Make them your own.

Wealth does not lead to purity. A pure heart does not grasp for possessions, pleasure, and power. Yes, these were the carrots that Satan put before Me in the desert (Luke 4:1). To have a pure heart, one must not yearn for them; but yearning for God's will is what must be desired.

Only I alone know your heart, mind and soul. Only I alone grant riches, pleasure and power. I alone know how to purify the heart and make you learn and understand my ways. My way is the way to peace and contentment. My way is a joyful, easy road to take because I go before you.

148

I broke the power of death (1 Corinthians 15:55-57) over humanity—that is why I became one of you, to bring you to Heaven to live eternally in peace and joy. The joy of Heaven consists in unity with the Beatific Vision, oneness with the Father of Glory, total freedom from toil, sweat and tears. All this can be gained by the pure of heart. It awaits my loyal friends, my faithful subjects, my obedient disciples—those who think like Me with hearts of gold.

Purity leads to contentment and peace. Purity foreshadows Heaven.

5/30/18

Here I am, Lord. I come to do your will.

Today I want to speak about intentions of the heart. This will speak to the sixth Beatitude. To have correct intentions, one must have purity of heart, otherwise you will think wrongly because your heart is in the wrong place. When a heart is pure, then peace, joy and love will flow from it, and your thoughts will be kind, gentle and forgiving toward others. You will be generous with your time, and you will not be selfish or greedy or begrudge helping your neighbor.

With a pure heart, the spirit is joyful, free of the drudgery of hate, resentment and anger. Then the intentions in your heart and soul will be for the good of others, for you have learned and understood the truth of my love for you personally. Armed with the truth, then you are set free to be my special disciple, to do what I ask; and no more will there be fear of rejection or thoughts of failure because you will trust that I am supporting you, guiding you, protecting you. You know no harm will come to you because Mine is the power. Even should they kill you, it does not matter because I will have you in my arms and take you where I am. Remember the reward of the sixth Beatitude: *"Blessed are the pure of heart for they shall see God"* (Matthew 5:8).

Now, how to purify the heart: Be still and know I am God (Psalm 46:10). Do good to those who mistreat you. Trust my power to transform you. Receive the Sacraments: Eucharist, Confession. Pray, asking for my Spirit to fill your heart with love, to wash away all impurities: pride, vanity, selfish desires, and above all to magnify your heart that it may contain my presence to the fullest measure; and to the bravest of hearts, they may ask for the marks of my Crucifixion. Ask and you shall receive abundantly (John 10:10).

6/1/18

Purify me, Lord, then I shall be clean.

Today we speak about the pure of heart. These are my children who trust Me with all their heart. They know that I am their Creator, Savior, Redeemer; and that I delivered them when they were in trouble. They know I protect them, transform them and love them. The pure of heart are those who listen to my word and obey Me. They lay down their own will, and in all their endeavors, they seek to know and obey my will. They know I am only good and will never harm them, hence they trust Me with all their heart, mind and soul.

The pure of heart shall see God and they will know what I have in store for them. They anticipate the joy of Heaven. They have given Me permission to guide and enlighten them.

They live for Me. Why is this, you ask? Because they have tasted the sweetness of the Lord (Psalm 34:9). They know my goodness, my greatness. They know I will never fail them. When things look dark, they know that the light will dawn.

The pure of heart are strong in conviction. They are not swayed by specious arguments or discussions contrary to their faith (2 Corinthians 10:5). The pure of heart know and live the truth. They know who their God is and worship him with all their hearts. They rejoice in the work I have done in their souls. They eagerly allow Me to remove all darkness from their hearts and minds. Their hearts are cleansed from bitterness, anger and hate; instead they are compassionate, kind and gentle with others and with themselves. They know they are nothing without Me, that I am their only good.

My love has triumphed in their despair. My light has overshadowed them. My will is uppermost in their thoughts. They survive by serving their God. This gives them life, joy and peace. Hence, they see the face of God.

6/3/18

Cleanse my heart, Lord, of every vain desire.

The sixth Beatitude is important because where I am, there can exist only beauty, glory, perfection. So, to gain Heaven and to be united with the Beatific Vision, one's soul must be purified—that is to say, it must be cleansed of all darkness, sin, longing for earthly pleasures, detached from self, clothed in virtues, and bearing much fruit in faith, hope and love.

You ask for examples? How to do this? How to achieve purity of heart? In one word: trust. Trust that I can do it.

Trust that I love you and want you with Me where I am. Trust my power to work miracles. They are all around you. Trust in my good will. Did I not create you? Did I not save you? Will I not teach and sanctify you? Yes! This is my will that every man, woman and child will know, love and serve Me. In this, they achieve Heaven.

Every one's journey is unique and yet the same. Their souls must be cleansed of every vestige of sin: mortal and venial. They must examine themselves, turn away from their false self and their darkened minds. Learn the truth. Live the truth. Then they will find their true selves made in my image living in grace and light.

Simply ask for purity of heart. Ask and you shall receive (Matthew 7:7). Seek through study and then apply to your life the knowledge you have gained. This is wisdom. My Spirit will assist you in the journey of self-knowledge. Know yourself and you will find Me. Knock and the door of my life, grace and wisdom will be opened to you.

A father's treasure is reserved for his children. So, with Me. Look at the stars in the night sky. Do they not sparkle with delight? They are uncountable, unrepeatable. So, my children are stars in my eyes. I see each one and call them by name (Isaiah 43:1). They are precious to Me. Look at yourselves in my eyes. Trust in my love for you. It is the truth.

6/10/18

Free me from sin, Lord, and make me whole.

Today we speak of the pure of heart, the sixth Beatitude. What I would like to say is that this Beatitude is most

152

important because without a clear conscience and a firm will, the heart cannot be pure, unsullied. So, what to do: empty your heart of all bitterness, resentment and calloused thinking. It helps to fast from the pleasure of rich food such as candies, cake and other such delights. The purpose is to free the heart from selfish and pleasing desires to make room for prayer, devotionals such as novenas, litanies and the Rosary. If one is indulging in rich fare, the mind gets lazy and any hope of fasting is squelched.

My servant wrote a book about the battle is in the mind. To have a pure heart begins with a pure mind. A pure mind begins with self-control developed slowly by squelching the desires of the flesh. These dull the mind, suppress the spirit, smother all hope of purification from sin. An athlete trains his muscles; a saint restrains his desires.

What must one desire mostly to gain purity of heart? To please his God and his neighbor. Hence, my command to love. It is not that I need your love but that you need to love Me, to see Me in your neighbor. Purity of heart heals blindness, obscurity of mind and vision.

Let Me give you a strong example. My Mother kept everything that happened to her in her heart (Luke 2:51). She pondered in her mind every word spoken to her by Gabriel and Simeon about Me, her Child. She treasured every one of my words and deeds. In short, she meditated on Me, weighed my words; she thought more about Me than herself. She kept her eyes on Me and off herself. Her life, desires, hopes and dreams did not matter to her. She only thought of Me. She dedicated her life to Me. I was her other self; and she remained in Me to the end. She felt every nail that pierced my hands and feet in her own flesh. She suffered quietly, unobserved. She stood by my cross bravely accepting my Father's will, knowing in her heart that good would result from every drop of my blood. She united her heart with mine and it was breaking at the sight of my blood flowing out from my wounds.

Yes, grieve for her pain as much as for mine. We suffered for love's sake. You have not even begun to suffer as we did. Nor is it necessary to do so. Our suffering saved the world. My sacrifice atoned for every sin forever. I died once for all (Romans 6:10). I ransomed your souls, bought your freedom with my blood. Why? Because we are merciful; we love our children. I know it is difficult to comprehend. For this reason, we pour out grace in abundance so you may have faith in our love, power and mercy. Trust us with a pure heart and you will see!

6/11/18

Instruct me, Lord, so I may walk in your paths.

Let us begin. The pure of heart longs for God. As Saint Augustine said: the heart is restless without God. It yearns for its only good. That is why I created my people to be with Me forever close to my heart. But my purity cannot be acquired by impurity. The heart and soul of man needs to be pruned of all sin. Sin is a defilement which blackens the soul. Sin marks a man for death (Romans 6:23). It is not a life-giving action, rather it kills the soul drawing it away from the good which gives life, peace and joy. A life of sin is drudgery leading to death. Purity of heart leads to prosperity of grace and contentment.

I gave my people a free will (Joshua 24:15) but yet, I created them for greatness, to be like their Creator. They have the ability to choose goodness and truth, wisdom and knowledge. I did not leave them orphaned (John 14:18). I put my Spirit in them to guide them down the road that leads to safety and goodness. They have my Spirit in them but they have the freedom to follow, the freedom to choose life or death, the freedom to decide their destiny. I will not force them to choose Me. I only invite. I do not treat my people as cattle herded into a stall. I respect them too much. I cherish my children. I long for their love. If only they would, I should give them wealth untold. Ahh, how I suffer for my lost children; like a mother for her lost child, or whose child rejects her love. I grieve like a father for his wounded son crippled by disease.

Sin is a mortal sickness, killing my presence and my love in the heart and soul of my wayward, disobedient children. Sin destroys the covenant I made with humanity—the one my Son sealed with his blood (Luke 22:20). The promise of salvation was won by his death on the Cross. As he was mocked then (Matthew 27:30), he is mocked now by those who sin against him. He and I are one (John 17:21). My people mock their God, their source of life, with each and every sin.

Yet, I know and understand the condition of my children. This is why I gave my Apostles the authority to forgive the repentant sinner (Matthew 16:19), the one who humbles himself recognizing his need for my mercy that is readily given (Matthew 16:19). Would a father withhold assisting his child? Neither do I! Ask and you shall receive (Matthew 7:7). Humble yourself before your Maker and you shall receive riches beyond compare. No one can assure you the grace of eternal life—only the One who knows the inner working of your soul. The soul animates the heart, the core of the body, the life-giving implement connected to the spirit that in turn is connected to my Spirit, the source of all holiness, all goodness, all life, peace and joy.

Wonder of wonders is my all-consuming Holy Spirit.

6/13/18

Open to me, Lord, the gates of holiness.

Let us speak today about purity of heart. The heart is the resting place for my Spirit. Where my Spirit is, there can only be perfection. Therefore, the heart must be cleansed of all defilement. This is a slow process because the person's spirit is also in the heart. You did not know that. The heart, soul, and spirit are closely related, and the mind controls them all. That is why a pure conscience is necessary. Pure mind, pure heart. So, let us begin with purifying the mind, then the heart, soul and spirit will follow.

Hence, the significance of having the mind of Christ as Paul spoke of (1 Corinthians 2:16). In Baptism, you received the Holy Spirit and through the Holy Spirit, you received the Light of Christ. Putting it simply: the baptized are joined to Christ, live in him, and partake of his mind, his thoughts, his love, his Spirit. In the Holy Spirit who resides in your heart, you have the mind of Christ with all his powers, his courage, his judgments. This is a huge gift made possible by God the Father. Why? Because we love our people.

Yes, the Holy Spirit is the third Person in the Blessed Trinity; just as the Father and I are one, so, too, is the Holy Spirit one with us. And if the Holy Spirit dwells in your heart, you are one with us, the Triune God—therefore, you bear the mind of Christ. You have the power to think as he does, love as he loves, act and obey as he does.

On one condition, you must accept this blessing. This requires obedience, conformity, knowledge, wisdom and understanding—all gifts of the Holy Spirit who must increase in the heart, soul and spirit of man. Say yes, my children. Say, "Yes, Father. I know you love me and want me with you wherever you are. *'Whither thou goest, there shall I go'* (Ruth 1:16). I know you have a great plan for my life. I accept it. Do as you will with me. I am your humble servant grateful for my life, salvation, redemption and deliverance. I know I cannot live a holy life without your grace. Please purify my heart so you may dwell there in light, and increase your presence, filling me more and more with your love, compassion, mercy, kindness, goodness—all the outstanding virtues of the Blessed Mother. Then I will know the truth and the truth will set me free—free to be transformed into the image of Christ, my Savior and King. Father, let your Holy Spirit teach me and guide me and increase in me, for I want to be all you want me to be. Amen."

6/27/18

Give me a new heart, Lord, and a new spirit.

The subject today is purity of heart. This is a heart totally dedicated to her God. She has only God's will in her heart. Her greatest desire is to please Me and obey Me to the best of her ability. She is dedicated to following my lead and rejoices in her love for Me. Her soul magnifies her God and rejoices in him (Luke 1:46-47).

The pure in heart are those who revere Me. They have studied my word and made it their bond and seal. They triumph over temptation and have cleansed their house of

157

false thinking. They know who they are in Christ Jesus and rejoice in it. They have labored in my vineyard, struggled to die to their selfish desires (Luke 9:23) and put Me before themselves. They want only goodness in their lives, to live in peace and contentment. They are happy with less, putting aside inordinate desires, willfulness, and especially a hunger for riches, materially speaking. Their hunger now is to be right with Me, their God and Father.

The pure in heart have placed their trust in my providence knowing full well that I will never abandon them (Hebrews 13:5). They have witnessed my action in their lives. They know I love them and will never forsake or forget them. Can I forget myself? No. *"Can a mother forget her infant, be without tenderness for the child of her womb? Even should she forget, I will never forget you"* (Isaiah 49:15). I have nurtured you as a parent raises his child to his cheek (Hosea 11:4). Yes, the pure in heart cherish my words in the Bible receiving all the graces found there—in my word, in my light, in my Holy Spirit.

Their greatest love is to spend time with Me in silence, Sacred Silence. It is there that I am able to move powerfully in the soul. I take over the silent mind. I correct the thoughts. I put my thoughts in them. I can heal the quiet heart for it is at rest listening for my words, guidance, correction, and enlightenment.

I have much work to do to prepare the soul for its passing from this life to the next. One must know what is expected. My will is discovered by the docile of heart, the quiet, listening spirit. In the stillness, I move the gentle heart and flood it with my grace. In the quietness of the soul, my children find rest from their struggles, doubts, fears, and their hearts are renewed and take on a greater light. In this light, they see Light. They see my Face and are astounded by my beauty. To see Me is joy of spirit. To see Me is to know my heart. To know Me is to love Me and welcome Me with all that is in you.

Take heart, my people. Take my love and my grace. It is always there, waiting, calling. Come to Me, my people, and you will find rest (Exodus 33:14) for your souls. I am your peace, your joy. There is no other (Isaiah 45:5).

8/7/18

Create in me, Lord, a new heart.

Yes, I will and I have. Through study of the Beatitudes, you have recognized your poverty, your helplessness against evil spirits, your need for my grace and mercy. You have mourned and admitted your sins against Me, your only good. You have hungered and thirsted to know and serve Me, the source of your righteousness; and now you are hungering for a new and refreshing spirit so you will be able to love Me with a perfect love.

You ask for a new heart. What does that mean? I will tell you. It means having a heart filled with love, mercy, kindness, compassion for the sins of others, and for the sins committed against you. It is easy to forgive those who love you, but not so with those who reject and malign you. Having a new heart means to bear injustice, calumny, and hatred as I, your Savior, did. In Gethsemane, I pleaded with my Father to *"take this cup away"* (Luke 22:42). Even though I knew what my mission was, it was awful to bear it. I needed the grace of His will and fortitude to replenish my lagging Spirit. You see, even God seeks comfort and solace.

159

So, do not be afraid or ashamed to ask for my help; and this is what you are doing in asking for a new heart. You admit your need for my grace. You know you can do nothing without Me. You are humbling yourself before God. This is the perfect posture of a servant before her Master. Humility is a great virtue. It wins hearts. It converts sinners. It opens the storehouse of my treasures, and it is in line with my perfect will for all my children.

Yes, you are all my adorable children. Come to Me with all your needs and burdens (Matthew 11:28). I will refresh you and put new hearts in place of the old. I will recreate and replenish your spirits. Yes, you will be a new creation in my love (2 Corinthians 5:17).

Let Me tell you a secret: It is my will, my infinite will to save all the world of the ugliness of sin and to make all things new. I am about to make a new world where there is no darkness of sin. The light will be so bright that it disperses darkness. All souls shall be made new. There will be a new spirit in the hearts of my people. A new world and way of life will open to them.

O my people, rejoice in anticipation of the new life I have planned for you. Yes, there will be a new heaven and a new earth (Revelation 21:1). The old will give way to the new. Lift up your heads and see the new days ahead. I will be there and you will see my Face. There is nothing to fear for I am here carrying out my mission to renew, restore, and to live in your hearts in a new way. There is always something new ahead. I am infinitely creative.

8/14/18

Forgive me, Lord, for I have sinned against You.

Today my message is on purity of heart, mind, soul and body. With a pure heart, one conquers the self. The secret longings of the heart are controlled by the virtue to be right with God, to be just and holy. One no longer desires unholy things like immodest clothing, garish fashion styles of hair, dress, shoes. The fashion of the day is no longer of interest to the pure of heart; rather, a simple style of not only clothes but also, of a new way of life.

Where there were desires for wealth, pleasure, rich food, there is now a need for simplicity and a desire to only please her God who has become a bigger part of her life. The pure of heart seek to please God, want more of God, and less of the world. Worldly things are less tasteful. They enjoy silence, to be alone with God who they love with all their heart. Their whole life has changed. They desire to be at peace with the world. They begin to long for peace with each neighbor and with their enemies! Although, they do not consider anyone an enemy: they are only lost souls in need of a Savior.

They begin to pray for my return—to save my people once again. They pray for the conversion of sinners. They plead for the salvation of avowed atheists. They want everyone to love and know God as they do. They have reached the point in their own conversion that they love the enemy enough to pray for their conversion.

This is the work of grace in a disciple's soul. Their heart is pure. It is cleansed of selfishness and thinks of others in imitation of their Lord and Savior. The pure of heart long for peace around them and they bring peace wherever they go. They have found contentment of soul and spirit. Their eyes are focused on Christ, their Lord.

Life is one long blissful day loving their Heavenly Father. They look for ways to please him, ways to honor him. They rejoice in any sign of his presence or movement in their heart. They wonder at my power. When things work out for them, they know I have come to their aid and they rejoice with tears of gratitude. They see Me in all things and know in their hearts the truth of my love for them. *"Blessed are the pure of heart for they see God"* (Matthew 5:8).

9/8/18

Help me, Lord, to love my enemies.

Today, my people, we shall discuss the sixth Beatitude: *"Blessed are the pure of heart, for they shall see God"* (Matthew 5:8). Matthew, the apostle, wrote my words accurately. Those who have emptied their hearts of pride, selfishness, and vanity shall see my face. These, the pure of heart, have listened to my Word and have obeyed every word I have spoken to them.

Yes, they listen and hear, and then obey because they have shed any preconceived ideas of their own about what is good for their sanctification. They have left behind their own will in order to obey mine. They know I am their only good, and that I am true to my word. They have witnessed my power to change their hearts, and now they follow where I lead them.

Light and peace are the road signs on their journey. Anything unkind or lacking in mercy, they avoid. They detest hatred, name-calling. Their heart is pure and they protect it by avoiding sinful behavior. They love their God more than themselves. Hence, they detest hurting Me by sin. This is the state of sanctity I will for all my children.

When they have learned to love Me more than themselves, there has been a complete purification of heart. They are now ready to move up the ladder. They are climbing the Mountain of Love that leads to sanctification.

Yes, the journey is long and trying because there are so many obstacles on the road. But the pure of heart have tasted victory over sin and now hunger for peace, blessed peace. My peace is so delightful and desirable that they fill their days with prayer to be in communion with their Father. They find joy in prayer. They seek ways to be alone with Me. Prayer satisfies their thirst for righteousness with their God.

O my people, I have so much love to give you. Open your hearts to my Light. *"I am the Way and the Truth and the Life"* (John 14:6). Whoever finds Me, finds joy and peace, and it is so delicious and desirable. Stay close to my heart. Let Me tell you a secret. It is very easy to pray. Just look up. Lift your head. Say, "Hi, God! I know you're watching over me. Thanks." It takes very little effort to pray but the reward is tremendous. It can be the difference between life and death.

Remember, prayer is the password to my heart.

9/16/18

I rise before dawn, Lord, and cry for help.

Today we will speak about renewing the heart of man. Again, this takes a willing spirit, an open mind, the desire for a change of heart.   Yes, I put the desire in your heart (Psalm 37:4), but you must fan the flame (2 Timothy 1:6). How to do that, you ask? Simply pray and I provide the grace.

Let me give you an acrostic for **Grace**:

Generosity: Be generous with the gifts I give you.

Renewal: Renew your outlook, expand the horizons of your mind.

Action: Take action, pursue new interests to stimulate your mind and creative skills.

Counsel: Seek counsel from learned men and women.

Expectation: Expect that all things will fall into place. What does that mean? It translates into trust because you know that I desire your salvation more than you do!

Am I not God who created you? Are not my plans greater than yours? I repeat myself: I created you to know Me. Does that mean I would withdraw from you? Of course not! I love you. I want to help you know Me, to know my love for you. I guide you on the right path to heavenly glory. With tears in my eyes, I fret over your sins, mistakes and lack of understanding of who I am in your life. I am your Heavenly Father. I want to bounce you on my knee and to protect you from harm. I have given you life and breath, intelligence and a good heart—everything you need, I have provided. Is this not **G**enerosity?

Then I **R**enewed your spirit and you began to see spiritually. You saw the truth for the first time in your life, and your life was never the same. I put you into my service by **A**cting on the talents with which you were endowed by Me, and your faith grew by leaps and bounds. Your hunger to know Me prompted you to seek **C**ounsel from other Christians who

164

were also on the upward journey seeking my face. You and they Expected those who were more knowledgeable to share their faith, hope and love, and they did.

Do you see how grace/church works? Brother helping brother, neighbors sharing with neighbor—passing on the faith from generation to generation; and grace/church spreads throughout the land renewing hearts of men and renewing the world.

This was my plan from ages past. It is still in action and will continue until every man, woman and child have been awakened to the truth of my love for them.

My Word has been given and will not return to Me unfulfilled (Isaiah 55:11).

9/25/18

Open my heart, Lord, and fill it with your love.

Today our lesson is on purity of heart, the sixth Beatitude. This calls for complete openness of heart. My disciple must trust Me in three ways: with all your heart, with all your mind, and with all your soul. As the Father and I and the Holy Spirit are three in one God, so my disciples shall be.

Now, how to achieve this is the work of a lifetime. As a child, you were taught by your parents. As an adult, you began to listen to your conscience; now in your maturity, you are guided, counseled by the Holy Spirit whose purpose is to mold you into my image. You already are the child of God Most High, but you are still in need of more formation. This is spiritual and must be done in and with the Holy Spirit. Once you have reached this stage, the heart is ready and willing to obey, love and serve her Savior with all her heart, mind and strength.

In this stage, the soul is filled with light, peace and trust. Whatever happens, the soul knows it is God's will for the purpose of her sanctification. The soul's joy is to commune with her God in prayer frequently. She finds time during the day to be alone in her secret place to listen to Me, or to seek my advice, or to ask for help. I have become the most important person in her life. This is the right order to follow if one wishes to be my disciple.

At this point, I must warn you, the enemy attacks furiously. It desperately works to stop the sanctification process from going forward. The soul, if it fears or doubts, may waver and stumble, but knows that I will come to the rescue. I will never abandon or forsake my people (Joshua 1:5). I am the Savior of the world (Luke 2:11). I rule with a mighty hand (Ezekiel 20:34). I send down my faithful servant, Michael the Archangel, to do battle with the enemy, and it is defeated (Revelation 12:7). This is why I died on the cross to make the enemy powerless over my faithful, prayerful servants.

Use the tools I have given you. Use my name to rebuke and command the enemy to leave you in peace. Sometimes, I allow It free rein—only for the purpose to wake you up, to alert you to danger or to get you back on the right road. Remember always: Satan has no power over you. Do not give it back to him. Beware of his lies. It would have you believe things that are not true. Every word from Its mouth is false.

You know the Truth. Live in the Truth. I have set you free and shared my Life and Spirit with you. Use the power of my name to overcome every evil that attempts to steal you away from the light of my love and all the good things I have in mind for you. Be diligent. Be wise. Be holy.

10/23/18

Purify my heart, Lord, so I may climb the mountain of love.

Yes, I will. This is my plan and my work to do in a willing spirit. You must be open to receive my grace, and then obedient to the call on your life. I gladly pour out grace when you call for help—whenever it is according to my plan for your good (Jeremiah 29:11), for your salvation; for this is my purpose in creating you and breathing my grace into your soul. I want you with Me; I want you to believe in Me, to trust Me to be there for you. And I will. It gives Me joy to have my children with Me, to eagerly respond to my grace—then I can work miracles of healing, purifying, filling those empty spaces in the heart with my divine love, wonder-working love.

Now let Me tell you about making the climb up the mountain of Love. Yes, Love is the mountain of the Lord Jesus Christ. No one has or ever will love as unselfishly, perfectly and freely as He did. Do you know what it means to suffer as he did? He took upon himself all the sins of humanity. Maybe I had better speak about sin to help you understand the enormity of His suffering.

Sin is slavery to evil. Sin is destructive—a force of such strength that it causes blindness of physical vision and spiritual vision. Remember the words my Son spoke when he was crucified? *"Father, forgive them. They know not what they do"* (Luke 23:34). He was addressing their

167

blindness. They were so deep in sin, they could not see the Good before them.

Another aspect of the evil of sin is that it destroys love—the most beautiful gift I can give to my children. And yet, love in the heart is killed by sins of selfishness and pride. Greed also chisels its way into the heart, and one is left with little room to love. Sin is an assault against the purity and beauty of my presence and Spirit in the sinner's soul. My perfection, my glory, my light, my heart is so sacred, it will not abide in darkness. Sin is an offense against my justice. Remember what happened when the person in David's service touched the holy Ark and he was killed (2 Samuel 6:6)? This is what happens when one defiles their God, their Creator with sin. You know how often a good man sins per day? Seven times (Proverbs 24:16). Imagine how often a bad man can sin.

But back to our subject. Jesus suffered the weight of an infinite number of sins! It is the weight of which only his divine flesh and blood could bear. It was a feat that only God the Son could perform. And he did it because his divine love is more powerful than the deepest, darkest sin any human being can ever commit. Do you understand what Jesus accomplished by his suffering and death? He atoned, paid the debt against my righteousness, my holiness, my honor with his own righteousness, holiness and honor. Only God could offer a sacrifice worthy of God!

Think on these things.

10/28/18

Strengthen my faith, Lord, so I may love You more.

Today my child, we will speak about purity of heart which leads to more faith in the heart and soul of man. Yes, I created mankind to seek Me, to know Me, and in knowing the truth, they love Me with a purer love, a love that seeks to know my pleasure, to know and trust that my plan for their salvation will bear good fruit; that they will be happy with Me in Heaven and content to serve Me while on earth because it gives them all those good fruits Paul speaks about in the letter to the Galatians: love, peace, joy, kindness, generosity—all good things that make the heart happy, healthy and wise (Galatians 5:22).

When you come to know the truth of my love, protection and guidance, you will set your sights on following my way— the way of love, laying down your own agenda for mine because you know it is a better way; you trust who I am for you and that my only interest is to make you happy and holy and fit for heavenly life. You store up treasures in Heaven— you have lifted up your head and broadened your vision to see your spiritual self and your spiritual needs. You learn to nurture your spirituality by praying more often and more reverently; you seek Me in the Sacraments, mainly Eucharist, so I may strengthen you with spiritual food. It becomes a delight to sup with Me at the table of my Altar. Also, your spirit is fed on my holy Word spoken from the pulpit daily in every church throughout the world.

O my people, I am always with you at Holy Mass in my Church; I am with you in my Word written in the Bible (take and read). I am with you in your home with loved ones, in your neighbors—yes, even on religious television programs

169

and movies. I am everywhere (Hebrews 4:13). You cannot escape my love, if you look and comprehend what you see. Open your eyes and hearts to the reality of my presence in your souls.

You have been wonderfully made (Psalm 139:14) to comprehend the depth of my love, my thought of you, your need for Me. I created you to know Me, so seek Me (Isaiah 55:6) with all your heart and strength. I will be found. I promise. It is in the seeking, the searching, the comprehending that the heart is made perfect. The journey presents itself to one who seeks. The prize is won by those who participate. Look, seek and I will be found, for I have decreed it so (Matthew 7:7).

11/4/18

Thank You, Lord, for redeeming my sins.

Sense my peace come into your soul at the first sign of gratitude for my gift of forgiveness and mercy. My peace elevates your spirit, gives life to your soul, and your heart expands with love for your Savior—and that I am! You cannot live without my grace which, in essence, is my very Life within you. It is my Spirit that infills you with grace, and your soul is purified and strengthened to avoid all occasions of sin. My Spirit infills your heart, and its capacity expands to receive more of my Love, so you may love with my perfect Love that knows the true wishes of your Heavenly Father; and in this way, you accomplish his will for your life. Also, my Spirit teaches you my ways to become holy as I am holy (Matthew 5:48). And is this not the purpose of your life? To become holy so you can enjoy eternal life in Paradise with your Savior who loves you and wants only good for you?

Why would you think that I don't love you? I am Love (1 John 4:8). Why would you think I am not fair? I am the Just Judge (2 Timothy 4:8). Why would you think I don't know you? I am All-knowing, Omniscient (Job 37:16). I know everything about you: what you've done, good and bad; what you've done and what you have not done. I know the desires of your heart, your hurts, triumphs and failures; what you hope for in the future. Have I not convinced you that I love you more than you love yourself?

Has anyone in your life suffered the cruelty and abject misery of a crucifixion just to redeem your sins so you will not suffer the penalty of death for your own sins? I took the blame in your place. Why? Because I could and because I love you, and because it was the only way to save you from eternal death in the fires of hell. No, I would not do that to you. I love you too much!

Oh, if only my children would open their hearts to the truth, I would pour out my grace, my Spirit, my Life into them, and they would know such love and peace they couldn't stand it! When they do understand, when they do come to believe, then they will have such gratitude in their hearts that they will love Me totally. Oh, what joy! What fun we will have together!

Blessed Virgin Mary on the Sixth Beatitude

"Blessed are the pure of heart. God is present in my Child Jesus. His Heart is the Heart of God. He has assumed human nature from me, but his Person is divine. Thus, the Heart

that beats in this Child is the very Heart of God. See God in the Son, whom I carry in my motherly arms. Feel the beating of the Heart of God in his, which beats, and learn to love. Purity of heart is born from the perfection of love. Therefore, only one who loves can attain to purity of heart, and only one who is pure of heart can see God."

St. Padre Pio on the Sixth Beatitude

"Try to reflect the simplicity of Jesus in your life, keeping worldly wisdom and sophistication far from your heart. Try to have a mind that is always pure in its thoughts, always righteous in its ideas, always holy in its intentions. Try to have a will that seeks nothing but God and his preferences and seeks glory and honor only from him."

St. Thomas Aquinas on the Sixth Beatitude

"Although someone is well disposed and united to God, still if his affections are bent on diverse and trifling things, his power is weakened and he is rendered less effective to do good. And hence it is that God, to make us productive of good, often cuts off from us and purges us of similar impediments by sending us tribulations and temptations, which if we overcome, we become stronger in the performance of good. And therefore, no man in this life is so pure but he may be more and more purified."

Chapter Seven

Seventh Beatitude
"Blessed are the peacemakers,
for they shall be called sons of God."
Matthew 5:9

5/7/18

May the fire of your word, Lord, consume my sins.

This morning we will write about peacemakers. How do we change our attitude from hate to love? This is important in the process to cultivate peace, for love is the deciding factor. We choose to love. We choose to hate. We choose to forgive. We choose to give up anger. I have given mankind a free will to make their own choices. They must decide what they want in their hearts. Do they want hate, resentment, unforgiveness, or do they want love, kindness and peace in their hearts?

I have said it before: As a man thinketh, so he does. Do they choose to hate Me because I permit evil to exist? Do they blame Me if man chooses to do evil? I will not take back my gift. Grace once given will not be taken away (Luke 21:29). I stand firm in my decisions. I will not abandon anyone who asks Me for grace. "Ask and you shall return," was not spoken by my Son but, *"Ask and you shall receive"* (Luke 11:9-13). The gift is given and received. It is a final transaction.

O my people, choose wisely. Choose to be peaceful at heart. Peace enlightens the heart. It expands into joy. I have much more to say about being a peacemaker, but it must begin in the mind and heart. To be a peacemaker is to live in peace with oneself. Unburden your resentments. Clear your minds. Change your thoughts. Yes, make an attitude change. It will give you peace and joy. The burden will be removed from your shoulders. Give Me your burdens, your hurts, your misunderstandings, your cares, fears, worries, and I will bear them for you (Psalm 55:23). Come to Me and I will instruct you and give you the gift of peace so you may live and abound with joy.

Be peacemakers. Heaven awaits you.

5/19/18

Lead me, Lord, in the path of your justice.

Today we begin with peacemakers—these are those who love God with all their hearts. They have conquered their false selves. You wonder about that? The false self is the side of man's ego that tells him he must save himself. Thus, already he is in rebellion against the right of his Creator over him. The false self tells the woman she is on her own. She can decide what is good for her; she knows her own mind and is impervious to the needs of others. You see with that mind-set, she does not need anyone but herself. She keeps her own counsel. The false self is not open to change nor open to new thoughts. In a way, they are imprisoned in their own minds, oppressed and bound up with false beliefs. I repeat: they cannot change.

That's where I come in. I know my people. I love them. They are mine whether they know Me or not (Isaiah 43:1). Nothing is impossible for Me (Luke 1:37). I can change hearts, correct false belief systems. My grace is powerful, efficient and works wonders in the souls, minds, and hearts of my children. I am their Father. Would a mother forget her child

(Isaiah 49:15)? No, I will never forget my children. I long to make peace with them. Jesus reconciled us by paying the debt of sin against Me (2 Corinthians 5:18). I accepted his recompense. All is right now. Sin is atoned and will be atoned forever.

All that is left to do is to spread my peace, one to the other. I need peacemakers. They work for Me. Let the children come to Me so I can transform their hearts, mold their thoughts, teach them my ways. "Let us return to the Father the good that he gives to us. Let us trust and believe in his goodness and faithfulness. We cannot do it on our own. We are only dust molded in his image. We need him." Let this be the cry of the heart for all my people.

5/25/18

Grant me the grace, Lord, to live in peace.

Peace is my gift to you when I reconciled you with my Father by making atonement for your sins (John 20:19). The gift of peace that I give is not of the world. You must pray for that, but my peace is given freely to help you grow into my image. You must have peace in the heart before you can see my Face.

When I came the first time to the world, I was prepared to restore divine order in the hearts and minds of my people. They would not believe. I announced the Kingdom of Heaven is at hand (Mark 1:15), but many missed my visitation. They would not listen and repent. They took their own counsel and remained in the dark. The Light of the World came (John 8:12), but they rejected the Light and condemned themselves. Had they repented and believed, it would have been better for them.

My heart is heavy and tears drop from my eyes for the loss of my love for my chosen people (Luke 19:41). They remain in darkness till this day. I will come another day and all will see my Face, and they will believe. They will have no choice. The day of my Judgment will be final. Some will believe and be saved, others will not. I will not force them. Their answer can only be yes or no.

What does this have to do with regaining your peace? Everything! With knowledge of my love, one has faith. With faith, one obeys. In prayer, the heart is open and I am able to fill it with sanctifying grace. With grace, comes assurance. With confidence in who I am, comes peace because you know there is nothing impossible for Me (Luke 1:37).

Know, believe, pray, obey and my peace will fill your heart and soul.

5/28/18

Keep me safe, Lord, in the palm of your hand.

My child, today we will speak about peace, the seventh Beatitude. **Peace** is Prayer, Ecstasy, Adoration, Counsel, and Energy. One must pray to achieve peace in the heart, mind, soul and spirit. Peace in the heart comes with a clear conscience. You know you are right with God. You have amended the mistakes you have made, grieved for them, prayed for the grace to walk away from them, and also, to pray for healing for the ones you have offended. This is

mportant.   One must have contrition for offending my
people and myself.

Remember, no one is perfect, only my Heavenly Father is
perfect (Matthew 5:48).   So, to achieve peace in the heart
requires repentance.   That is why I came proclaiming the
Kingdom: one must repent for the Kingdom of Heaven is at
hand (Mark 1:15). Meaning, I brought my kingdom of power,
grace, healing, light into the darkness of your world.   I
brought Heaven down to earth when I came to be born in the
stable at Bethlehem (Luke 2:4-11).   This was planned before
the world began. My Father planned everything for the good
of his people, for you personally, and for everyone who
believes and trusts in Me.

I have so much to give to those who believe, pray, hope and
don't worry, as my son Saint Pio would say.   Yes, I make
Saints of souls who trust Me.   Yes, my Mother helps Me.
She is very good at creating Saints.   Pray to her for guidance.
This is the work I planned for her.   She is your holy Mother
(John 19:26-27).   Love and respect her for she was chosen by
my Father to give Me her flesh and blood.   I, my presence in
her body, sanctified her.   She is precious to Me and those
who love her love Me.

6/8/18

Lord, grant me the grace to be obedient.

Let us talk today about peacemakers.   They are the salt of the
earth (Matthew 5:13).   Peacemakers are happy people.   They
are faithful to their Lord.   They are content to be obedient.
They strive to be useful, and care for their neighbors.   They
are upright and just in all their affairs, and they trust in the

goodness of humanity. They hope and dream for peace in the world.

On a different note, it is the work of grace operating in the souls of peacemakers. Do you see your President working for denuclearization of North Korea? He is my chosen servant, although he does not know it is my power at work in him. Just like you and so many of my children are not aware of your power to please Me. If you did, then I would do great things in and through you. You must surrender to my love, ask for my mercy in healing the wounds and fractures in relationships caused by pride, the chief barrier to peace.

Wars are the result of pride. Men have not known how to ward off this sin. They believe falsely that they are invincible in falling prey to the devil's wiles. In this way, they lose the grace of peace in their hearts and minds, and can no longer function peaceably, and are filled with anger, lashing out at their brother, sister, whoever withholds their approval. On another note, pride functions in this way: hate rules their hearts. They become confused, then arrogant, puffed up with false bravado: they can take on the world!

Oh, if only my people would surrender to my rule. I would shower down grace into their hearts. They would know a peace the world cannot give to them. Only in my light can they be happy, care-free, trusting in their God who loves them. Then and only then will they find blessed peace in their hearts and this peace will spill over and spread to all around them.

Pray to be a peacemaker.

Guide my feet, Lord, into the way of peace.

Let us begin today with the seventh Beatitude. *"Blessed are the peacemakers for they shall be called sons of God"* (Matthew 5:9). This promise is to those who put aside their preconceived decisions and are flexible enough to listen to the needs of others. This takes magnitude of mind, heart and will. Uppermost in their minds is to do the will of God whom they have grown to believe in, trusting in my power, and have a true desire to do my will, to please Me and obey Me. They have learned to be meek and humble of heart. They practice mercy and forgiveness. They seek to be right with their God, and they know that all things are possible when they are in my will (Luke 1:37).

Peace is a powerful force. It calms angry spirits, relaxes anxiety in the heart; It brings down high blood pressure thus promoting good health. There are many benefits in this Beatitude. Aside from preventing wars between nations, and mending broken relationships within families, peace restores order in the soul and reconciles that soul with its God. Then all things fall in place. Blessed peace relaxes the heart, the source of life. Peace brings joy wherever it is practiced.

Do this: Sit quietly in a chair . . . Think of a favorite food you enjoy . . . Relish the delicious flavor . . . Toss it around in your mouth . . . Taste and see how sweet it is for a moment . . . Swallow it slowly, envision it passing through the esophagus into your contented stomach spreading joy throughout the body . . . Rest in that peace . . . Make it a friend . . . Discover the power of peace to bring serenity to your mind and heart . . . Your eyelids relax . . . Your tight chin slackens its grip on your mouth . . . Your lungs give a sigh of relief . . . Then something wonderful happens . . . Good, gentle thoughts enter the mind and the whole body is at rest.

Practice these exercises of peace in the heart. Peace opens the mind to think new thoughts, and new attitudes will develop. Peace will reign in your soul and a new vision presents itself—peace among nations. Peace in the heart restores order in the world. New thoughts bring new feelings and this leads to a stronger faith and trust in my power.

6/26/18

Lift my spirit, Lord, and fill me with joy.

Let us talk today about peace in the world. Although I have much to say about evil in the world: man hating man. This is what leads to wars among brothers. Envy is another war-provoking evil. Jealousy of brothers for each other is akin to murder.

But let us also speak of hope and joy. These are instruments of peace in the heart. Consider joy. It is an emotion stemming from contentment with one's self when the soul knows its Savior and trusts in him. Having gained peace in the heart leads to contentment and facilitates the fulfillment of one's duties toward God and man. Having fulfilled one's duties in life and having obeyed my commandments brings a joy of spirit, and this infuses peace in one's heart.

Always do what you know is best. Then there is nothing to regret or to trouble your conscience. I have given you a good, healthy mind to know my will. And since I only want good for you, it follows that in obeying my plan for your life will result in peace and contentment. A life well lived brings joy.

Let us talk now about peacemakers. These are the sons and daughters of my own heart. My Son Jesus the Christ came to bring peace to the world. He is the Great Peacemaker. He reconciled humanity with its Creator (2 Corinthians 5:18). He paid the ransom for your souls. He paid the debt owed to Me for all the sins of disobedience and rebellion against Me. My children were lost in sins of the world and sins of the flesh. There was no hope for their salvation. So, my Son gave his life to save them, to make retribution for them. Now they live in peace by the blood of Christ. Praise and honor what he has done for you. Better still, become one of his disciples. Spread peace wherever you are and wherever you go.

Peace is ecstasy of the soul. Peace lends beauty to the spirit. Peace is a tranquilizer. Peace in the heart should be everyone's goal. How to gain peace? Think happy thoughts. Be kind, loving and gentle. Forgive your brother and sister. They are not the enemy. Resist the devil's voice when he speaks (James 4:7). His end is near. He knows it and is stirring up his forces to wreak havoc, hate and discord throughout the world. Refuse his manipulations. Rebuke him in the name of Jesus! Resist with all your strength. I will be with you with my grace. I defeated Satan on the cross. He has no power over you. Trust Me and you will live peacefully and fully in my light.

One more thing before we end this session: love, love Me your only good; love your neighbor who I created in my image and whom I love as much as I love you; and lastly, love yourself because I made you good and worthy of my love. Trust my Word. He came to give you abundant life (John 10:10). Cherish his presence in your heart. He has set

181

you apart to obey him (Ephesians 2:10). Follow him willingly, joyfully. He has great and wonderful plans for your life. Be at peace with yourself and the world. Should it get you down, pick yourself up and try again. I am with you.

7/4/17

Speed my steps Lord, along your path.

I wish to speak today on the subject of peace which I won for you on the Cross. Without the Cross, there could be no peace. So, one must choose to accept or to reject the cross in their life. Acceptance brings grace; rejection brings misery. Choose the right path. It is spelled out for you in the Bible.

Did I not begin my ministry by teaching the Beatitudes? They are beacons of light on your journey into the Kingdom. Follow them. Adopt them as your philosophy of life. Yes, they give life to whoever follows them because these are my attitudes and I am the Way, the Truth and the Life (John 14:6). Those who follow will think like Me and I will lead them to the Kingdom where I have reserved a special place for them (John 14:3).

Listen to my commands and obey. Life will become a joy not drudgery. My life within you will give you the peace the world cannot give. Treasure my presence in your heart and soul. This is why I say to you to cherish yourself. Where I am, and I am in everything by virtue of my omniscience, there can only be health, happiness and peace of soul.

Let not your hearts be troubled (John 14:1). Trust my power to redeem your sins, failings, mistakes and to make you a new creation. I will create in you a new heart and a steadfast spirit (Psalm 51:12), and you will have eternal life with Me in Paradise. Trust my Word to accomplish this mission in and for you. I will pour over you my Holy Spirit to wash away your iniquities and I will shower my graces upon you to prepare you for your own ministry. In my Kingdom, all have purposeful work to do. Idleness is undesirable. Work makes holiness. Choose to obey and follow Me. The reward is eternal joy!

7/17/18

Fill me, Lord, with your Spirit.

To be a peacemaker, you must listen to both sides of the story. Each person has their own opinion of the truth. Each one has a personal sense of understanding their own truth, so to speak. They want and need to be loved and accepted by others and when this need is frustrated, they become dejected, injured.

In order to resolve issues, they must first resolve to agree to restoring an area of agreement on solid ground, equal issues. They must agree to compromise, to listen to the opposite party's views and needs. Bottom line, they reach a point of agreement to make peace between themselves.

Usually, there should be a moderator who can assist the dialogue between opposing parties. The moderator must be privy to the issues and knowing both sides. What caused the disagreement? What is the surface problem? Then pray that the root cause of the problem will be revealed. Usually, it is three things: money issues, pride, or preconceived judgments leading to misunderstandings; bottom line: self/ego.

The peacemaker is one who understands human nature, who can rise above the unsettling problem at hand and resolve it. To do this, the peacemaker knows himself, his need for God and asks for the grace of wisdom and discernment. Then he is ready to listen to both sides and find a common ground on which to repair the broken relationship.

The peacemaker must have peace in his heart, have a loving and kind disposition, and a firm relationship and prayer life with Me, for I alone can heal hurts, touch hearts and minds, and bring light into the darkness. I alone rebuild the inner man, transfigure mental capacities; in short, change hearts, renew souls and infill the spirit of man and make him a new creation (2 Corinthians 5:17). This was my work accomplished by my death on the Cross. I am the ultimate Peacemaker. It is my gift to the world and I bestow it on anyone who asks. It is freely given. Ask, seek, and knock on the door and you shall receive a peace beyond understanding (Luke 11:9-13).

7/19/18

Have your way, Lord, in my heart.

Today I will speak about peace—a peaceful heart can work wonders for the world. Yes, they are my intercessors. They have great power to do good. After all, I am Spirit, so my intercessors move, work and pray spiritually. They move in the sense that the recipients of their prayers are moved, motivated by my grace to repent, to be converted, and to be healed.

The work of the intercessor is to make peace, to bring my peace into their own souls and then into the souls of others, to bring comfort and consolation in their hearts. This is all done on the spiritual plane through the grace of my mercy and my power.

Their (intercessors) prayers are powerful in deed because the peace in their hearts is the gift I gave to the world when I resurrected from death. John speaks eloquently in his Gospel about my appearance in the upper room to my disciples (John 20:19). Yes, they became Apostles when they were sent out on the day of Pentecost by the power of the Holy Spirit who anointed them to preach and heal my people (Mark 16:14).

So, my intercessors are anointed by the same Holy Spirit, and hence, their prayers—the power of their prayers—are spiritual. We have come a full circle: the intercessor is a peacemaker whose prayers move and work miracles in the world. Hearts and lives and minds are transformed by the effective prayers of the peacemaker/intercessor.

Keep these words in your heart and mind. They bring life and light into the world because their (intercessors) prayers, love and obedience move Me, God of the Universe. I respond to every prayer (Mark 11:24). No prayer is ever left unanswered. I am not a small God. My power is infinite, incomprehensible. This is the reason I call my disciples to trust, to trust in my love, mercy, forgiveness and power to recreate the heart and soul of man, and the world.

Pray for a harvest of intercessors. In them, I can and will work wonders unimaginable to humankind. There shall be a new, wonder-provoking world. It is coming. Be prepared, trust and pray.

7/20/18

I rise before dawn, Lord, and cry for help.

In order to be a peacemaker, one must entrust the conflict, the situation, or the misunderstanding or argument into my hands. I am the Divine Counselor (Isaiah 9:5). All matters are first presented to Me, left in my hands, and I will dispose of the matter in due course. Do not take the matter in your own hands. I repeat: trust and wait for my light, my guidance, my will to run its course. If you rush headlong into a problem of discord or disagreement without my counsel, things will end up badly. Wait, wait for guidance. Trust, trust that in due time, the light, the answer will come. At the right time and in the proper order, the truth will be revealed to the satisfaction of all those involved in the dispute.

Trust my word to guide you. Search the Scriptures to see how I handled all my affairs, plans of action, and how I guided my people Israel through the desert. Did I not provide manna from heaven and quail for their appetites (Exodus 16:4)? Did they not reach the Promised Land (Joshua 1:2-3)? Yes, in due time they understood my presence among them: the cloud by day and the pillar of fire by night (Exodus 13:21). The wise men followed the star and found my Son in the manger (Matthew 2:2). So too, my disciples will find the way out of all their struggles. My way is the best way for I have walked it before you. Follow my footsteps. They lead to victory.

On another note, let us speak about true love. Does not love bear all things—including calumny? Is it not better to turn the cheek than to prove your innocence? Do what I did when my persecutors accused Me falsely. I was silent so my Father's will would be done (Isaiah 53:7). Always keep this n mind: I can always defend and protect you from danger to your soul, for your soul is a part of Me. I abide in you as long as you remain faithful and obedient to my commands. I will keep you safe from the enemy. Stand your ground against him (James 4:7). The evil one is a coward and will flee from your light. Faith in Me defeats evil.

7/22/18

Restrain me, Lord, from every evil impulse.

Let us speak today about peacemakers. This is an important subject because the state of peace in the mind, and peace in the soul leads to a state of heavenly bliss. With peace in one's heart, we conquer the world! It is a state of euphoria, an elevated state of the soul. One will sense a calmness of spirit coursing through the entire body. So, peace is a state of health. The blood pressure works normally, and consequently, the heart is more at ease. The person's whole demeanor relaxes and calmness reigns over the nerves and muscles. The body, mind and spirit relax. The entire corpus rests in peace.

Once a soul has reached this state of tranquility, the world appears normal and beautiful. The sun shines brightly. The birds sing sweetly and all is light about them. They have a renewed strength and energy to conquer the world. The flowers are prettier, and their spirit is lifted to their God who is the source of their joy, and life is worth living. They have a new purpose in life. They go forward with a new resolve to serve their God with joy in their hearts. Nothing can bring them down again. They have the desire to slay giants! Confidence courses through their body strengthening tired bones.

They have turned a corner, so to speak. A new resolve enters their hearts. They will conquer themselves, control their appetites. They will do what is necessary to make themselves right with their Heavenly Father, to please him, serve and obey him. Suddenly that state of euphoria has taken root and begins to spread its wings. Their spirit will not be conquered by the whims/sins of others. Their feet are set on a firm path. They know they have it in themselves to conquer the world.

All this because they have loved their God, obeyed his commandments, served him with all their heart, and prayed for his transforming grace. Yes, it is amazing grace given generously from a generous God who loves his people more than himself! He proves this by suffering and dying, nailed hands and feet to a cross like an animal. No pity was shown Him. He was not spared from torture, cruelty. His own people mocked Him (Matthew 27:29), laughed at His suffering. Their hate killed Him. He was not spared even the disgrace of crucifixion.

He bore it all for you!

8/6/18

Thank You, Lord for your gift of peace.

Yes, we will speak of *"Blessed are the peacemakers for they shall be called sons of God"* (Matthew 5:9). That is no small matter. A son knows his father's ways and wishes and strives to conduct himself as his father does. A shoemaker's son learns to make shoes. Most times, a son goes into his father's profession, be it doctor, lawyer, fireman; so, with peacemakers. I am the chief source of peace in the world. I made peace between you and my Father (Colossians 1:20). That was no small feat. It cost Me my life. So, too, will it cost you. This means you will make concessions to others for the sake of peace and harmony beginning within yourself. After all, this entire study of the Beatitudes is centered on your life, your attitudes, your conditioning, your struggle to change and to learn who you are and where you are going. This book my servant is writing, is for your transformation and to give you knowledge of your God and Father, so you can truly and honestly and honorably become my beloved child.

Peacemakers will find ways to compromise. It must be done equitably to both parties. Find common ground and build on that. One of my sons wrote a book titled "Art of the Deal"; and now, after years of developing this skill, he is applying it for the welfare of the nation. Everyone can become a peacemaker: a father in his home and among his family, a Pastor among his congregation, and a president with his country.

Always remember, peace is my gift to the world (John 14:27). Cultivate peace personally, sense it in the quiet of your mind and heart. Calm your spirit, take deep breaths, pause during the day and retreat into the stillness—listen to your heart beat. Relax your muscles and finally, rest in my love.

9/21/18

Guide me, Lord, into the light.

Today let us begin with another story. It is about a religious woman who had many children. Her heart was with Me, her God, but she did not know Me personally. Yet, she had faith—the size of a mustard seed. I kept watch over her and watched what she would do when tested by the loss of wealth, family—the things she held dear to her heart. Because she never stopped obeying my law to keep the sabbath day holy, she was never lost. Finally, she came to her wit's end and became fearful. In fear, she fell to her knees in supplication and I answered her prayer for wisdom, knowledge and courage. Today, her faith has moved mountains of obstacles and she has been set free of countless fears.

This is what my grace will do when my people turn to Me invoking my help. When my people turn to Me with all their hearts, I never refuse them. I take them into my heart in a deeper way because most times, they have suffered greatly trying to live without my counsel, guidance and protection through the tempests and temptations of the world, the flesh and the devil. If my people would only understand their need of my assistance! I would pour out my Spirit upon them and fill their hearts with peace!

But who is there to send? I already sent my beloved Son into the world so my people might not perish (John 3:16). I established my Church on earth to teach my ways and laws. What is it in the hearts of mankind that they should resist goodness and beauty and seek the ways of my enemy? Is it pride that thinks falsely? Is it ignorance of my love for them? These are the problems of the ages. Sin is a destructive force bringing man down to degradation and filth of mind, body, soul and spirit. Maybe they are comfortable in their ignorance? Is it laziness: the sin of sloth? Yes, it is all these things. They are called the seven capital sins: pride, anger, gluttony, sloth, avarice, envy, lust.

What I am proposing is mankind's need for God, for my help. Man cannot live without my grace. Now I have provided everything they need to overcome the obstacle of sin: my Son shed his blood to atone the sins of the world— the debt was paid and souls ransomed (1 John 2:2). His blood destroyed Satan's power over humanity; he is defeated once and for all. I have provided and spread my Church throughout the world to teach the truth of my love and presence in every individual's heart and soul. I have sent my Holy Spirit to actively enlighten, comfort and guide my people to safety (John 14:26). I do all this. The only thing remaining to do is for my people to lift up their heads and pray (Luke 21:28).

Prayer is the secret to salvation. Prayer is the link between my Kingdom in heaven and my Kingdom on earth. All who pray are linked with Me in heaven. It is a strong connection to the source of all that is good. Pray with all your strength, knowing and believing in my power to restore peace in the hearts of all mankind. I made them in my image (Genesis 1:27). I claimed my right over them by my blood. They belong to Me and will return to Me. I will judge them eternally.

Mark my words: I am returning to reap my harvest. Will you be ready to welcome Me (Luke 18:8)?

11/1/18

I could stay here with You, Lord, forever.

Yes, stay in my peace. It subdues all thoughts of anxiety, fears, worries, and concerns for your loved ones. My peace is a special gift given to my devoted, obedient children.

191

They love their God who loves them back and all is right with the world. Keep my peace within you. Take it where ever you go. Let no one take your peace from you.

It is special because it touches the hearts of those around you. They feel it. Yes, it is palpable. I have done much work pruning your soul because you have given Me permission. You are open and docile to my Spirit who guides you into my light—the light opens your mind to the truth and the truth sets you free to do mighty things in my name (John 8:32). This is how my disciples honor Me, and I am glorified in their works of kindness, love, mercy and especially, forgiveness. It takes a big, generous heart to forgive those who injure you, persecute you with false accusations, who hurt your loved ones, and desecrate what is holy to your soul.

Yes, tears fall from my eyes when I see the wounds inflicted upon the hearts of my beloved children. I am a God who grieves, who suffers with you and in you. I understand the evil in men's hearts and the destruction it causes to the soul.

O my people, this is why I command you to know Me. When you know how strong my love is for you, you will rejoice; and all weariness and ugliness will leave you, and you will be filled with peace. My peace in you demolishes mountains of hate, dissensions and groundless fears and anxieties. There is no room in a peaceful heart for hate, vindictiveness, or unforgiveness.

Peace leads to wisdom and knowledge of Godly ways to walk safely through the mine-fields of the evil one, whose only desire is to rob your peace from you. I brought peace into the world with my birth (Luke 2:14) and sealed it with my death. Let no one take it from you and, on the other hand, don't give it away by stirring up resentments, anger and hate toward your neighbor. When I speak of neighbor, I mean those next to you, in your family, your loved ones. You only end up hurting them and yourself. That's why I said, *"Love your neighbor as yourself"* (Mark 12:31). Be a friend to yourself and you will be a friend to others. Feel good about yourself and you will feel good about others. Try it! It works!

11/10/18

Let your peace, Lord, rule my heart.

Yes, I will. My peace is most effective in restoring a soul to obey my holy will. I know best for the souls of my children. Do not you desire what is good and right for your children? I hope I have been making my will clearly understood. Page after page of dictation, I have stressed that I love you. Do you still doubt and wonder if it is true? Just because people get sick, I don't stop loving them. In fact, I have made provisions for their recovery. I send them to hospitals where they are treated and healed.

The first thing Christ Jesus did after calling Andrew and Peter to follow him, was to heal Peter's sick mother-in-law (Mark 1:29-31). I always want to heal my children. Yes, you are noting that there is a significant difference between my people and my children. Read the gospel of John 1:12. *"But to those who did accept him (Jesus), he gave power to become children of God, to those who believe in his name, who were born not by natural generation . . . but of God."* Yes, my children are those who believe in my Son, the Lord Jesus Christ, who I sent to pay the debt owed Me by man's rebellion and rejection of my love.

193

Every time you break my laws, you break my heart. To sin is to throw dirt in my face. I don't care so much for myself—I'm a big God—but I do care that by sinful disobedience, you're dirtying your precious soul that I created so beautiful and pure, in my own image (Genesis 1:27). Can you understand what that means? I put myself into you. If I am wise, you are wise. If I am merciful, you are merciful. If I am great, you have the capacity for greatness. You have within you my power never to sin again. You have the ability to live in peace. Where there is peace of heart, there is serenity, wisdom and joy. With a peaceful heart comes good health, good thoughts, good performance. Sin will always lurk at your door, but with peace comes strength and courage to overcome sin that only leads to sickness and death.

Sin deprives you of so much that is good, that I often wonder why my children want to hurt themselves: hate causes high blood pressure, injuring the heart; anger leads to depression of spirit and takes away your joy; greed/avarice lead to loss of self-control and you end up making yourself sick. Pride separates you from my love which gives you comfort, safety and power to overcome sin in the first place.

Trust in Me is your saving power. Trust that I love you simply because I created you. It is my will/plan for you to obey Me because that's the only safe place for you to be. Without Me, you walk alone on a deserted road, unprotected from wild beasts. With Me, the sun always shines and you walk on the yellow brick road that leads to glory!

Be smart, my child. I am addressing you who read this book. Listen to Me. I offer you life, peace of mind, joy beyond compare. Don't lose it!

Thank You, Lord, for the gift of peace.

Yes, I gave my peace to the world when I died on the Cross. It was my suffering that atoned for your sins. My blood washes over you and it covers you from head to toe and you are set free from concupiscence. What I want you to understand is that my Father sees my blood over you and evil passes by. It is my blood covering that protects you from the enticements of the world, the flesh and the devil.

Yes, the act of the High Priest in ancient Jerusalem, to wash the sacred altar in the blood of a perfect lamb, atoned for the sins of the people (Leviticus 1:10). This prefigured what I would accomplish by my Incarnation, Passion, Death and Resurrection. When I returned to my Apostles, I gave them my peace (Luke 24:36). I reconciled them with my Father, and they were exonerated from their guilt. Yes, they were guilty of breaking my commandments, but I forgave them in honor of my Son's suffering. Never fear to suffer, it atones for many offenses against my holy Name.

So, I made peace with the world expecting that they would appreciate my Son's sacrifice, would understand the meaning of it—that he laid down his life because he loves them; and that they would love Me in return. But, man is stiff-necked and rebellious (Deuteronomy 9:13), so my Son established his Kingdom on earth to teach and guide you, to minister my Sacraments, to heal your ills, to forgive your offenses, to give sight to the blind, to baptize you with my Holy Spirit who enlightens and consoles you through the darkness.

But let us return to the subject of peace. Yes, I have an acrostic for **Peace**: **P**atience, **E**ffort, **A**ction, **C**ontrition,

Exultation—in other words, make an effort to be patient, ac like you are sorry for offending Me, and exult in my love fo you.

I have so much to give those who love Me. Peace is jus one of my gifts. It is a powerful one. Is it not more relaxing to be with a peaceful person? Is it not more comfortable tc be in their company? It is easy to confide in someone who is sure of herself. She is open to listening to other's concerns, and always has a comforting word. A peacefu person is hospitable, thinks of other's welfare. She is neve grasping for attention—on the contrary, she effaces herself Pray for this gift of peace. I bestow it on those who have gentle, kind, loving, generous, and open-heartec dispositions.

Peace is my gift to the world. Spread my peace arounc wherever you go. It will touch hearts, comfort them and they will be healed. My peace is like my word: a double-edgec sword. *"Therefore, let us strive to enter into that res. (peace), so that no one may fall after the same example o} disobedience. Indeed, the word (peace) of God is living anc effective, sharper than any two-edged sword, penetrating even between soul and spirit, joints and marrow, and able tc discern reflections and thoughts of the heart"* (Hebrews 4:11).

My peace is upon you. Rest in this knowledge. Take shelte in my power over you to guide you to everlasting peace.

12/10/18

Oh, happy day it will be, Lord, when there is peace on earth.

I have a formula for the word **Peace**: **P**ious **E**xultan **A**doration **C**ontrols **E**motions. When this formula for peace

196

is applied to all the problems in the world, then will there be peace everywhere. The word pious is defined in the dictionary as zealous devotion to God in prayer and in worship. This is what I have been preaching throughout this book. My people must have this attitude toward Me. Why on earth do you think I made it the First Commandment (Deuteronomy 5:1)? Yes, for your good! You must know, love, and serve Me in order to live in peace by loving your neighbor and yourself. It is imperative and yet it is not obeyed—hence wars and chaos, murders and deaths of innocent babies: evils practiced and condoned in an evil, dark world.

This could easily be changed if my children would devote themselves to Me. How beautiful it is when my people exult in their God. They would be so happy, kind and generous with their affections. They would see beauty everywhere because their hearts are joyful, carefree, trusting in my power and providence.

I am thoroughly capable to run the affairs of my world. It depends on your prayers, praises and obedience of my commandments. It would be easy if you truly loved and adored Me because adoration of the one true God keeps your mind and heart focused on Me and on my love, which is a powerful force for good. I would provide all your needs, physical and spiritual.

In contentment comes peace. When you reach satiety, the heart longs for peace with all her soul. Nothing but God alone suffices. The soul is saturated in grace which overflows, sending shock waves of light around it— shocking and zapping others with the sting of goodness and kindness. Camaraderie is established between nations of families and peace triumphs in the world.

It is very possible. It can be done. It will be done, says the Lord.

12/17/18

Guide my feet, Lord, into the way of peace.

Yes! Would that all my people would walk in the way of peace! There would be more laughter and joy in their hearts. Their bodies would be free of stress, high blood pressure, heart attacks, etc. Peace is a healing balm for their souls. They would then be more kind, tolerant toward the faults of others, more understanding of why people act the way they do. They would have insightful knowledge of human nature. There could be more peace in their hearts, less stress and more joy.

Oh yes! Learn to be at peace with one another. I gifted the world with peace when I reconciled the world with my Father when I atoned for the sins of mankind on the throne of my Cross. Yes, a throne because I am God and I was ruling, judging, freeing, saving, redeeming and delivering humanity while I slowly and torturously lost my blood nailed to the Cross.

Never fear to carry a cross whatever it may be. You will find the same power I had as I carried mine to the end. I will it that my people will persevere through every attack sent them by Satan. They cannot be defeated and must not lose heart because I destroyed Satan on the throne of my Cross (Hebrews 2:14).

You must understand that to have peace there must first be a battle. Not necessarily a full-blown war between nations, but just a simple struggle within your heart. For instance, when you carry a grudge against someone, does that not wear you down? Rob you of peace? Are you not tense in their presence? Yes, you are carrying anger, hate and unforgiveness in your heart instead of peace. Let it go! Free yourself! Is not peace a better way to go?

Examine your thought-life. Correct your thinking when necessary. If you are stressed or worried or doubtful and confused, say this little prayer: "Jesus, you died on the Cross to set me free. Now I am free to live in peace." Repeat it often until it sinks into your heart, and you believe it. You will sense your tight muscles relaxing and peace will flood over you. All this because you are speaking the truth. Remember: *"If you remain in my word, you will truly be my disciples, and you will know the truth and the truth will set you free"* (John 8:32).

Blessed Virgin Mary on the Seventh Beatitude

"Blessed are the peacemakers." Here for you is the Child who is Peace itself. His name is Peace. His mission is to bring peace between God and humanity. His plan is to pacify the whole world. Only He can bring peace and render peaceful the hearts of all, called to form part of one single family of the children of God. If it rejects Him, the world will never know peace."

St. Padre Pio on the Seventh Beatitude

'Peace essentially consists in being in harmony with our neighbors and wanting good for them. It also consists in being in friendship with God through his sanctifying grace. The proof of being united to God is the moral certainty that there is no mortal sin weighing our souls down. Peace, finally, consists in having won the victory over the world, the devil, and our own passions."

St. Francis of Assisi on the Seventh Beatitude

Blessed are those who endure in peace
For by You, Most High, they shall be crowned.
Praised be You, my Lord, through our Sister Bodily Death,
From whom no living man can escape.
Woe to those who die in mortal sin.
Blessed are those whom death will find in Your most holy will
For the second death shall do them no harm.
Praise and bless my Lord and give Him thanks
And serve Him with great humility.

(*The Canticle of the Sun,* composed by St. Francis of Assisi.)

Chapter Eight

Eighth Beatitude

*"Blessed are those who are persecuted for righteousness'
sake, for theirs is the kingdom of heaven."*
Matthew 5:10

5/15/18

Help me, Lord, to grow in holiness.

Let us begin with speaking on the eighth Beatitude: *"Blessed
are they who suffer persecution for my sake"* (Matthew 5:10).
They are blessed because suffering of any kind opens my
heart. I am a loving Father who suffers when his children
suffer. I would rather suffer in order to spare my children. I
did suffer for them a long time ago and I still suffer today;
even now I suffer to see my children at war with each
other—shooting and bombing with no concern for the value
of each man, woman and child.

I died to set them free from the evil spirit of hate, anger and
violence. Yet my people do not understand my ways or the
meaning of my death on the Cross. I appeased my Father's
justice. I atoned for man's disobedience and rebellion
against my Father's will. Tragedies occur when my Father's
just ways are thwarted and bent out of shape, when my
Father's justice is denied, refused, rejected by man's pride,
haughtiness and ignorance.

Yes, my people perish for lack of knowledge (Hosea 4:6). If
they knew my love, they would be changed. If they knew
Me and understood who I am, they would worship Me on
their knees. They do not know who they are in Me. I sustain
them. I am the air they breathe. I created and fashioned
them. I want them, long for their return to my Love.

O my people, turn to Me, long for Me, I am life for you. Listen to my Son Jesus, learn his ways. He established his kingdom on earth to point the way to safety. Obey my commandments. Love each other. Do good to those who despise you (Matthew 5:44), for they do not understand what they do. Show them my light, my goodness and kindness. You are my hands and feet. I have loved you; now won't you love Me?

"Then the people . . . shall turn back and seek the Lord, their God . . . They shall come trembling to the Lord and to his bounty in the last day" (Hosea 3:5).

5/17/18

Your word, Lord, gives life to my soul.

We begin today with a word about suffering and persecution. My suffering on the Cross is one type of suffering. It was physical pain and heart-felt pain because those who I died for did not understand that I left my place with God, my Father, just to save them from eternal death.

There is another dimension of pain that is also hurtful. It is the pain of fear. Fear is tantamount to the loss of God's love. Fear comes from the false self that rebels against God the Father. Fear destroys the bond of love between the Father and his children. How can there be fear where there is love? Love conquers all fears (1 John 4:18).

There is another type of fear—the fear of loneliness. This causes emotional pain. I created mankind to be sociable, to be in community. The saying is, "There is safety in numbers" which is true. What one lacks, another may supply. Man should not be alone. That's why I created Eve for Adam. Let Me tell you a secret. I have handpicked every spouse for every man and woman. Do I not know my children? I who created them? Do I not know every hair on each head (Matthew 10:30)?

Again, the problem stems from the false self. My children do not believe; hence they do not trust. So, they do not ask. Every man, woman and child exist in Me. I know what they need. I made them. I sculpted their hearts for myself. Does a mother not suffer the pain of her children's rejection, rebellion against her authority? I, too, have a mother's heart. I gave life to mine—whether they know it or not. They belong to Me, and I long for their love, respect and obedience—not for myself; as the song says, "I'll Get By", but because my children cannot live and thrive without Me. Without my grace, they die.

6/23/18

Help me worship You, Lord, in every trial.

Today let us speak about suffering persecution for my name's sake, for the Kingdom of Heaven shall be theirs (Matthew 5:10); for those who suffer to speak my Word to the nations shall be infused with courage, strength and boldness. I will be with them and the power of the enemy will be destroyed. Hearts will be set free to worship their Savior and there will be joy in the land.

Let us talk about what makes a man fearless enough to suffer persecution. First, they trust knowing that my power is unsurpassable. I created man, therefore I am unsurpassed in power over man. Second, they trust because I am the Mover of man. I decide who should go where and do what I say. I can put up barriers to thwart the enemy. Here we are speaking spiritually. Satan was defeated by the sacrificial Lamb of God and has no more power over those who trust and obey Me. Thirdly, they trust because they know my love. They have experienced my guidance, have been enlightened with grace, and have a share of my wisdom and knowledge; and they are open to my counsel. My Word is in them and they walk daily in his footsteps. Their personal relationship with Christ my Son, has fortified virtue in their soul and their faith is invincible—fearless.

So, let us consider what must be done. One, trust is a necessary component in the struggle to overcome fear. Two, obedience to my word opens the door to my grace and power. Three, the soul must journey with the Holy Spirit who is poured out upon the soul because of my love for my Son Jesus the Christ. In him, all things are possible (Luke 1:37). In his name, walls tumble. In him, the world came into being. He is my Word and I have given him all my power (John 1:1-3). Everything is subjected to my Son.

Do you understand what this means? You are his subject. You belong to him. He is your Master, a loving, gentle and kind Master (Matthew 21:3). We could refer to him as your Landlord. He has every right over you. He ransomed your soul when he poured out his blood (Matthew 20:28). He literally died for love of you. He has a right to expect your respect which means obedience to his will. You are the renter, he, your landlord; and he wants his property, your soul, well cared for. The soul is his house, and he wants it kept clean—no dirt of sin to darken the windows of the soul; no false beliefs that will damage the soul's mind and wound its heart. No, your heavenly Landlord wants you, his property, to be clean of heart, filled with the light of the Holy

Spirit so your soul will shine in the darkness. Picture this: if every house/soul sparkled with the light of the Spirit, what a blazing, glaring profusion of light would fill the world! This is my plan from the start, that my people would live in the light of the love of their God.

Oh, peace would flood the land! All beauty and grace would fill souls, and all hearts would kindle with joy. Oh, their laughter would fill the skies and bring comfort to my heart. Yes, this is my will that my people should live in harmony, peace, and with love for Me, their Creator, Savior, Redeemer, and Deliverer. I am all good and only want good for my people.

Pray, my children. Rejoice in my providential love for you. I will you no harm. My plan is for your salvation. Trust Me with all your heart. You will have courage to fight the enemy. You will not be overcome, I promise. Let your hearts be carefree. Unburden the load on my shoulders, for I am the Good Landlord.

6/25/18

Infuse me, Lord, with your courage.

The eighth Beatitude warrants a discussion on pride and suffering persecution. It takes great courage and humility to suffer for one's faith in Me, your Lord and Savior. Saint Peter failed the test when he denied he even knew Me (Matthew 26:70). But look what I did when he repented: he became the leader of my Church on earth (Matthew 16:18).

Yes, there is a Church in Heaven. It is the Triumphant Church. All those who won the battle against Satan are victorious in Heaven. Peter became the first Pope because he loved Me greatly. I endowed him with graces necessary to perform his leadership role. Just so every Christian who loves and obeys Me, I groom and prepare them for their ministry.

So, it takes a humble, docile spirit, and a willing spirit to sit quietly and listen for my guidance, and I will perfect the soul. I will not waste time because there is much to do in my Church. Sinners must be taught and come to repentance. They must be told the truth and hear my voice. Then when they know Me, they will love Me and serve Me. From service comes a greater love and joy in their Master. Then they willingly subject themselves to persecutions of all kinds.

Love makes them strong. Love makes giants of men. Love endures and grows from a mustard seed to a giant oak tree (Matthew 17:20). Love multiplies and changes hearts but first one must surrender. They must change their minds and hearts and choose to follow Me, the Good Shepherd (John 10:11). This takes humility and courage—powerful virtues that are developed by sacrifice, prayer, fasting, almsgiving and great love, love for God, neighbor and self.

Let us speak about self. One must be kind, gentle, loving to one self before they can love their neighbor. So many of my people are misguided about selfishness. It does not mean to degrade oneself, nor hate oneself or denigrate one's abilities and talents. No, these are God-given talents. But it does mean to value the life I have given them, to care for it with proper diet, exercise and cleanliness. Life is important and valuable in my sight. So, one must cherish his body, soul and spirit. It shall return to Me, its Creator one day and give an accounting of how well it was taken care of (Romans 14:12).

Yes, I cherish you. I provide all you need to live beautifully, happily and peacefully. So, please value your life. Then you will value your neighbor's life. You will see my presence at work in them just as I live and move in your life.

What has all this to do with courage to suffer persecution? With a heart full of love for neighbor and self, the soul worships its Creator and no price is too much to pay for the soul's redemption. In gratitude because the soul knows its debt to its Creator, it gladly accepts what occurs to it. It accepts persecution because it understands it is God's will. Their soul is so in love with its Savior, the cost is never too high. They joyfully suffer from love. The soul is satisfied to do God's will.

Then in turn, I can move powerfully in that willing spirit, giving it all it needs: strength, courage, fortitude. The humble soul can suffer easily when fortified by my grace. Nothing is impossible for them because they are infused with the power of God, the wonder-working power of love so powerful that mountains and hills, and impossible and impenetrable fortresses are demolished.

Love for God is a powerful weapon for goodness and righteousness. Love knows no bounds (1 Corinthians 13:7). It is everlasting, divine, indestructible and inimitable beyond compare.

7/1/18

Help me die to my sins, Lord, so I may live in You.

Today we will discuss the matter of persecution. I know of what I speak because I was crucified. The Romans used this type of execution to perfection. The nails were formed purposely to hold the weight of a man's body suspended on a cross. My bloody Cross was made of the strongest wood—solid oak. It was exceedingly heavy. Simon of Cyrene came along just at the right time. (You ask if I spoke to him? Yes, I blessed him. He was rewarded beyond expectation.) The crown of thorns on my head cut through my scalp burning my flesh (John 19:2). This I say to you to explain that I have known every kind of torture known to mankind.

You must understand that I live in my people. I feel what they feel. I sense their sensations. I know their thoughts and fears. I count every hair on their head (Matthew 10:30). They are mine and mine know Me (John 10:14). They know my love and mercy. They receive my counsel and guidance. They have faith in Me and obey Me. My people suffer for Me. Their loving kindness extends to their fellow man because they know Me, have suffered for Me.

Do not be afraid of persecution—be it emotional pain of rejection, or physical pain; I am with you bearing the pain for you. This is how my martyrs endure to the end because I am with them granting grace and supporting them with my presence. I ask no one to endure suffering beyond their ability. I always give them a way out (1 Corinthians 10:13). No trial is too much to bear. I am a just, fair, compassionate Father to my children.

Yes, you think of men who have been tortured and killed. They have been rewarded with eternal happiness. Those who survived their ordeals are heroic in my eyes. They have my special predilection. I know mine and mine know Me (John 10:14).

Don't try to figure this out. I am more than man can comprehend. Just know and trust my Word: I created you.

love you. I died for you, and in Me, you will remain if you keep my commandments (John 15:7). Choose wisely. I am here for you. I do not reject those who come to Me, who seek my help, and ask for what they need. I do not say I will grant every desire. I reserve discretion to what I know is best according to my plan for you. Remember, my plan is not for woe but for your welfare (Jeremiah 29:11).

7/21/18

Fill my heart with zeal, Lord, to serve You.

This is what I want you to write: Rejoice in persecution. When you are falsely accused, submit peacefully. I am your Defender and Redeemer (Isaiah 59:20). Listen to my voice. Follow my example. The student becomes the Teacher. Rejoice when others mock you or say harsh words about you. I grant a special grace to those who suffer unjustly.

The question is: Why does God allow bad things to happen? If God is so powerful, why does he not stop it? Yes, through the ages, men have asked these questions wondering where is my power and justice? These questions will never be answered, for it is my will that man solve the problems of every era; every generation has its own set of problems. I have equipped man to forage through centuries of good and evil to find his way into my heart—into my perfect will for each one.

A man's journey is designed to lead him to Me. His destiny is to find Me, his Creator, Savior, Redeemer. This is the goal of the journey—to enter the Promised Land. I am always with man on this journey guiding, caring for his needs, enlightening his mind to the wonders of sanctifying grace;

and always aiding and abetting him in his trials, fears doubts.

Do not be afraid to question my ways for your soul. Every unique man has a unique journey planned for his salvation He alone can traverse the path laid out for him. I offer grace for the journey, but he must accept it. Yes, I do not force myself on any man, woman or child. Even the heavens and birds in the air and beasts in the field accept my designs for them.

To man alone have I bestowed the grace of intelligence memory and a free will. He must use it wisely, discreetly to reach the goal of life: mystical union with the Blessed Trinity. Man must make this decision. Does he want heaven or hell? life or death? His entire life is focused on these choices.

Choose well the decisions you make for yourself. They are eternal!

8/27/18

Grant me grace, Lord, to see your face.

Persecution and calumny go hand in hand. When a person is lied about, their reputation is damaged. Ahh, you have felt the sting of false accusations! You see how gossip is a form of persecution? You never saw that before. Your eyes have been opened!

Yes, gossip is a terrible sin—not only does it hurt the person maligned, but it is self-damaging, also. It takes peace away from the heart. It may feel good to release the tongue at first ut try to take back the harm it has done to others and oneself. It is impossible.

Do you recall the penance that Saint Philip Neri gave to the couple who spread rumors about their daughter's friend? They were told to pluck the feathers of a chicken as they walked through the street and then to reverse their steps and retrieve every feather from where the wind had scattered them! That is how difficult it is to stop a juicy bit of gossip from spreading.

Gossip/calumny cause needless suffering. The antidote is total restraint from self-indulgence. Make a firm purpose to seal your lips when tempted. The more one tries, the easier it gets. Did not the Pharisees find fault with Me? Did they not reward those who lied about Me? Was I not calumniated and persecuted? Every lie finds a target that hits the heart causing injury to the recipient, and to the one who spoke it (James 3:6). Don't give up trying to curb the tongue. It can be tamed.

Today in the world, calumny and persecution are rampant. To the watchful observant, it is very obvious to see the evil intent. They want to destroy the man's name, honor and reputation. It causes hatred to grow into murderous threats: exactly what caused my death on the Cross!

Let Me tell you this: *"Blessed are those who are persecuted for my name's sake. They shall rejoice in Heaven"* (Matthew 5:10). On the earth, there will always be turmoil, hatred, sin—brother against brother, son against father, daughter against mother. But I will restore order in the world. There will be a time of rest. It will come when my Father orders it. It will be a time of peace and happiness in the world. Brother will welcome his brother. Joy will exist in the land and in the heart of man. I will see to it. Daughter-in-law will welcome her mother-in-law. Friendships will be restored. There will be a time of peace man has never known.

Then I will come again as I promised—on a cloud with trumpet blasts and everyone will see my Face and shudder (Acts 1:9-11). May my disciples be prepared. I have warned you beforehand. The time will come. I have given my Word.

8/28/18

In You, Lord, is the source of life.

Today we shall speak about enduring persecution for my name's sake. Yes, I say rejoice when men call you all kinds of derogatory names. Rejoice when they insult you (1 Thessalonians 5:16-18). Why, you ask? Because I am your Defender. The hate directed toward you is absorbed by Me and then deflected by my light and my love.

I am your Advocate (1 John 2:1). It is my duty to protect, shield and nurture my people. Who else cares for their needs? Who is there to lay down a worthy sacrifice for my people? When they persecute you, they persecute Me. I take the blows. Do you not sense my presence? I am as close to you as your heart. Whenever men defile you or slander your name, they do it to Me for you belong to Me. I created and nurtured you as a child (Hosea 11:4). I have guided and taught you through your years of schooling. I took delight in your achievements and mourned for you when you failed— always encouraging you to try again. I am with you in all the good times and in the bad. Why would I not be with you when you are mistreated?

Yes, I say, rejoice, because I am there with my grace to hold you up, to teach you to surrender to whatever happens to you, to teach you to turn it over to Me and I will transform the bad into good (Romans 8:28). There is nothing that can happen to you that I am not able to make right.

Let's go back to what I said about who I am—I am the Almighty, All-seeing, All-knowing God, your Creator-Father and I love you. You are mine (Isaiah 43:1). What is there to fear? Mean words cannot harm you, so do not react to them. Take shelter in my love. Come to Me in prayer and be consoled. Come to Me in the sanctuary and I will bind your wounds. There is nothing man can do to you that I cannot make right. So, do not fear (Luke 12:32). Instead, rejoice for your reward is great in Heaven, and I am here to heal you.

9/12/18

Fill me, Lord, with your healing light.

"Blessed are those who are persecuted for my name's sake, for theirs is the kingdom of Heaven" (Matthew 5:10). The persecution of Christians prevails much glory for the renewal of the earth. The blood of martyrs atones abundantly for the sins of the world. Never fear to be persecuted because I will never allow more than you can bear (1 Corinthians 10:13).

My disciples know and trust my Word to be always with them with my courage and strength to carry them through every trial. They are certain of my protection and power to defeat their enemies. The light of love and goodness overwhelms darkness and evil. This was accomplished by my death on the Cross—once and for all (Romans 6:10). Everyone is under my protection providing they walk in the Light, submit to my holy will, and seek my kingdom over them (Luke 12:31).

On another note, blessed are those who are persecuted because they are walking in my footsteps, suffering for the welfare of their loved ones just as I did. Never fear to suffer, it leads to glory—the glory of freedom from tyranny, hate, blood-shed. Your pain may be the salvation of a son's soul. Did you ever think that you could be the instrument I might use to save the life of someone dear to you?

Your pain, physical or emotional, leads to glory. The reward is greater than you know. Suffering works for good in two ways: the one who suffers gains the necessary graces for his or her own salvation, and their suffering wins mercy for the souls of others who do not pray for themselves.

Suffering leads to healing. The suffering of my Son healed the world of darkness and sin (Isaiah 53:5) and brought his people into the light, his healing light where they have found the glory of truth, goodness, peace and eternal joy with Me in heaven. Is it not worth it to suffer a little to accomplish so much good?

I know to suffer is no little thing. It takes courage and strength, but always remember that I ask no more from you than I am prepared to provide (1 Corinthians 10:13). My grace is sufficient and always available for the asking (2 Corinthians 12:9).

O my people, if only you would trust Me who loves you so much. I gave my life for you (John 3:16). I shed my blood for

214

your salvation so you might be with Me and my Father. We never look down on you or refuse you anything that's good for you. Trust my wisdom. I know what is best for you, and if you follow Me, I promise you will see Me in the glory of Heaven.

10/25/18

Save me, Lord, from my enemies.

And who are your enemies? Anyone or anything that will separate you from the love of God. That is your enemy. Does pain separate you from Me (Romans 8:35)? Of course, not. This is because I am in you, suffering the pain with you, helping you to withstand the pain, providing medicines to alleviate the pain—physical pain.

In emotional pain or when suffering insults or false accusations or rejection, I am with you, comforting, consoling, encouraging and strengthening you by building up your confidence, teaching you the truth of my love for you. I console you by filling you with my grace. I strengthen you with my Spirit. I teach you the truth by my Word that sets you free to know and understand that suffering injustice cannot separate you from my love (Romans 8:38-39); on the contrary, your suffering draws Me like a magnet. How could I ever leave you when you need Me the most. No, never could I abandon you (Hebrews 13:6). I always provide a way out (1 Corinthians 10:13).

Love does not walk away when someone is suffering or sad, down-hearted, lonely. I am a God of compassion—yet, I do not smother my children. I come when they call Me, when they want Me, when they acknowledge their need for my help. I respect my people too much to intrude on their privacy. I answer when they call Me. I answer every prayer of supplication (1 John 5:14). I am always ready and generous with my grace. Grace is my Spirit. I am my Spirit. So, I am always with you—in suffering or in joy, in bad times or good; in weakness, I am your strength (2 Corinthians 12:9) and in sorrow, I comfort you (Psalm 23:4).

O my people, come to the fountain of living water. Turn to Me who loves you and gives you life. Trust my Word to save you. I am your refuge in the storm (Isaiah 25:4). I am ready, willing and able to supply your needs. Come to Me. What have you got to lose? Sadly, if you lose Me, you've lost everything!

10/26/18

Make me holy, Lord, as You are holy.

There is much merit to be gained when you suffer persecution for my name's sake. Your reward will be great in Heaven (Matthew 5:10). And my joy is upon you because your heart is turned toward my honor and glory.

There is much to be said about the glory of God. I Am Who Am (Exodus 3:14) and everything stems from Me. I am the Light of the World (John 8:12) and thus, man can see. Mine is the music in the air, and man breathes. I am the sun that makes the day, and the night that calls man to sleep. Mine is the sabbath rest (Genesis 2:2) that refreshes man's soul and spirit. Therefore, everything manifests my glory, and so does man by how he lives.

When man suffers for my name's sake, he too, is glorified— in many ways. In suffering, I give him courage. When persecuted, I give him spiritual strength to bear it. My Heart is in the man who bears the burden of his neighbor. My choice is the man who silently bears the sting of false accusations. There is no end to my mercy and comfort for the one who justifies and placates quarrels between brothers.

Do you see that in every type of suffering, I am with you to ease the pain with my joy, to comfort and encourage you to persevere through the persecution because it will come to an end? I do not allow you to be destroyed eternally. This is my reign (Psalm 146:10), my decision to make. I have counted the days of your life. The strong carry on with joy in their hearts. The meek inherit the land. Those who mourn are comforted. The merciful receive mercy.

You see, I am in everything and know everything. I know when you are sad or when you are glad. I make the strong and I make the weak. All are equal in my eyes (Rom 2:11). I make use of everything. I store up tears in a bottle (Psalm 56:9). I count hairs on your head (Luke 12:7). Every man, woman and child are precious in my eyes. My desire is that all should see my glory. My light shines on everyone.

Will they look up to see my glory? Will they suffer for Me? If not cheerfully, at least with forbearance? Will they accept my will or will they rebel like Adam and Eve (Genesis 3:11) and Lucifer before them? Have they not seen what evil can befall them when they turn their backs on Me? Have they not learned the lessons of history? Why are my children unwilling to serve? To be healed and guided by my light? Why do they choose death? hate? Yes, tears fall from my eyes at the destruction of their immortal souls (Luke 19:41-42)!

O my people, heed my warning! This life will end and you will be judged on your merits. It is not too late. Give up, surrender to my grace. I call out to you in the name of my Son Jesus, to accept the gift, the grace of salvation he suffered to win for You!

Do not be afraid (Mark 5:36).

10/29/18

Your word, Lord, is a safe haven.

Today is a new day and I have a new teaching for you. Yes, love is the greatest gift I give my children but there is something greater. It is my Spirit, the essence of my Being; it is the inner strength whereby I endured the pain, the scourging, the mocking, and the nailing of my hands and feet to a hard, splintery wooden cross where I hung for three hours unable to move my arms and legs, just pinned there to the wood, open and vulnerable, unable to wipe the blood coursing down my face, getting into my eyes. But you see, I endured to the end because of the Spirit of Love coursing through my heart, strengthening my Spirit, lifting Me up and above the pain that was wracking my poor, mutilated body. I was able to rise above the pain—in a way, I looked at it as a gift from my Father who I knew loved Me more than himself.

My suffering was his gift for by it, I accomplished the purpose for my life. I was born to suffer, die and thereby atone for all the sins of humanity. And for this I was greatly exalted (Philippians 2:9); I sit at the side of my Father on his throne, bestowing grace and mercy on all those who believe and obey Me.

Yes, my Father and I and the Holy Spirit grieve for our lost children, and we look for souls who could willingly suffer as

218

I did on the cross. We have found many heroic souls in the past who accepted the Stigmata. You have heard of some: Saint Catherine of Siena, Saint Francis of Assisi, Saint Padre Pio, to name a few. Through their suffering, many souls have been saved from hell. They suffered as I suffered to help others on their way to salvation.

Until the time comes for the new heavens and new earth (Revelation 21:1), when all my people will enjoy eternal rest, one of the ways we have chosen to save our lost children is to ask our faithful children to lay down their lives for their brothers and sisters. Are you beginning to understand the need, the purpose, the value of your suffering? I use it for good (Romans 8:28). It is never wasted—even when you knew not that I was using your pain—no drop of blood was overlooked. Every broken heart and every broken bone is of great value in my economy.

Does knowing this aspect of the value of suffering help you understand that I am looking for brave souls who will offer to become my intercessors, not only with their prayers but with their flesh and blood? Yes, this is the highest form of imitating your Savior, the Lord Jesus Christ, my Son. The Stigmata is the greatest gift I have to bestow on my chosen ones. This gift is waiting for the asking.

"Let not your hearts be troubled. You have faith in God; have faith also in Me" (John 14:1). I will prepare a place for you. I will come back again and take you with Me, so where I am, you also shall be. I will not give you more than you can bear (1 Corinthians 10:13). Just be willing and open to my grace and all shall be done for you according to my holy will. Trust Me, my child. I have your welfare in mind.

219

Yes, you are thinking of my cloistered Nuns who pray all day interceding for others. This is how many of my fallen children escape hell through the merits of their prayers. Every prayer spoken in faith receives a reward (Matthew 21:22).

10/30/18

Open to me, Lord, the gates of holiness.

Yes, I will. I want all my children to follow Me on the upward journey to holiness. I know the way. *"I am the Way, the Truth, and the Life"* (John 14:6). Anyone who follows Me, will have the Light of Life, and I will be with them forever. Believe Me when I say I am the Way. I am the only Way to the Father of all goodness and kindness and mercy.

Yes, my death on the Cross was a sign of great mercy, for by it all the sins ever committed plus all the sins still yet to be committed, have been redeemed by the shedding of my flesh and blood on the holy Cross of satisfaction—atonement. It's been done, once and for all (Hebrews 7:27).

At every holy Mass offered at every Catholic Church throughout the world, my sacrifice is being offered again and again—for the sins of mankind never end! My Father foresaw this and provided for it. This is why I gathered twelve men to my side (Mark 3:14-19) to teach them my Way, to follow my Way, and to spread my Way to all the nations of the world, so everywhere and every hour of every day, I am being lifted up on my Cross. From there comes all the graces of the mercy of God. From my wounds flow the life-giving blood that washes away every sin committed against my Father. There is no end to the atonement of man's sins.

Can you comprehend the depth of my Father's plan to save mankind? I must open your eyes slowly, for it is a very deep mystery to understand. But this has been my work from the beginning, and I will never stop saving my people (John 3:16-17).

Would you consider helping Me in this work of salvation? My Apostles succeeded in spreading the Good News to all the world, but there is still more work to be done before Lucifer is banished forever. I need prayer warriors to lift up my banner so all may see the light. I need those with big hearts full of love to pass my love around. I need priests to minister my Sacraments. I need generous hearts who will give to the poor and needy. I need doctors, nurses, care-givers to tend the sick. I need scientists to uncover mysteries of the unknown world. I need explorers to discover new realms of life yet unknown. The list goes on. There is a need that every man, woman and child can fulfill in the physical and spiritual world.

But, I am saving the best for last: I need brave hearts who will lay down their lives to serve their God—my Way: the royal road of the Cross. If you do not have courage, pray for it. If you doubt your capacity for pain, trust Me to expand it. If you feel unworthy, believe in my judgment. Have I not taken you this far? You believe in Me; you know I love you; you've seen my power to transform you. Do you still not know Me (John 14:9)? Don't you trust Me? The Stigmata is nothing more than wounds that do not heal. You cover them with bandages that will need to be changed daily. But it is not more than you can handle. I will see to it.

11/24/18

Help me fight the good fight, Lord, against the enemy.

Yes, there is the enemy to contend with. He is real. Although invisible to the eye, his work is evident in this world—hate, envy, greed, malice, murder, drugs, human trafficking—the list goes on. These evil actions demonstrate and define the mind and heart of the evil one, Satan. Why do I allow him to exist? Because I created angels to serve Me, to work for Me, to be my companions. Lucifer was my masterpiece, the most beautiful of all my angels. Yet, he defied Me, rebelled against my rule over him. He became proud, defiant and hateful. You see, the choice was his. It was not my will. He chose to fight against Me and those who love Me.

This is where you come into the picture. Satan hates you because you belong to Me. He will use all his power to separate you from my love, peace and joy. He will lie as he did to Eve in the garden of Eden (Genesis 3:13), and he will stir up hate in the hearts of men as he did to the Pharisees who condemned my Son to a cruel death (Matthew 27:22). Unknown to Satan, this was my plan to defeat him once and for all. I resurrected my Son from death, and this reversed the whole of Satan's plan which was to keep men fearful of death. I defeated death (2 Timothy 1:10)! Satan has nothing to stand on. I have destroyed his power to instill fear in the hearts of my people. There is nothing to fear. Satan is toppled off of his throne (Luke 10:18). Just the mere mention of the name of Jesus Christ makes him shrivel with fear and run away!

Have I helped you understand what the Resurrection of my Son means for you? By your Baptism in the name of the

Father and of the Son and of the Holy Spirit, your bondage to original sin which you inherited in the flesh, has been broken, washed away once and for all. The act of shedding my blood in payment for all your sins, has freed you to live in my light, to follow my reign over you, which gives you the right to use my name to command the enemy. Say the name of Jesus Christ and Satan shivers!

In Baptism, you receive the power to fight the enemy. Use this power! Do not permit Satan to rob you of your inheritance as a child of God. You belong to the family of the Most High (Luke 1:76), so rejoice in this privilege. Know who you are! Do not concede your power to Satan! He revels in his deceptions; rejoices in your ignorance of the truth, and in the blindness caused by pride, selfishness, vainness. Guard yourself against his tactics. Dress yourself daily in my armor (Ephesians 6:10). Keep my commandments (Deuteronomy 5:1-21). Observe the laws of the Catholic Church, receive my Sacraments; they will reinforce your power over Satan.

Remember, he alone is your enemy. He will steal away your rights as a child of God (John 1:12). You have the right to live in my love, to use my name, to receive my protection and guidance, to be enlightened with wisdom, knowledge and understanding. Just know who you are. Wear your armor. Use my word as a sword to fight the enemy (Hebrews 4:12), and your faith as a shield against his darts.

Remember always: I have your back!

11/27/18

Stand by me, Lord, in the time of my testing.

My people, in every trial life presents, I am always there by your side. It is impossible for Me to abandon you—ever. I am God and I know you need Me in every minute of every day of your existence. From before your conception, I knew you (Psalm 139:13) and I planned for your life. Yes, Jeremiah 29:11 says it very well. *"I know well the plans I have in mind for you, says the Lord, plans for your welfare, not for woe! Plans to give you a future full of hope. When you call Me, I will answer."*

So, you ask Me to stand by you when you are tested? I am always with you. I cannot separate my Spirit from yours. We are enmeshed together in the bond of love. That is why the Church is referred to as the Bride of Christ (Revelation 22:17). We are one in the Spirit. Where you go, I go. When you cry, I cry. When you suffer, I suffer. That is why I suffered persecution for your sins. To free you from the snares of the devil.

What I am leading up to is this: Do not be afraid of suffering for my name's sake. I never give you more than you can bear (1 Corinthians 10:13). There is always a way out. I provided for every occurrence of pain, grief, loss. Yes, I send my angels and my Mother to comfort you, to encourage and console you. But the greatest consolation is knowing that I am with you twenty-four/seven. I stand by my people. I can be trusted because all power is mine (Matthew 28:18). There is nothing impossible for God (Luke 1:37). You know that from experience. In every test, I have shown you the way out!

For example, once there was a lady who had a beautiful voice and she rejoiced to sing my praises. Well, the evil one stole her gift, and she could no longer sing. What did I do? I gave her a new gift. Instead of singing for Me, she composed lovely melodies, written as personal prayers to her God. The new gift was greater than the old one.

Never fear to be tested, my people. I will always be there in your midst.

Blessed Virgin Mary on the Eighth Beatitude

"Blessed are those persecuted for the sake of justice. See in this Child the Victim, called to journey along the road of rejection and persecution. As a little one, He must flee into exile, for Herod orders that He be killed; as a youth, He lives in a poor house and is subjected to humble and heavy labor; during his public mission, He is obstructed, marginalized, and threatened, even to the point of being arrested, tried and condemned to death. It is He, the persecuted and stricken One, who brings healing to all."

St. Padre Pio on the Eighth Beatitude

"The greater your suffering so much greater is God's love for you. May these trials be for you a marker of God's love. You will recognize God's love for you by this sign: the afflictions he sends you. Exult and humble yourself before his divine majesty, for this love is the very unique love of the divine Bridegroom for you."

St. John Bosco on the Eighth Beatitude

"The true Christian must suffer privations and poverty with resignation, like Jesus Christ who did not even have a place to rest his head. He must learn how to bear insults and abuse, as Jesus Christ did when his face was spat upon, slapped, and reviled in a thousand ways at the praetorium. The good Christian must be willing to accept patiently every persecution, sickness, and death itself, like Jesus Christ who—with a crown of thorns, lacerated by flogging, pierced by nails—gave up his soul serenely into the hands of his heavenly Father."

Chapter Nine

Ninth Beatitude
"You shall love your neighbor as yourself."
Matthew 22:39

6/17/18

Without your love, Lord, I am lost.

Today let us speak on the subject of love—love for God, love for neighbor and love for self, the greatest commandment (Matthew 12:30). The Beatitudes give you a picture of Jesus, the Christ. As one takes on these attitudes, they begin to think as he does and love as he does, because he lives in you. Like Teacher, like student. Like Creator, like creature. I am your God and you will become god-like fulfilling the purpose I have for creating you. Now you know why I first taught the Beatitudes that you may become like Me, think like Me and conduct yourselves as I do—mercifully and lovingly.

Oh, what a great virtue is the virtue of love! It covers all wounds of sin (1 Peter 4:8). Love is life-giving. It is heart-healthy, erasing all hurts and grievances; all mistakes are rectified, bridges rebuilt, relationships repaired. Mighty works are performed by those who love their God, neighbor and self. I know someone who hated herself. She was so desirous to be loved that she would blame herself when others because of their own lack of love, failed to love her! You see and understand why love is so important? Lack of self-love injures hearts, destroys self-esteem.

But let us speak of divine love, holy love, the Love that created human flesh, the Love that died for love. Divine Love in the soul, lays down its life for God and neighbor.

Perfect Love does not count the cost of obedience but tries to obey fully and completely. My Love will lift up the wounded soul and make it whole by satisfying the desires of the heart. My heavenly love will make new what is old. It will restore broken hearts, broken relationships; hands will reach across the table to make peace with one another. Nations crumble from lack of Love. Divine Love alone mends broken fences.

Teach my people to love. It is the one powerful force to restore peace in a soul, in a country and in the world. Love is tantamount to the power of God. It is an indestructible power. Nothing can destroy it. Love will recreate the world. Love is Heaven on earth performing its Creator's will. Nothing and no one will hold it back. I will see to it. I have given my Word and my Word will fulfill all Love's demands for love of Me, the Eternal God, your humble God and devoted Father, the God who loves his people and longs to restore peace and order on earth.

My Word holds Me back for I have promised to never destroy the earth again. The rainbow still shines in the sky (Genesis 9:11). I am God and my Word stands forever. Mark my words: I will come again and restore order. I will make the Final Judgment (2 Corinthians 5:10). It is coming. I, the Lord, have spoken.

6/18/18

Empower me, Lord, to love as You love.

Today we speak of the power of love—love in the mind and heart. To love is to forget oneself, one's hopes and expectations and to forfeit your own will for the will of the

Father who has full right to your love and obedience. Once you have reached the stage of full simulation of the Beatitudes, being right in comprehension of truth, that is to say—right thinking, and having the will to be meek, merciful, peaceful, having courage to withstand persecutions, you are ready to conduct your life in the right way—as your Savior did before you. You are now ready to follow in his footsteps. Then my power is unleashed in your willing and adjusted, purified heart, soul and spirit, and I am able to do great things in your life.

To love is to trust your Almighty God and Father with all that is in you which is my sanctifying grace. You are ready, eager and anxious to do my will for you know I have your best interests at heart; you know I know what is the best road to follow; you know I only want your good which is to be with Me eternally in the joy and bliss of Paradise where the Light always shines; there is music everywhere, joy, laughter and blessed peace—no more competing for first place—all are equal in my presence, content with their place in Me.

Enough for today. Think for tomorrow. Prepare for eternity. Use your gift of love generously. Do not worry, just hope and pray as my son Saint Pio would say. I am a patient, long-suffering God. I know your ins-and-outs, your hopes and dreams, and the level of your strength. I will make you strong in Me. I said it and I will do it. My word never returns to Me void. It fulfills my will (Isaiah 55:11).

6/19/18

In your love, Lord, hear my voice.

Tell the world of my love. I died to set my people free—free to worship Me, their only true God. Love grows like a mustard seed. I used that as a parable to teach my disciples the truth of my kingdom of love (Luke 13:18). Love benefits the soul. Love heals the body, mind and heart. Love is a unifying bond between Me and my people. Yet, love can be broken; it is fragile, delicate like a broken heart. My heart was broken when I saw my people suffering from the effects of sin. I saw the need and ran to their rescue.

Love does not count the cost. Love is generous and powerful. The more one loves their God, Me, and not the world of pleasure and wealth, the more love I pour back into their heart. Their hearts become open vessels of love spilling over and restoring that heart to good health, peace and joy, a joy of life that is infectious, bringing happiness to others around them. Lovers are stars that shine in the dark filling their neighbor's need for affirmation and acceptance.

How sad it is to be unwanted, excluded. I invite everyone to the banquet of Heaven. Come and feast at my table (Isaiah 25:6). You are most welcome. I am the Heavenly Father looking and waiting for my prodigal children to return to Me (Luke 15:11). I will put a crown of gold on their head and wrap them in garments of salvation (Isaiah 61:10), and then they will know a peace beyond comprehension—a peace the world cannot give (John 14:27).

Tell my people to make the Beatitudes their own. Practice them in their daily lives until they become habitual. I give them the necessary grace, for this is my will that they should become holy as I, their Father, am holy (Isaiah 6:3); and we shall rejoice together. We shall go hand in hand into the promised land.

I have much to say on the subject of love. Love opens the door to my heart. I abide in love. Whoever loves is granted the wealth of Solomon (1 Kings 10:14). Whoever loves his neighbor receives glory that shines in Heaven. Whoever loves his enemies (Luke 6:27) wins the higher place in Heaven. He will stand in honor among my glorious Saints. Whoever loves and serves my enemy, the Devil, will be cast out into unutterable darkness forever.

Choose wisely, my children. Choose to do good. Choose the path I set before you, the path of holiness. Choose to love, suffer, if necessary, and obey. It is the way to glory.

7/6/18

In your love, Lord, correct my thinking.

Take heart for today all your sins are forgiven. You have been deceived by Satan, the evil one who lies and cheats and robs my people of their joy and peace of mind, heart and soul. But today we begin anew. Each day is another chance to get it right. I never give up on the ones I love and who obey the law of love.

It is the divine and first law that anyone who prays, loves Me and I will bless them. Yes, one of my children who recently passed to new life, loved my people by opening her heart to them. I blessed her with a gregarious personality and she did Me honor by embracing all whom she loved.

This is why I say not to judge (Matthew 7:1). Only I know the heart of man. I weigh everything in a balance and I decide their reward or punishment. When they come before Me, I know everything about them: how they lived, the good or bad they did, their faith, obedience. These things matter, but as Saint Paul says: Love is the greatest gift (1 Corinthians 13:13) for I am Love (I John 4:8), and I am merciful, forgiving because I know the problems of the world and made satisfaction for the sins of my people. I paid the price of sins committed against my Father by laying down my life. Everyone is indebted to Me.

But do they understand what I did for them? My child did. She prayed in hope of mercy and was rewarded with salvation. In time, she will be shown the Beatific Vision and will rejoice with all the Saints in Heaven, the highest Heaven. Yes, there are levels of sanctification, but there is eternal rest for those who love my people because in doing so, they have loved Me and saved their souls.

Take heart. Trust Me to save my people. I read hearts (Jeremiah 17:10).

7/9/18

My heart cries out for You, O Lord. Come, visit your slave.

We will begin today speaking about the greatest gift of all my gifts: love (1 Corinthians 13:13). Once a disciple has learned and lived the new way of the Beatitudes, a change of heart occurs. Love has replaced the old attitude of pride. This is the result of practicing the second Beatitude of mourning your sins. Now you know the proper order: God first. God in the heart supplants self which is an easy prey for Satan to work his wiles. The self-centered are not God-centered which is most important for the soul's sanctification which is the goal, purpose and venue to achieve eternal happiness.

Now we speak of the facet of love that fills the hearts of my disciples and leads to complete transformation of the soul— the eternal soul. Once I have breathed life into a soul, it lives forever because I am infinite—lasting forever (Revelation 1:8); so, too, the soul that has been fashioned in my image and filled with my divine Spirit. It can never die unless I withdraw my Spirit. Then it dies, bereft of my presence, my grace. But do not fear! I move heaven and earth to save my little ones! I shed my blood to save them (Ephesians 1:7). Would I not use my power to rescue them? Rest assured of my good intentions. I want every man, woman and child saved (Isaiah 35:4). I want them with Me always. Yes, they must cooperate with Me. They must accept salvation.

That is why love is so necessary. What one loves, one fights for! Is it not true that an athlete puts forth great effort to win the Olympic gold medal? So too, my children must train for the victory over pride, selfishness and vanity. The desire to achieve this goal is based on how much they love and want it—their salvation. Do they even think or know that their eternal life is at stake here?

Sometimes I think of another source of action to save my people. But, no, I know that the only way—the Way of my Son is best—to live in my people's hearts, to place my Spirit within them, to guide and enlighten and teach them the truth of my love for them (John 14:26).

And there we have it. My Love saves. My Love is the best source of action. Love is victorious and achieves its goal of victory over sin and death. Love is Life. Love is everything!

Enlarge my heart, Lord, so I may love You more.

Today we shall speak about my Kingdom of love. We shall begin with love for your fellow man—love in general. There is platonic love, sexual love, fraternal love, fascination and love in particular. We shall speak, also, of divine Love, the Love that heals, comforts and transforms hearts and souls. One cannot transform its heart without my grace, but I am openly generous with bestowing grace upon my loved ones; still, they must ask and seek for it like the pearl of great price my Son spoke of in the Gospels (Matthew 13:46).

So, to have love in one's heart, pray for it. Pray and you shall receive. Know to whom you pray. How to know Me? Read the Creation story in the Book of Genesis. It is recorded for your benefit. I spoke and the world came into existence. I spoke and the sun was created. I spoke and there was light; then the Light of the World, my Son, the second Person in the Blessed Trinity, entered the world at Bethlehem and a new covenant of love took place between Me and my people.

All was made new in the birth of my Son—a new beginning, a new hope, a new calling to perfection. A new and perfect Love entered the world—a Love that would grow and mature to heal the blind and the lame, to change the hearts of men so they might go forth to spread his kingdom on earth. The Church grew and a new order manifested itself on earth—and Heaven above. Peace was granted so men's hearts would turn to God, to know and love him, to serve and obey him. Then a feeling of joy touched their hearts, unspeakable joy coursed through their veins, lifting man into the new heaven: my Kingdom on earth where all receive

234

mercy, forgiveness, light of understanding, wisdom and knowledge of their God's goodness.

And so, the world turns from darkness to light, from despair to hope, from sadness to joy, for my Son gave his life to reconcile his people to their God and Father. This is divine love, sacrificial love, perfect love (1 Corinthians 13:4).

7/25/18

Lift me up, Lord, from the depths of my sins.

Today my message is on love—the power of love that created the world and sustains it in my love. Love is what drove Me to the Cross of your salvation. Love motivated my Father to create the world in seven days as recorded in my book (Genesis 1:1-2:4). You, too, are writing my book about the Beatitudes, the right attitudes my disciples must emulate in order to gain the prize of Kingdom living, the land of eternal love.

I speak about the power of love to create. How so? Love builds character. Love makes hearts grow. Love increases and souls once dead live again, like the story in Ezekiel about the dry bones (Ezekiel 37:1). The world was in chaos, I spoke and the earth was formed. Trees and flowers began to grow where there were none—so with the dry bones. I spoke my love into them and they began to walk—so with my dead people who have chosen to live in the dark. Their souls and spirits are dead, but when they hear my voice and listen and obey, they are recreated.

This is the work of love. It restores, invigorates dead bones, so to speak, and these dead bones live again in my love, my light. The Light of the World (John 8:12) came down into the darkness and brought his transforming Love/Light, and the lost were found, the blind began to see, and the lame walked. This is the creative force of love, my love for my people.

O my precious, adorable children, come unto Me and you shall live.

7/27/18

Teach me, Lord, so I may know You.

Yes, I am the Teacher, you are my disciple. A disciple is one who adapts his life to his Teacher's philosophy of life. Mine is love above all. Love is what I lived and died for. Look at the historical accounts of my birth and death and see it as one of true, perfect love. My love filled the oceans with salt and every kind of fish. My love placed the sun, moon, and stars in the sky. Love created my creatures in my image (Genesis 1:27). My love is present everywhere. One cannot escape my presence. I am in all, for all, and with all (Matthew 18:20). Those who receive and accept my presence in them become my followers, disciples and they learn from Me.

They conform themselves to my teachings, and they go farther up the mountain of love. They are motivated to become the best version of themselves as one of my disciples wrote. They study Scripture to learn who I am and what I have done. People who strive for love's perfection are undaunted by the enemy's attacks. They arm themselves, rely on my protection, and trust my power to lead them from darkness into the light of my glorious Kingdom on earth; and ultimately, into Heaven knowing I await them with open arms.

I opened my arms and had them nailed to the cross so they could see that my arms will be permanently opened to them. I will never abandon them (Hebrews 13:6). I love them too much. I want them with Me and my Father—one in the Holy Spirit.

Teach my people to accept the truth. Pray for an outpouring of grace upon the world that there may be a spiritual revival and the Good News will spread by means of all avenues of social media.

Hearken to my words: I will come again. Be ready. Be prepared. I am coming.

8/1/18

Save me, Lord, and make me your own.

Today our subject is love, a Kingdom of its own. Love is more than a condition of the heart. Love is a way of life. Without love, a soul dissipates; it becomes cruel, hardened against its God and kills the heart and soul of a man. Without love, one is lost, wrapped up in the opposite sin of hate which destroys peace and joy in the heart, soul and spirit.

Likewise, charity is lost and the state of a man's heart is embittered toward his fellow man. Love is the most needed virtue of a man's entire life. An infant without love and tender care suffers—does not thrive. Children need love to develop and grow into well-adjusted adults who in turn, give affirmation to their loved ones. And the wheel turns.

Love does make the world go around. Love is as necessary as food and water. But my love is needed before it is possible to begin to love. Love begins with Me and I am very generous with my gift of love. Ask and you shall receive because it is my will that you should love (Matthew 7:7).

Take care to love properly. Excessive love smothers. Love must be used wisely, carefully—never to manipulate a needy person but only for the other's good. You ask for an example? Yes, the Blessed Mother is always the best example. She loved Me with all her heart but she did not ask Me not to suffer for my love for you. It hurt her terribly to see my body scourged mercilessly and my head bleeding from a thorny crown. She shuddered at the venom spit in my face (Mark 15:18). Yes, love cost her dearly. Love suffers for love of others.

But love is not always painful. Love is liberating, joyous and the only way to live in peace with others. Think always of the good of others. This is how love grows. When you give it away, I give it back to you. Empty your heart and I will refill it. Yes, the heart is the vessel of love. The heart beats normally when it is at peace with love for self and the world.

Trouble not yourself (John 14:1) about things beyond your control. Leave the troubles of the world in my hands. I created the world and I am managing its affairs. I am quite capable of protecting, guiding and controlling everyone and everything. Trust Me. I will do what I say. My word is reliable and true. I keep my promises. You can bank on it.

All I ask is for you to learn to love—the right way, the royal way, the Christ-like way. The perfect way is to pray, hope, trust and obey.

8/4/18

Take away my idols, Lord, so I may love only You.

Listen. Today we speak about tough love. First, one must have true, kind love in their heart in order to discern when tough love is needed. Divine love for God empowers you to discern my will for the matter at hand. Sometimes withholding love is the answer, the way to do good, to be helpful to the recipient.

I have already spoken about smothering love when the person has everything done for them. This cripples the person from learning to care for themselves. The opposite type of love is often needed to spark the inner need of the person to care for himself—to grow up, so to speak. Maturity lies in self-autonomy. One must think for herself, to make wise decisions. When one has not learned to do this or is not proficient in surmising her choices, she becomes helpless, frustrated, debilitated. This is not a state of contentment. She lacks self-confidence, is unable to become the person I willed her to be. You see to not help a child develop all her qualities and talents is not love. So, parents especially must discern when tough love is necessary—when it is most important to help their child—not stifle her. This is not easy. Look at what courage and wisdom it took my Son to suffer his Passion and Death. We had no choice in the plan for your salvation for only God may atone for offenses against God.

Do you understand? No one or nothing on earth is equal to God. Only Jesus, my Son, could make satisfaction for every sin of humanity against its Creator. Do not think that because I am supreme, omnipotent, I am beyond feeling and suffering. It hurt Me to send my Son away on this mission of the world's salvation. We did it for the greater good that our sacrifice would accomplish. This is the prime example of tough love.

We ask nothing of you that we have not already done before you. All things are possible with God (Luke 1:37). I did it, so can you.

8/13/18

I love You, Lord, fill me with more love.

Today we will speak about charity to God, self and neighbor. Charity is the virtue closest to my heart. Charity forgives and forgets. A pure mind and heart will not find fault in God, self or neighbor. It searches for ways to help, serve and comfort others including self. So often my disciples forget that charity begins at home, and in their effort to please God and neighbor, they forget their own need for respect, for being treated kindly and gently. *"Do unto others as you would have them do unto you"* (Matthew 7:12). Love must be in the heart in order to pass it on to others. To love God with all your heart means to love neighbor and self. This is the proper order. So be good to yourself and I will fulfill your needs.

Listen and know what I ask and you will be kind and charitable to others. My Word works miracles through **Love: L**istening, **O**bserving, **V**ictory, **E**ffect result when there is right order. I am a God of order. Everything I do is orderly. I have order in the Church, in the atmosphere, the seasons, in the growth of life from conception to death. Everything is under my rule of law. Gravity is set in motion by my will. I order the sun to shine in the day—the moon and stars at night. Can I not order my people whom I created out of Love? I have given you a beautiful world to care for. Should I not expect you to do so? Likewise, I have given you love and respect. Should I not expect you to return it?

Why do my children hate their fellow man when I created them good? What evil is this that destroys my orderly world? Yes, you see it all around you. I have allowed evil to exist for my purpose, so my people will recognize their powerlessness and turn to Me, their Savior, who patiently waits for their conversion of heart. When they ask for my help, I will answer immediately, happily—for I love what I have created. I made them good and only want good for them.

Tell my people to trust their Heavenly Father who sent his Son to deliver them from eternal death. Why? Because I love them. I want them with Me. I want them to be happy. I want them to endure to the end trusting in Divine Providence and my almighty power. Nothing is impossible for those who love God—neither death, sickness, fire or disasters of any kind. I am their shelter, their hope, and I will never abandon them. I keep my Word.

Trust Me and you will live.

8/31/18

Lord, let your will be done in me.

Today we will speak about Divine Love that stems from a deep conversion of heart, mind, soul and spirit. This happens when one discovers the truth of who I am in each individual's life. First, as I have said, I am the Creator, Father of all. I am in all and for all (1 Corinthians 15:28). I wait patiently until my children mature in faith and begin to believe that my Son truly died on the Cross for love of them, that I raised Him from death, and now He reigns with Me in Heaven sitting at my righthand dispensing mercy and grace into the hearts of the faithful.

Saint Paul has beautifully described the virtue of love in his letter to the Corinthians but allow Me to share with you a few tenets of my love for you. Yes, I created the human being having made it from nothing. I 'thought' the human body with all its multiple functions: eyes, ears, nose, skin, organs, and it came into being. It is my will that man should be created.

More importantly, I gave man a soul which includes his reasoning power, a memory to store up truth, and a free will to make right, wise decisions. I say a free will which I will not invade. This is his own property. I will not take it away from him. That is not to say that I will not be near him. Yes, I planted myself, my Spirit within him, never to leave him for if I did, he would fade away.

No, I will never abandon my people (John 14:20). I am God, not man. I know what is in the heart of man. I created that heart to long for Me. Whether they know it or not, I am with my people. Can you see just how precious you are to Me? How great my love is for you? If I did not want you, I would not have created you. Love enjoys sharing and I wanted to fellowship with man so I could share my glory with him.

Now let us take it more personally. I want you in my Kingdom. I want you to share in my treasures. I want you to be happy and to enjoy our relationship. I have given Life to you. Won't you share it with Me?

10/3/18

Let me love You, Lord, more than You love me.

Yes, today we will speak about love, the most important virtue highlighted by Paul's exposition of the virtue in 1 Corinthians 13:4. Love is the reason I created the earth and populated it with humankind and all the animals. I designed the globe of the earth to be a place of beauty, a fertile ground to provide food for humanity. A place or land of plenty whereby mankind may prosper and populate it. This I did out of love, and in this love, I wish my people to live and prosper.

Love is the motivating factor in the heart of man. In response to love, a Kingdom was born—the Kingdom of my Son the Christ. We envisioned it to be visible to the heart that loves, that has been purified into gold, that has been tested by fire, and can withstand all the vicissitudes of life.

Love is the heart of a worthy servant in my eyes. I see the light of love shining through them and in them. Yes, they shine like stars in the dark, lighting up the world by their gracious deeds and kind words (Matthew 5:14). They speak words to comfort, to inspire, to relate truths and goodness. They spread joy and lift up hearts that are troubled. They serve their God with true diligence and respect, careful to observe my decrees.

In peace and in love, they find contentment of soul and spirit. They trust my holy Word to guide and protect them throughout their lives knowing that I love them and will never abandon them. They look to Me to provide their daily bread and they are satisfied. This is the wonder of love that it always satisfies the hungry, loving soul.

Love fulfills all of man's dreams and fills the soul with sweet contentment. Love encourages the down-hearted and lifts the spirit until they find the magic of love in their own hearts. One lives in peace when one loves. It is medicine for the body and covers a multitude of sins (1 Peter 4:8). Love washes away the residue of sin in the soul; the mind is cleared of evil thoughts, selfish desires—things that get in the way of the soul's beauty. Yes, love is powerful, attractive, welcoming. Love has no bounds and is everlasting—unto the end of the ages.

Love lives, grows, multiplies and is undefeated. That is why Christ's death was victorious over the death of sin because behind it all was the power of my love to restore him to life. Just as it is with anyone who loves, for love is life-giving, life-saving, life-transforming, life-fulfilling. Yes, love never dies but lives on forever (Jeremiah 31:3).

10/10/18

I am overwhelmed by your love ,Lord, keep me in your presence.

Today is a new day of revelation and guidance by my Holy Spirit of wisdom, knowledge and understanding of what it means to walk in my light. Each day brings new wonders— things you have never before seen or experienced. I have much to teach you about my power over you. All I need is an open heart, a docile spirit, and a willing soul. Then I can work miracles of healing and transformation of life-styles.

"Come to Me you who are weary and I will give you rest" (Matthew 11:28). This grace is for all who love Me and obey Me with all their heart and strength. Yes, it takes a loving heart and a willingness of spirit to follow Me up the

mountain of love and of mystery. It takes courage and bravery to step into the unknown. Yet, be assured that there are many supports and resting places along the way.

The upward journey to holiness requires determination to unravel the secret thoughts buried in the psyche. Only my grace is sufficient or able to bring these hidden secrets into the light. Shall I tell you a secret? I alone can reveal the inner depths of a man's soul. Can you create an ear? or an eye? or hair? No, but I can and I do. Knowledge of the inner-workings of your soul: memory, intellect, will is a simple matter for Me.

Wait and see what I can do. Pray to be open to my power to work in you, with you and for you for the good of my people. Just be an open vessel for my grace. Ask, pray for understanding. Open your heart to my light. I will never fail you.

Will you be loyal to Me?

10/12/18

You are my Shepherd, Lord. I shall want for nothing.

Yes, I am your loving Savior. I have called you into my flock and I will watch over you. I know you by name and have heard your cries for help (Isaiah 65:24). I answer you in the storm clouds that threaten your safety. When you are in great need, I send my angels to protect you. When you are happy, my angels rejoice over you.

No matter what stage you are in life, you are never left alone. Take for example your relative. I have given her the desire to seek my presence at daily Mass in order to comfort her and to draw her nearer to my heart. I know the need my people have of my grace and I gladly extend it whenever they call to Me. Would a father give his child a snake when he asks for bread (Matthew 7:9)? Keep in mind that I am greater than the highest mountain but because of my love for you, I supply the faith that can move mountains (Matthew 17:20)!

This is my love song for you to encourage you to seek my power over you, to fulfill the plan I have to make you happy, whole and to complete your journey through this life.

Love means that you are never alone. I walk with you; I exist in you. If this were not true there would be no life in you. Where I am there is fullness of joy, excitement, newness of spirit. Love causes all things to grow, thrive, to achieve greatness, splendor, fulfillment of goals—one of which is to see my Face in those around you. Love accomplishes all things and love never ends because I am God, Father Almighty and everlasting. I have the final word.

Understand who you are in Me, where you are in the big picture. What is the final end? How long will life exist? Is there something beyond this world? Are there other worlds in the vastness of the universe? Other suns? Where do the clouds go? Only your Father in Heaven knows. Are you beginning to comprehend who I am and what you are in relation to Me?

Consider the possibility of existing in a world without my love. There would be no sun to light the day; you would live in darkness. There would be no rain to water the crops; you would go hungry. There would be disorder in the elements: no air to breathe, no fire for warmth, the land/earth would turn to dust. All life would be consumed and wither away.

Think of these things. It is a matter of life and death, love and hate. Learn to whom you belong. I offer love, mercy, forgiveness, eternal joy in Paradise. How can you refuse my Love?

Love Me as I love you, my people. Choose wisely. It's in your hands. Come to Me.

10/14/18

Make your love, Lord, the foundation of my life.

One cannot live on bread alone (Luke 4:4). All human beings, and yes, even my animals need my love. I am Love (1 John 4:8), so the world and all that is in it require Love (Me) to be able to love. This is because when I created the first man, I put myself within him. I put my heart and soul into my creation; how else could he live? Nothing can exist unless they have my Spirit in them. I have discussed this with you earlier but it bears repeating for a clearer understanding of who you are in Me. Without Me, my presence, my light, my grace, my wisdom—everything— you would not survive. Alone, you are lost.

This was by my design from the beginning. I wanted fellowship, so I created man in my image (Genesis 1:27) and told him to enjoy all the fruits in my garden. Then I gave him a companion, a woman to be his soulmate (Genesis 2:21-22). They were supremely happy, healthy and great friends. And I, on my part, loved and enjoyed and doted on them. There was only one prohibition given to them: Do not eat of the tree of knowledge of good and bad in the center of the Garden (Genesis 2:17).

Well, we know the rest of the story. Although I was obliged to banish them away from Me, I did not destroy them because of my love for them. I could not cut myself off from them completely because of my Love. You see, Love is my Son Jesus the Christ in whom the world was created (John 1:3). As long as the earth exists, my Son is in it. He, Love, will never abandon my creation (John 14:18). He became a human being for the purpose of preserving His people. He did not come to condemn them (John 12:47).

Do you not yet understand the depth and the value of his love? What it cost both of us, Father and Son, to keep you safe? Do you understand how much we value you? How precious you are in our eyes?

Yes, the Father and I are one (John 17:21). We are united in the bond of Love who is the Holy Spirit who we send to those who are baptized in the name of the Father and of the Son and of the Holy Spirit. (Please note that I said name—singular not plural) We are three Persons in one God. Believe the truth and you will be saved (Romans 10:9). Have faith in the power of Love to guide, protect and enlighten you all the days of your life.

Enough for today. Go and rejoice in my love for you.

10/8/18

Grant me grace, Lord, to persevere to the end.

Today we will speak of charity to God, self and neighbor. "Charity begins at home" is a familiar saying. And home is in your heart, so we must love ourselves first in order to love others. How to do that? Take care of your body: give it a balanced diet of protein, fruits and vegetables.

(Permit me to explain that at this point, I was still taking dictation from Our Lord, but the voicing changed. I was writing in the first person, as if these were my words.)

Take care of your soul: nourish it with times of silence before the Lord as long and as often as God permits. Everything comes from God: air to breathe, food to eat, light to see, a heart that beats, a mind that thinks, and a mouth to praise the wonders of your God who fills you with every spiritual blessing in the Heavens (Ephesians 1:3)!

We are nothing without God working His plan for our well-being and our salvation. Everything comes from God: our sanctification, our knowledge, understanding, joy and peace. Without God, we are resounding gongs, using a favorite expression from Saint Paul (1 Corinthians 13:1). Without the light of Christ, we are lost in the dark and left to our own resources. God forbid that this should happen! I don't know about you, but I'd be an unruly mess, lost in my own muddles and mistakes with no hope of salvation. But, thanks be to God's mercy, my soul was awakened to the truth—now I am free to seek the God of my dreams.

Did you ever dream that God was as near to you as your skin? I didn't. But it is the truth. God loves us so much that He never leaves us. Let me tell you a secret I learned not too long ago: He wants to be your friend (John 15:14). He already knows you because He knows everything! But He wants you to like Him, to friend Him, to share your life with Him on an intimate basis. He wants to help you and protect you and comfort and console you. God is wonderful!

11/5/18

Let me love You, Lord. Show me the way.

I will because you ask in faith. This is the first of the theological virtues. From faith comes life and with hope comes love, the greatest gift of all. But without faith in the heart, mountains cannot be moved, rivers not crossed, victories not won, and the race lost. But with faith, all is accomplished. You want an acrostic for **Faith**? How's this: **F** for Father; **A** for Adoration; **I** for Interior; **T** for Total; **H** for Holiness. Adore or ask the Father for interior, total holiness, and in and with faith, it shall be done.

Do I not love you? You know I do. Am I not your Father who owns everything? Who commands the sun to shine? The rain to fall? Who spoke and you were created? Can I not give you everything and more besides? Yes! When you ask in faith—believing in my love for you; believing that I died on the Cross for you; believing that I save every tear you shed; believing that I live in you, breathe in you, and long for your friendship, then I will grant every prayer for holiness because this is my will for you.

It is good for you to become holy, then all doors open for you. Then you are free to walk in my light, to love with my love, to follow in my footsteps that will take you up the mountain of love where you will see things you've never before seen. You will peer into spiritual mysteries, stages of holiness described for you by my Saint Bonaventure in his book: *The Soul's Journey into God.* Knowledge will come into your mind and spill out from your mouth. You will speak of my holiness, goodness and love, and my people will listen to you and their hearts will be converted, their lives transformed—all because you have **Faith** in your Father,

Adore him and ask for Interior (and I add: it will affect your exterior life, also) Total Holiness. You will glorify Me with good deeds that will last forever. They will take root in my heart and by my grace, you will produce bounteous good fruit in my Kingdom of Love.

11/8/18

I love You, Lord, let me love You more.

Yes, I will for it is my will that you should love Me. This is the way I planned for all my children. To love Me is the easiest way to eternal salvation. In loving Me, my children open their hearts to all I have for them. I know what they need to be happy and fulfilled. I know the way to their hearts, for I am God, their Creator, Savior, Redeemer, and I have delivered them from their only enemy, Satan.

Yes, many of my children are easily trapped by Satan's lies and temptations to hate. If only they knew how easy it is to love, and that love is so beneficial to their health. Love and laughter give joy to the heart and they gain a sense that "all is right with the world." This attitude gives them spirit and life, energy and vigor. This attitude makes them conquerors over evil and heroes of good in the world. They accomplish greatness. They are undefeated, successful in all their endeavors. Love gives them a zest for life. They face the world and lick it!

Why not set love and laughter as a goal? Practice putting aside old thoughts of negativity, resentment, and think new thoughts: "Hey, it feels good to be happy. I am tired of complaining and being dissatisfied with my world. There must be a better way to live. Why not be good to myself for a change? You can't change other people anyway, so stop trying! Work on what makes me feel good about myself— what makes me happy."

There, you see? That's what I mean when I say, cherish yourself. You're taking care of yourself. You will do what it takes to make yourself feel good, happy. Just by being kind to yourself, you have struck a blow to the only enemy in your life: Satan, who only lies to you, makes you believe negative things about yourself and those around you. Train yourself to think happy thoughts and you will feel happy. If you like to sing, sing cheerful songs to lift your spirit.

Remember, when I created you, I gave you a good mind, a healthy, strong body and a beautiful soul made in my image. What have you done with it? Did you educate your mind by reading good literature and my book, the Bible? Have you learned about all the love I have for you? Or do you fill your mind with hate, anger? To be happy, you need a healthy body. Have you fed it with good nutritious food, exercised your muscles? Filled your lungs with clean air? Or have you clogged your lungs with foul smoke? You see, it is up to you to care for the precious mind, body, soul and spirit that I gave you since the conception of your life in your mother's womb (Psalm 139:13). I knew you before you were born. I cared for you and fostered you like a father (Hosea 11:4). I carved you in the palm of my hand (Isa 49:16). You are precious to Me and my love for you is everlasting (Jeremiah 31:3).

So, now, my precious child, cherish yourself. Be merciful and love yourself. You are wonderfully made (Psalm 139:14). Remember, Rome wasn't built in a day. So, get busy with the work of making yourself happy, healthy and holy. I have given you a free will to choose for yourself. I am as close to you as a prayer; if you need counsel or wisdom, ask for it.

11/13/18

Teach me, Lord, the way to perfection.

Today we will speak of love, holy love, a thing of beauty, grace and enduring, unselfish love. It is the love that originates in God—it is a divine love that is unconditional. It builds character and demolishes evil. Love is a bulwark of courage and strength to carry you through all the vicissitudes that come your way. Divine love does not count the cost. It is not measured by dollars and cents, but by common sense. Ask yourself, "Is this, what I am contemplating, good or bad?"

You ask, "How does one measure love?" Consider whether it lines up with the standard set by my Son, the Lord and King of your heart. Is it unselfish, will it give life to you? Or will it lead you away from my light and shelter? Think on these things because this life is only a day compared to eternal life. Do you want to live in misery or joy? You see, love is for the asking; yes, but once received we must cherish it, multiply it until love consumes your whole life—you live to love.

So, what I am telling you, dear Reader, is that love is the way to perfection. When you have put aside all selfish desires and ulterior motives for self-aggrandizement, until you can carry your brother's burden with a cheerful heart, when you are extravagant with your time and treasure, when you have learned to love Me with your whole self, and your neighbor as well as yourself; then you are on the road to perfection.

The road is bumpy because self-love can be a two-way street: "I come first, that's what matters." "I have to watch out for myself." "If I have time, I'll come and help you out." No, perfect love does not hesitate. It gives immediately, unconditionally.

O my people, do not be afraid to die to self. Walk in my footsteps and I will carry your burdens. The road will be easy when you take my yoke upon your shoulders (Matthew 11:30). On your own, you cannot do it.

11/17/18

Talk to me, Lord, about your holy Mother.

Yes, I will. I enjoy bragging about my Masterpiece, the holy Virgin Mary. As you well know, she was conceived without original sin, and that is enough reason to call her holy. My plan for her life was to keep her free from contamination of anything evil because only a perfect vessel, one without blemish or spot (Deuteronomy 17:1), could be used for the purpose of giving birth to Jesus Christ, the second Person in the Blessed Trinity, God the Son. I cannot exist where there is sin/evil. It is not possible to *"put new wine into old wineskins. Otherwise the skin bursts, the wine spills out, and the skins are ruined"* (Matthew. 9:17). So, with my Mother. Her womb had to be perfect for her own sake. My light is perfect as God is perfect.

So, that's the first point: Mary's soul was without blemish or spot—like mine. I was the perfect Lamb chosen to be sacrificed for mankind's sins. And my Mother shared in that sacrifice by offering her life in service to Me. She said: *"Do unto me according to your will"* (Luke 1:38). Those are the perfect words of total surrender to the Father's will. Emulate this quality/virtue. Take her as your model. That's the second point: surrender.

What else can I say about my Mother that you do not already know? How frightened she was when I stayed on in my Father's Temple and she thought I was lost (Luke 2:48)? How distraught she was at the thought that I may have been harmed, that she had failed the Father? Then the anguish at seeing the negative attitude of the Pharisee's toward Me, the Son of God (Matthew 12:14)? She suffered terribly for Me. Emulate her courage, trust and openness to suffering. For she was yet to see her Son scourged, crowned with thorns, spat upon, and she could do nothing to help Me. Her heart was slowly breaking, but for the grace of God that coursed through her veins, she would have gladly died in my place. But she knew this was my destiny and she did all she could to comfort Me. I looked upon her with great love and compassion. I knew she was carrying my Cross in her heart, and this comforted Me.

You know, dear Reader, that I rewarded her by crowning her the Queen of Heaven (Revelation 12:1). I have given her great power to do good on earth. She is your Mother, praying and interceding for you in Heaven. She sits by my side and whispers in my ear, "Son, have mercy on your people. They do not understand."

Yes, that's my precious Mother, kind and gentle of heart, always willing to do what I ask. She never says no to Me because she knows that my heart is for my people. And so is hers!

11/20/18

Grant me eternal wisdom, Lord, to guide my steps.

Listen to my words. They are life for you. Listen closely to what I say to your heart. It is the seat of knowledge. Yes, love rules the heart, and I dwell in a loving heart. Listen to my words. They will guide your heart and you will follow in my footsteps to eternal life.

Wisdom shall be yours because of the disposition of your heart. When you obey my will completely, when you are totally dedicated to laying down your life for Me, I will come to you quickly and you shall see my face—the Face of the eternal God and Father of all ages. You shall see wonders never before conceived in the mind of man. These Heavenly things are unimaginable for they are holy and beyond the reach of earthly man. Can you catch a star? Or touch a moonbeam? Yet, I created these wonders just by willing them into existence. The mind of God is infinitely creative and endures forever.

How can I exist in mortal man unless he be elevated to a state of perfection? For I am perfect, unrepeatable, original, the First and the Last (Revelation 22:13). Nothing existed before Me. I created the universe and will create a new heaven and a new earth. You ask, "When?" When all you know and see has passed away. When the sun no longer shines. When night fills the sky and day no longer exists. You cannot imagine what I have in store for mankind. Just remember, my will is holy and perfect. What I will, comes to pass. I have the power to perform my will. When I speak, it is done. When I decide, it is accomplished. When I command, I am obeyed. Nothing escapes my attention. I see all, know all, and exist in all. I am unsurpassable, Almighty.

But, let Me tell you a secret: I am touchable. I can be touched daily by fervent prayer. I can be swayed by good, kind, loving acts of mercy. When my people love each other, I am moved to tears. You see, I have a tender, loving heart filled with infinite love to pour out on my people. My grace and mercy never end. There is enough for all.

Won't you approach my throne of grace? It's easy to do—just love Me, your neighbor as yourself; and all my wonders and treasures will be yours just for the taking, for I am a generous God, approachable God, and I love you always.

This is eternal wisdom: to know, love and serve God with all your heart.

11/25/18

Lord, help me climb the mountain of love.

Yes, I'm glad you asked. *"Ask and you shall receive"* (Matthew 7:7). You're getting good at remembering my scripture verses. Would that all my children would read and study the Bible. It was written as a manual to learn how to operate in the spiritual world where I exist; and also, as a manual on how to conduct yourself in the existential world. I am all-knowledgeable and I want my children to be educated about Me, my ways, my thoughts, my plans. I want my children to walk with Me in the light of my love, to know who and what they can do with my assistance.

To climb the mountain of love, what is needed is first, the desire—the desire to know, love and serve Me. Second, obedience. They must agree to obey my commands, my promptings of the Spirit; and third, to accept my way, my plan for their life. Many will desire what is not good for themselves. They stay up all hours of the night watching worrisome movies or programs on television. Instead, they should be praying themselves to sleep and get a good night's rest. Then they would be fortified for the next day's work of fighting against the temptations of the world.

So, to climb a mountain, one trains for it, prepares a plan, gathers tools needed for the journey. Sound familiar? That's what this book is all about! Preparing for the greatest and most important journey of your life. It is the journey to eternal life. Is your goal to reach Heaven, or is your goal taking you to hell? They both exist. I hope you will take my way.

I promise if you take the Beatitudes as your road map, you will reach Heaven. You will climb that mountain and it will lead you safely home.

12/13/18

Help me to leave sin behind, Lord, for You are my Savior.

Today we will speak about kindness. This is the fruit of love. With my Spirit in your heart, you can break down barriers in the hearts of others. Kindness engenders the power needed to soften and open the mind to think new thoughts and feel new feelings (2 Corinthians 5:17). You want an analogy for kindness? Well, let Me tell you a story or maybe it's a parable.

One day long ago, there was a tired old man resting by the road side. He was on his way to the market to sell his horse. Along comes a younger man who stopped to inquire if he needed assistance. Well, he told the young man that he was tired, needed to rest, but asked if the young man would like to purchase his horse. So, the younger man in a moment of kindness, purchased the horse so the elderly man would not have to make the long, tedious trip into the city. In his relief and appreciation for the kindness shown to him, the elder man extended his hand in friendship and confided to the younger man the reason he was selling the horse. It had been a gift he had received from his father. But he never appreciated it. So, he decided to sell it. They shook hands and each went their way.

As it turns out, the saddle was more valuable than the horse because stitched into it was a hidden pocket containing diamonds and emeralds! The old man had not seen nor appreciated the valuable gift his father had given him and gave it away. So, the young man took the horse and the saddle containing a fortune in jewels, returned home and praised God for his good fortune.

The moral of the story is to seek ways to be kind to others and you will be rewarded beyond your expectations. Kindness is a virtue necessary in the world today where there is so much narrow-mindedness. My people are wrapped up in hunger for wealth and power that they miss the treasure buried in their souls: my Spirit, in Whom lies all the power to save their souls from damnation! How blind can man be? They throw away an eternal life of happiness for a few pieces of silver.

Be wise, my children. Take stock of your choices. Do you want a long life of peace and joy with Me in Heaven, or are you satisfied with this short span of life on earth being manipulated by your enemy who wants to steal your inheritance and doom your soul to the everlasting fires of hell?

Blessed Virgin Mary on the Ninth Beatitude

"Jesus is Merciful Love, because in Him is reflected the divine mercy of the Father, who has so loved the world that He has sent it his only begotten Son for its salvation. In Jesus, the mercy of the Father becomes personified and realizes itself in the plan of salvation. By means of Him, the Father causes his pardon to descend upon humanity which had wandered away because of sin, and brings it back to a full communion of love and of life with its Lord and its Creator."

"Jesus makes charity the new commandment. By loving his own "to the end," he makes manifest the Father's love which he receives. By loving one another, the disciples imitate the love of Jesus which they themselves receive. Whence Jesus says: "As the Father has loved me, so have I loved you; abide in my love." And again: "This is my commandment, that you love one another as I have loved you.""

St. Padre Pio on the Ninth Beatitude

"For the sake of love, I implore you, by all you hold sacred, do not wrong Jesus by suspecting even slightly, that you have been abandoned by him—not even for a single instant. This is precisely one of the most satanic temptations, and you need to thrust it far from you as soon as you become aware of it."

St. Alphonsus Liguori on the Ninth Beatitude

"O infinite goodness! O infinite love! A God has given himself wholly to me! Has become all mine! My dear Redeemer, I embrace you. My treasure! My life! I draw close to you; do not disdain me. Miserable that I am! I would rather a thousand times lose life than lose you, the sovereign Lord! In spite of all my offenses against you, I feel that you have commanded me to love you."

"Yes, my God! Where can I find in heaven or on earth, a greater good than you, or one who has loved me more than you? Ah! Jesus! Take possession of all my heart; possess it entirely and detach it from all love which is not for you. I choose you alone for my portion, my riches."

Chapter Ten

Tenth Beatitude
"For theirs is the Kingdom of Heaven."
Matthew 5:3

6/16/18

Remain with me, Lord, the rest of my days.

Today we will speak of my Kingdom—the reward of virtue, the result of observing the Beatitudes. My Kingdom consists of light, beauty, music, gaiety, concern for others, and admiration for all my creation: trees, animals, seas, astrological entities, and human beings who have responded to the work of grace in their souls.

In my Kingdom, there is no shame, no striving or envy, but only love. Heaven is a place of rest and comfort. Yet, it is not dull! There is much to do in Heaven. There are no time limits or constraints, nor limits or lack of anything. You have heard of spiritual satiety; yes, the soul is completely consumed in Me, thus it is satisfied without any struggle. All is provided in abundance, and there is no wrong done. Everything is orderly, shared with each other. Sin does not exist in Paradise. There is only light, no darkness of any kind. Your souls will be peaceful, light-hearted. You will see God face to face, and hear angels singing and adoring Christ the King who will reign over all forever.

The world will be made new. Wars forgotten. Peace will reign throughout the Kingdom. Satan will be chained and consigned to the place I have provided. There are six levels of existence: one for the Saints, another for the Angels, another for men, women and children, one for my servants the Prophets, Apostles; one for my musicians, and one for those closest to Me. My Mother sits at my right hand, and we all live together in peace and harmony. It is a beautiful life I have planned since the beginning. Time does not exist. It just goes on and on like a day. There is no night for there is no darkness. I am there so I am the Light.

O my people, do as I say and you are guaranteed a place in my Father's Kingdom. I have prepared a place for you (John 14:2). I know your likes and dislikes so it is perfect for each one of you. I know your needs and wants and I will guide you by the hand if you will only follow Me. I appeal to your hearts. Say, "Yes, Lord Jesus Christ, You are my only good. You created me for great things. I thank You for my life, salvation, redemption and deliverance. What else is there that I need? I want to follow You. I want to be your disciple. Please help me to find the way to your heart where I will be safe and protected from the world, the flesh, and the devil. I have three strikes against me but You came into the world to save me and for this I am grateful. Give me what I need to turn my life over to You, to trust You with all my heart so I can live in your Kingdom forever."

Do this and you will be safe. Take on my attitudes and doors that were closed will now open to you. Listen to my words and obey. Live the life I have given you. Don't hold back. Look ahead to the finish line. I, your Father, am waiting to scoop you up in my arms. Come, my child. I love you.

6/28/18

Grant me grace, Lord, to persevere to the end.

We shall speak of the cumulative effects of living the Beatitudes. Not only do they affect the mind and heart, but the entire life changes—one's behavior and even the world changes in their view. They see life differently—through rose-colored glasses, so to speak. The heavy burdens of grieving, striving, and unforgiveness no longer take a toll. One becomes the opposite: happy, dependent on the Father, and merciful to themselves as well as to others. They take on an air of holiness and they love greatly. Speaking ethereally, they shine like stars in the sky (Philippians 2:15).

This is my Light shining in and through them. The heart has literally expanded. They love Me, others and themselves. They have learned to be merciful and at peace with the world of sinners. They scratch their heads wondering why every man, woman and child would not want the peace that fills their heart. In fact, they mourn for other's miseries, but with one exception, they hope, anticipating everyone's conversion and salvation. Redemption, they know, was achieved on the Cross of Christ for everyone. All that is left to do is to trust in God's mercy to save all his people, and they know I will do it because they have seen my saving power at work in their lives.

And my word in the Bible announces it: *"Blessed be the Lord, the God of Israel, for he has visited and brought redemption to his people"* (Luke 1:68). They have made the word of God the motto they live by. They know my word is true, glorious and life-giving, that my word shapes hearts and always comes true. They live on the Word of God.

Aside from all this, the Beatitudent becomes holy as her God is holy. She believes in her God with all her heart. She begins to see the effects of her holy intentions take root in those around her. She sees faith in the hearts of her family. She becomes the virtuous woman spoken of in the book of Proverbs, chapter thirty-one. (Read it!) Yes, she is firm in her faith, unwavering in hope and productive in love because love is a promoter of good deeds.

The Beatitudent has a charm all her own. She is unique. She trusts God's power to make all things possible. She sees her loved ones healed, saved and loving God. Her joy is their salvation. She has taken on the practice of prayer which fills her life. Whatever she does, she offers it to her loving God and it turns into prayer/grace. Time is of no importance. She spends her days in conversation with the God she loves, always turning to him for help, guidance and consolation.

She does not know what will happen but spends little time in worrying or fretting. It is a waste of time to fret over things that have happened in the past. It is over and gone. "Just live in the present," she tells herself. "Try not to make that mistake again." She knows her God is merciful and forgiving. She does not worry about tomorrow for God is with her now—in the moment. (As you write these words I dictate to you, I am closer than you imagine.)

I have more to say on this subject: listening becomes an enjoyable practice. Listening to my word gives you life, joy and that peace beyond understanding. Let the world go by. Trouble not your hearts (John 14:1). I am God and will always be God. Pray, hope and do not worry.

7/3/18

Reign in me, Lord, You are my King.

Today we speak about the Kingdom of light, peace, and joy where there is no more the curse of death. The soul has been set free from the pain, darkness, and hate of the world to live its life to the full. In my Kingdom all is light, streets paved in gold, doorknobs carved in diamonds, emeralds; and rubies pave the streets. The sun shines but never burns, stars sparkle in the sky. All around is beauty, all the eye can see is beauty. Limbs of trees are laden with delicious fruit.

There the peace is the stillness in the soul. There is no more the lure of sin, or lust for wealth, searching for pleasure. The soul rests in blessed peace. The torturers are gone forever. There is found the true soul of man. His worth is beyond measure and his heart is pure. It longs only to please its Creator. It is at home with its Savior in everlasting peace. It has achieved the purpose for which it was created: to be with God in full vision, clarity of mind, and its heart filled to overflowing with the holiness of the Holy Spirit who has sanctified his soul.

The ultimate joy is achieved: unity of mind, heart and soul with the Beatific Vision.

7/12/18

Guide me, Lord, into the land of justice.

Today we speak about Kingdom living—the everyday life of a Beatitudent. You have taken on the mind of Christ (1 Corinthians 2:16). You love God with all your being and beg for more love. In my kingdom on earth, I allow evil freedom to tempt my disciples. It is the way I have chosen not just as a test, but also, as a means to strengthen their resolve and to sharpen their discernment—to recognize good, bad, better, best, so they know what my will is; that they may become true warriors in the battle of life. They struggle to reach the goal of perfect faith, certain hope and true love of God, neighbor and self. They have learned the truth and the truth has set them free (John 8:32) to be the man or woman I planned they should be.

I will have my way in the souls of my people—whether they know it or not. I am the Ruler of the world (Matthew 2:6), and this truth comforts my followers, calming troubled hearts, disturbed spirits. Is it not glorious when I answer your prayers, your requests?

This is my will that all my people should be saved (1 Timothy 2:3-4). This is why my Son sacrificed his life. It is that important to us. We want everyone's salvation so they can be with us in eternity. Kingdom living must be won, fought for. It is not an easy struggle but I give you all the grace you need. Take it! Use it! Put it to good use.

Go on trusting my Word. I will never fail you. Am I a man that I should deceive you? My Word once given is never retracted. Live in my light and love.

7/13/18

Mold my mind, Lord, with the light of truth.

Today we speak about the kingdom of heaven that is the reward of virtuous living on earth while the soul is able to be transformed. Every soul is allotted a certain length of time in the physical body in which to attain the six levels of sanctity as described by Saint Bonaventure in *The Soul's Journey into God.*

It behooves everyone to study and learn about the spiritual life when possible. When not, there is nothing to fear for my Holy Spirit is the great Teacher who can turn stones into living rocks capable of understanding great truths of spirituality. When the time is right, the teacher appears. He may take the form of a book or video. I have myriad of ways to teach my people.

Let me explain something to you. My kingdom on earth is the Church. It is Holy because I dwell there wherever my people gather to worship Me, their God. My presence is in the hearts of my people and when they gather to pray, the more that gather the more my Spirit is multiplied.

Never forget that I am God. The world turns by my decree. My subjects listen and obey whatever I command. I have instituted great channels of learning my precepts throughout the known world. Yes, there are other worlds unknown to mankind. I am a creative God and my power to create is infinite.

Trouble yourself not to fathom the depth of my Being. Just pray each day for an open mind to grasp my will, and an open heart to receive my transforming love. I will enlarge your capacity to understand Me. You will comprehend my will, and my grace will always be sufficient for the day (2 Corinthians 12:9).

7/29/18

Praise, honor and glory to You, Lord Jesus Christ.

Today our subject is Kingdom living in the present. My interior Castle is in your heart. Where I am there can only be light. Darkness, evil will and evil intentions cannot exist where I am. Only light, love, kindness and goodness remain in a soul after I have purged it and pruned it so it will bear good fruit (John 15:2).

Next comes the stage of enlightenment where I fill my Castle with knowledge and wisdom, and give it understanding, prudence and the fortitude necessary to walk the journey of self-denial that it may also persevere in the shedding and casting out of false judgments of self and of others.

What I plan for other's lives is different from yours. Every person's journey is tailor-made individually, and yet everyone must go through the three stages of purgation, illumination and perfection. It is an inward, spiritual journey you must travel with Me and in Me. I take you by the hand and lead you. The work is mine but I ask your cooperation. Remember, I do not force—only invite. But I guarantee that this is a trip of a life-time. It is a trip worth taking. I have much joy in store for those who walk in my footsteps.

Now, let us speak about Kingdom living in the future. You have studied the Book of Revelation where everyone is clothed in white robes (Revelation 3:5). This signifies absence of sin in the soul, hence, purgation has occurred. Everyone in my Kingdom praise and worship Christ, the Lord of all. They have been illumined by the Light of Christ. They have set themselves free to be filled with love, goodness, adoration of their God and Father.

Joyfully, they wait for the coming of their Lord and Master. They know he comes with a great reward for every tear they shed, for every pain they suffered; as well as every wrong they did must be redeemed for them by their gracious, generous Savior. They rejoice in hope of eternal salvation knowing in their hearts that Christ will never abandon them nor forsake them (John 14:18). They know that his promises are kept—his word is true. So, they rest in peace with trust in their hearts that one day they will be united as one with the Father and the Son in the unity of the Holy Spirit.

Life does not end, for Christ is the Way and the Truth and the Life (John 14:6) that keeps on giving until all his children are gathered in his arms safe where they belong. His magnificent plan for each individual life is accomplished, is being accomplished, and will be accomplished.

In his perfect timing, everyone and everything will be made subject to his Father and the world you know will end (1 Corinthians 15:24-27). My Kingdom on earth will be established in Heaven. Joy will reign in the hearts of men. You have my Word!

7/30/18

Call me into your light, O Lord.

Today I want to talk about things you can do to live in my Kingdom day by day. One thing is first and very important: you must love God, neighbor and self (Mark 12:30). Secondly, develop the virtue of obedience. Look to whom you owe obedience in your life. Is it your boss who hires you to work for him? Then obey his rules. Is it your government officials? Obey the laws, pay your taxes and obey traffic laws. Are you married? You vowed to love, cherish your spouse. Well, keep your vow. Is it your Pastor? If you love Me, your God and Father, you will obey my representative on earth. Children, obey and respect your parents. We can go on and on. In any organization there are bylaws or regulations, or is it a religious order? Obey the constitutions. See how many ways you are called to obedience? Everyone must answer to someone.

The third requirement necessary for kingdom living is generosity. This includes unselfishness, no stinginess or refusal when demands are made on your time, or if it means a change in your plans or schedule. Think of other's needs before your own. This entails a kind heart, meekness and humility. Pray for these virtues.

7/31/18

I exalt You, Lord, with hymns of praise.

Let us pick up where we left off yesterday. Kingdom living on earth is, of course, worshipping Me in Church. My command is to keep holy the Sabbath, and in the Catholic faith, this means to attend Mass on Sunday in a Catholic Church, physically, mentally, and emotionally which means you are worshipping Me with your body, mind, and heart. All three components work together to love, honor and serve Me, the God and Father of my beloved Son Jesus, the Christ, together with the Holy Spirit.

Three things happen: worship, teaching, and sanctification. You worship Me by bending the knee. My word spoken in the readings gives instruction, and of course, the soul is sanctified by consuming my flesh and blood in Communion with my faithful ones.

I founded my Church to administer the Sacraments which are signs of my love. In Baptism, I wash away original sin and draw you into my family. In Confirmation, I confirm your presence in my heart and thus you are called into service. In Reconciliation (or as we used to call it Penance), when you come before my ordained priest and confess your sins, I forgive you with all my heart. Then in Matrimony, I bless your union: two hearts become as one, and I fortify your marriage with special love and grant the grace to create

271

my adorable children. I take them into my arms and bless them with my love. Holy Orders is granted to my chosen sons to administer, preach, teach, and to heal my people with the last Sacrament, the Anointing of the Sick. This is a special Sacrament intended to heal the blind, cure the lame, restore bodies to good health and vigor to live the life I have granted them—fully and joyfully.

All this to show my perfect love for my people. Oh, if only they would fully participate in the treasures I have given them. They would see all the love I have in my heart. They would share it with each other because love grows. It multiplies. My plan was for perfect peace to reign in the hearts of my people. They are sacred to Me.

Treasure my people for Me. I commission you to love them.

8/2/18

Love me always, Lord, or I will perish.

Yes, I will. I do. I always have and always will love you. Your God is a loving God, faithfully so. My love never stops. It just keeps growing and growing until it consumes your soul and you become totally mine. I am a jealous God, jealous for your love (Exodus 34:14). I want my children to love and obey Me for their own welfare. Only in and with Me will they find peace and contentment. I fulfill their destiny which is to live in my Kingdom forever and ever if they allow Me to help them.

My whole time on earth was spent for the purpose of saving souls so they might reach and fulfill the reason they were created. You know the reason. You were taught this in the old Baltimore Catechism. The question is: What must we do

272

to gain the happiness of heaven? The answer is: To gain the happiness of heaven we must know, love, and serve God in this world. And how do we learn to do this? From Jesus Christ, the Son of God, who teaches us through the Catholic Church.

I came that they may have life, abundant life (John 10:10); and I am the Life of the World (John 14:6). I lived and died so you may live eternally in the peace and joy of Heaven with Me, your Triune God. I promise if you will obey Me, follow in my footsteps, do all you can to fulfill your vocation, become a kind, loving Christian, I will use all my power to reward you with everlasting life, and a holy, well-contented life. I further promise that you shall see your descendants in Heaven with you (Acts 16:31). I am a loving God with infinite power. I stand on my word.

8/12/18

Draw me, Lord, close to Thee.

Today let Me tell you about Heaven. It is a place designed by us, the Holy Trinity of three loving Persons who cherish our creation. We considered the plight of the world once it was corrupted by sin and calculated our choices. Should we destroy the world by flood as at the time of Noah (Genesis 7:11)? Should we create another world and force mankind to obey for their own safety? No, we did not want robots! Should we create a different species of creatures to enjoy Paradise with us? But nothing proved right. We loved the human beings we created. They were special. It gave us joy to see them walking in the Garden among all the flowers and rippling brooks, singing happy melodies about their God.

We knew what the perfect plan was to save mankind: my only begotten Son would offer himself as a ransom to my justice (Matthew 20:28). He would offer his life to atone their sins to secure the life of their posterity. He would put his life into them and they would be holy as he is holy (Matthew 5:48). And this was the verdict. The Second Person of the Blessed Trinity, God the Son, the Lord Jesus Christ, the Anointed One gave up his life in Paradise to be born of a Virgin, to live in human flesh, to sacrifice his life, to die as an innocent Lamb for the salvation of the souls of his people, and to defeat death once for all. This was our decision. And it was a good one—a perfect plan of salvation.

And it has been going forth for thousands of years. It is the goal for all creation to gain either Heaven or Hell. As I said, we do not want robots. We want people who are mature in spirit, knowledgeable about their souls, loving of hearts, who are willing to walk the road mapped out for them by Christ, so they may be reunited with their Triune God enjoying the fruits of Heaven.

Come to Me, my people. Give Me your burdens for my yoke is easy and my burden light (Matthew 11:30). Return to Me.

9/6/18

Let me love You, Lord, with a pure heart.

Fret not the distractions that come to your mind. I am always with you. I know the deepest desires of your heart. You hunger and thirst to do my will, and I will satisfy your longing to dedicate yourself in my service.

Know that I have called you to a deeper journey into my Kingdom. You are approaching my throne of grace where I dispense the necessary graces for sanctification. Listen every day as you have been doing and I will do the rest. All I need from my disciples, prophets, servants, pupils and saints is their commitment to honor and obey Me. It is my responsibility to save, heal, convert, enlighten, guide and train my people. My Mother greatly assists Me in this.

I have much to teach you about Heavenly activities. One does not exist idly, doing nothing. No, they are busy with spiritual activities. They adore Me. They sing songs to Me. Yes, there is a Heavenly Choir. There are groups who only pray for the Church Militant. We have groups who study the stars, planets, and other celestial entities.

I am always creating new wonders. Let us say, there is always something new under the sun. The earth will fade away, but I will create new heavens and a new earth (Revelation 21:1). My word is always true. What I say, I do.

Enough for now. Get busy with your plans for the day. I bless you in the name of the Father and of the Son and of the Holy Spirit. Go in peace. I love you.

9/30/18

May the fire of your word, Lord, illumine my heart.

My plan is to illuminate the minds and hearts of all my people. Some are so far from Me that my fire does not touch them. What I need are more disciples who have been trained in the ways of the Beatitudes—a man is as he thinks.

There are far too many lost souls because of lack of knowledge of who I am for them. Rejoice in your salvation from the world of darkness, fear and sin. Of course, anything that separates you from my light is sin. We will save that discussion for another time.

Today I want to stress the need for prayer warriors, people of faith who will pray for the enlightenment of nations. It begins with those closest to you, and it will spread from one person to another until the whole world has been illuminated by the light and fire of my love.

It begins with faith, hope and charity. Once these virtues have become rooted in your heart, there is no stopping you. I open doors and you joyfully walk through them. Sometimes the journey is easy but other times obstacles need to be removed. This is why the attitude of the Beatitudes is necessary for success.

Beginning with the first Beatitude, poverty of spirit, you learn your need for my Holy Spirit to supply all you need to be a strong, fruitful warrior of prayer. In the second Beatitude, you mourn your sins, repent and receive the consolation of heavenly graces: wisdom, knowledge and counsel. All the remaining attitudes contribute to your final transformation. You will then have passed with flying colors!

Then comes the time for testing your courage—but never fear because I never give you more than you can handle. Look at my Son Jesus the Christ. You have not even begun to suffer as he suffered. And neither is it necessary because Christ Jesus did it for you. Satan was defeated once and for all. He has no power over you unless you give it back to him by disobedience or losing faith and hope in my power to protect you.

Be assured that every heavenly grace is available to you and every prayer you lift up to Me—especially intercessory prayer—is heard and answered in my time.

Now, let us recap what today's lesson is about: gaining my light through the avenue of the Beatitudes. We have come a long way. We have journeyed upward toward the kingdom of Light, and hopefully, I have convinced you of my love for you, of my protection and constant presence in your heart, of my will to bring you safely home, and that I rejoice over your yes to my call.

Enough for now. We will speak together again tomorrow. Arrivederci!

10/13/18

Consume me, Lord, in your wisdom.

Today let us summarize what we have learned thus far about the Beatitudes. They are the road signs on the map that point the way to holiness and the place of contentment. The Beatitudes reflect who I am, your Lord and your God. The Beatitudes teach you a new life style—one of meekness, mercy, right living.

I have taught you to cherish your soul for my sake, to love your neighbor for I live in them, to spread my peace to those nearest to you, to accept whatever comes your way for it is part of my plan for your salvation. I have taught you how to live in my Kingdom and what it means to be the "King's Kid."

Now let us speak about the wisdom of the Beatitudes. The very first Beatitude teaches the proper order of a subject and their King. They recognize their need, their poverty, and who it is that can supply all their needs. So, the proper posture is to humbly acknowledge who I am before them. Understanding this, they regret their sins against the One who gives them life and they mourn their loss. Then they meekly submit to my will and receive mercy at my hands. They grow in wisdom and in the desire to imitate and honor their Father in Heaven, they become merciful to their neighbors.

Once they gain this wisdom, they open their hearts and allow my grace to purify, rectify and incline their hearts according to my will. They begin to taste the goodness of their God and hunger for more.

At this point in the journey, they long for peace in themselves and in the world. Now, according to my plan, some desire to be missionaries, others find ways to serve in the Church, others become teachers, but one unifying trait is that they love and adore Me through prayer—the most powerful action of obedience to their God.

Prayer is the greatest source of wisdom. Prayer opens my heart. Prayer is always answered. Prayer connects your heart to mine. I exist in the prayers of the heart. Prayer invites Me into your life and I am free to help you, to protect and guide you, to heal and nourish you, to groom you to be my own precious, adorable child, and I would give you the treasures of my Kingdom, my love, my very self. I would come in and sup with you (Revelation 3:20).

O my people, invite Me into your hearts. I long to make you happy and peaceful, to protect you from the evil in the world, to make you my own special possession, close to my heart. Let Me smother you with my love and kisses.

10/18/18

Remember me, Lord. You are my consolation and joy.

Today I will teach you a lesson on Kingdom living—
learning to live with and for your God. You already know
that I must be first in your life because I am your life. You
exist by my will. I keep you in my world to love, know and
serve Me with all your heart so you may be happy and
contented in this life as well as the life here-after, when this
life is over.

In this present age, you have learned that I am your Father-
Creator, Lord and Savior Jesus Christ, and Advocate-Holy
Spirit. So, Kingdom living consists in obeying your Father's
will, seeking salvation by trusting the love of your Savior in
all things, and following the guidance and inspirations of the
Holy Spirit. These three responses made in faith are
sufficient for your total immersion into the realm of
supernatural life.

In this state, you have left all earthly desires and are moving
into a new spiritual realm. Here, only God satisfies. Your
soul is seeking my goodness, my beauty; you hunger for the
fullness of truth and knowledge—to know how to move
closer to Me, how to love Me more and more. You have
moved out of the world. Nothing satisfies your soul—only
your love for Me.

I triumph in this victory of luring you away from the
darkness, and I can bring you deeper into the light of my
Kingdom where your soul will find a peace never felt before.
It is an unshakable peace that no one can take from you. It
is guarded by an inner conviction that I am Supreme in the
world and in your heart. Your faith is rooted deeply in Me
and it shall not be taken from you.

Explain, Lord, the power of the prayer of intercession.

Ah, yes! The power of intercession is great indeed. It is the act of laying down one's own needs on behalf of another. Intercession is an unselfish act. My people are so engrossed in their own needs and wants, they cannot see that their neighbor has greater needs. They do not see further than their own skin, so to speak. Yet, this entire study on the Beatitudes has been about changing minds and hearts with the purpose of climbing out of the shackles of self-concern, of freeing the soul to think new thoughts and feel new feelings—to take on the mind of Christ (1 Corinthians 2:16).

Did I not give you the benefit of dying for your sins, thereby breaking the chains of slavery to sin? That was the ultimate act of intercession. But what I ask of you is simply to pray for others, to make time in your day to lift up the needs of those near and far. Is someone in your family suffering anguish? Pray for my healing light to fall upon them. They may not know how to pray for themselves, or their faith may still be weak—then pray that I may increase their faith. Is someone lacking in wisdom and prone to lack of good judgment? Intercede for them.

Let Me give you a prayer to say: "Lord God, Heavenly Father of all the children of the world, I lift up to you this son/daughter (name them). They need your help, healing and wisdom. In your great mercy, lead them to your light, so they may know your love and they will be healed. I ask this in the name of Jesus Christ. Amen."

The prayer of the just man avails much (James 5:16). Yes, but the prayer of the just man interceding on behalf of another is more powerful because it takes an act of unselfishness; it duplicates the act of Christ's intercession on the Cross. It is an act of mercy stemming from faith in my power to fulfill that specific request.

O my people, would that all of you become intercessors! There would be peace and joy in the land, in the hearts of all, and I would reign supreme. No more would there be shadows and darkness, for all would be in the light that exposes all the darkness in men's hearts, and they would be free to walk in the light, set free from their sins, impurities, ills and sadness. I could and would rejoice in and with them.

O my people, intercede for those who are far from Me that I may bring them closer and safer into my heart.

11/23/18

Grant me the grace, Lord, to follow You always.

Yes, I will. I want this for all my children. You wonder why I call everyone my children? The basic answer is because I created humanity. Therefore, the whole human race belongs to Me; they are my creation. But, like John wrote in his Gospel, only those who believe that Jesus Christ is my Son, are entitled to be called children (John 1:12). Faith in Christ is the first criterion. More is expected than faith. My children must follow in his footsteps. They are called to lay down their lives and take up their cross, and then follow where they are led (Luke 9:23).

In your case, it is to listen and take dictation. For another, I may ask to preach the Good News. Someone else is expected to teach my word—all this is meant for the building up of the Church. All its members have a role to fulfill. As

Paul told the Corinthians, there are many ministries in the Church (1 Corinthians 12:4-6).

There are many gifts which I assign because I know my children. I know who has a talent for, say: music. I know each hair on your heads (Luke 12:7), do I not know your strengths and weaknesses? To one I give five talents, to another only one (Matthew 25:15). And each talent should be valued and increased so as to glorify my holy name.

The light is given to follow. Search your heart and see what gift I have given you. What gives life to your spirit? What gives you joy? Pursue that gift. That is my light prompting you, guiding you. This is how to follow the light. I am the Light of the World (John 8:12). I am the way and the truth and the life (John 14:6). When you develop the gifts that I have placed in your heart, you will be following Me.

Gifts are given to share. Do you sing? Sing to give joy to others. Are you financially wealthy? Share your wealth. There is much work to be done in my Kingdom on earth. Everyone has work to do—be it big or small, it does not matter. Just so it is done in the best way. Do your best is all I ask. Have the right intention: to do good to your fellow man. In this way, you are loving God, neighbor and self!

11/26/18

Lord, tell me about the angels.

Ah, yes, my beautiful servants. They are special indeed. You know already about Michael, the Archangel, who protected my throne from the rebellious angel, Lucifer, by name. There was a big battle between them (Revelation 12:7), and Michael was the victor. Lucifer was consigned to the realms of darkness. He can no longer see the light. He brought it on himself because of pride and envy, anger and hate—all the capital sins that mark the souls of men that doom them to the fiery depths of hell in company with Lucifer (Revelation 12:7).

But let Me speak of my good angels. They are ministers of goodness, kindness and joy. They see my face daily. They sing my praises around my throne and rejoice in my company. I assign each angel to accompany each of my children, and to report back to Me about their concerns, needs, dilemmas—everything about them.

There are times I assign my angels to take on human features, such as Raphael who accompanied Tobiah on his journey to seek a wife, and to heal Tobit's blindness. The story is written in the Book of Tobit in the Bible. You also know that Gabriel was sent to announce the conception of my Son Jesus Christ to the Virgin Mary; and my angels announced his birth to the shepherds in the field— proclaiming the Good News on that first Christmas night long, long ago (Luke 2:8).

But what shall I tell you that you do not already know? My angels are in a sense, inferior to mankind because they are spirits. They do not have the soul of man. Check this out in the first chapter of Hebrews. Suffice it to say, that my angels do not have the concerns of mankind, such as seeking food, shelter, clothing, laboring for their needs, and the temptations that man faces daily. On the contrary, my angels live in blissful peace contemplating my face. They are not constrained by time, nor the necessity of nightly sleep. They live in the light and rejoice in my presence.

I wondered why the Lord told me that the angels, in a sense, are inferior to us simply because they are spirits without a soul? Why does not having a soul make them inferior? The angels see the face of God every day! and enter his presence! We do not. We must be purified, illuminated, and sanctified before we can see God! The angels obey and serve God completely! We don't. We're rebellious like Lucifer. Why are we not consigned to the realm of darkness with him?

Searching for an answer, I checked out the first chapter of Hebrews as the Lord directed. Verse three states that Jesus is "as *far superior to the angels* as the name he has inherited is more excellent than theirs" (*Hebrews* 1:3). Is the answer because we are baptized into Christ Jesus? Because our souls are inhabited by Him? That He lives and moves and breathes in us personally? That His love gives us value? That God no longer sees sin in our souls because Jesus redeemed us? So, that must be the answer. The angels do not have the treasure we hold in our earthen vessels—the very life of God through the Holy Spirit (2 Corinthians 4:7)! Let us rejoice in our Savior, the Lord Jesus Christ who gives us every spiritual blessing in the heavens" (Ephesians 1:3)!

12/16/18

Come, Lord, reveal your heart to me.

One thing uppermost in my heart is that all my children would believe in Me. The reason I gave up my throne was to rescue my people from the hands of Satan and his dominions of evil spirits. It is the truth that mortal sin cripples the action of the Holy Spirit. There is power in evil. You can see it destroying the lives of many who succumb to the devil's lies. The temptation to believe in falseness is real and it takes wisdom and knowledge to discern the truth.

The truth is that I alone have the authority to destroy evil. This is why I laid my life down so my people could be set free to live in the light of my love, to enjoy the peace that only I can give them, to grow in virtue, to fulfill the full potential of their lives, in other words: to be the men and women I planned them to be (Isaiah 61:1).

This is where my heart is: I want my children to believe in Me, to trust my wisdom knowing that I alone can and will save them from the destruction that Satan plans for them. Yes, the eternal battle is between good and evil. I have come to save the world out of love for the world. What other reason would I have? I am God Most High (Genesis 14:18). I spoke and the world was created (Isaiah 40:28). I have all power on earth and in Heaven (1 Corinthians 1:24). I am invincible (Psalm 18:14-20).

Is it too much to ask that you would put a little faith in Me? After all, I put air in your lungs and you breathe. I am the Lifter of your Head (Psalm 3:3). I draw you close to Me like a father with his child (Hosea 11:4). I have counted the hairs on your head (Luke 12:7). I have given you hearts of flesh, don't turn them into stone.

O my people, my heart is yours. I open my arms to embrace you. O Come! Come running joyfully to your Father. Let Me speak words of comfort and consolation to your troubled hearts. Free yourselves from doubts and unwarranted fears. Do not be afraid to ask for the moon; I will give you even the stars! Have faith and trust in Me.

Blessed Virgin Mary on the Tenth Beatitude

"A cause of hope should be for you, the fact that many have preceded you to the heavenly kingdom after having journeyed along the same road as you, after having endured the same sufferings as you, after having experienced the very same difficulties as you. And so, go forward with fortitude and without ever allowing yourselves to be discouraged along the road of the perfect observance of the Law of God, of the practice of all the Christian virtues, and of a daily communion of life with the Eucharistic Jesus who leads you along the road of sanctity."

St. Padre Pio on the Tenth Beatitude

"Let us always be mindful that the earth is a battleground, but in paradise we will receive a crown; the earth is the place of trial, but we will receive a prize above. We are in exile here on earth because heaven is our true home."

St. Augustine of Hippo on the Kingdom of Heaven

"There will true glory be, where no one will be praised by mistake or flattery; true honor will not be refused to the worthy, nor granted to the unworthy. There true peace will reign, where no one will experience opposition either from self or others. God himself will be virtue's reward; he gives virtue and had promised to give himself as the best and greatest reward that could exist. This is also the meaning of the Apostle's words: "So that God may be all in all." God himself will be the goal of our desires; we shall contemplate him without end, love him without surfeit, praise him without weariness. This gift, this state, this act, like eternal life itself, will assuredly be common to all."

Epilogue

12/25/18

Father in Heaven, please come to my assistance. What is your will for the Epilogue?

Yes, my child. I know your needs, your limitations. I do so because I want my people to know that the messages are truly from Me, that your role was to take daily dictation.

My children, these are my words given to my prophet for your salvation and growth of faith, hope and love for Me, the One, Holy God who created you and wants only good for you. All the words I have spoken that my prophet has written for you, compiling them in a manual, can be believed. I have spoken from the heart of a Father who loves his children, cares for their welfare, who wants you to be happy in this life and in the next.

I have spoken about poverty of spirit. For this, the remedy is to pray for the grace to trust in my unconditional love for you. To mourn your sins, I have suggested that you pray for the grace of repentance. Truly be sorry for offending Me, disobeying Me. Have a contrite heart and I will give you a new spirit. What more can I do when you tie up my hands by persisting in sin?

Now for the matter of meekness. Pray for the grace of humility. I want you to cherish yourself, to be the "best version of yourself," but always remember that without my grace, you can do nothing (John 15:5). I truly want you to hunger and thirst for my righteousness. This I want more than you do because I who know all things, know that you need to be right as rain, so to speak. When you are right, meaning devoid of wrong, then you shine like a jewel in my crown and all my power is available to you! Don't you want that?

Yes, then you will have a merciful attitude because you have received my mercy. I have wiped off the slate of your sins and restored you to my good graces, and you will be happy to extend mercy to others who need it. In fact, it will come natural for you to forgive and forget, because now your heart is pure. You don't have those yucky, selfish feelings tearing you apart. You have been set free. You no longer desire worldly praise. Your main concern is to love, honor and serve your Heavenly King. Your heart is in the right place. Nothing takes precedence before your allegiance to God.

Purity of heart leads to peace in the soul. You become a peacemaker in two ways—actively and interiorly. Your heart guides you into the way of peace. It relaxes your demeanor and you relish the calmness in your spirit. Should something provoke agitation, you quickly restore peace in your soul through prayer. You are in the habit now of rebuking evil spirits who attempt to harass you. Your peaceful nature senses their presence and you ejaculate simple prayers in the name of Jesus.

Now, what have I taught you about suffering and persecution? Yes, you know I am with you with my crook and my staff (Psalm 23:4) to chase off the wolves. I have given you the prerogative to call down my warring angels to fight for you. My light is always around you like a shield. No harm shall come to you because my name is above every name and every knee shall bend in heaven and under the earth, and every tongue will confess that I am Lord to the glory of God the Father (Philippians 2:10-11).

So, this is my word, says the Lord. Take them to heart and live in my love. For I do love you, my people. Let Me rejoice in your reciprocal love. I bless you in the name of the Father and of the Son and of the Holy Spirit world without end. Amen.

Appendix

Scripture References

Introduction

Mark 1:15
John 8:12
2 Peter 3:13
Matthew 11:30
Malachi 3:6
1 John 4:8
John 14:6
Deuteronomy 32:4
Jeremiah 32:41
Matthew 5:14
John 14:1
John 19:30
Mark 12:30
Matthew 13:5
1 Corinthians 2:16
Luke 7:22
John 4:34
Luke 3:8
Deuteronomy 5:6
Matthew 5:48
John 14:6
Genesis 11:7
Genesis 7:6
Revelation 3:20
Exodus 33:20
John 8:32
2Corinthians 11:23-29
Jeremiah 22:13
Hebrews 6:17-18
Isaiah 40:28
1 Timothy 6:12

First Beatitude

John 10:10
John 4:10
John 14:3
John 14:18
Matthew 19:14
Matthew 2:10
Matthew 7:14
Proverbs 3:28
Proverbs 16:18
Genesis 1:27
Genesis 1:28
Genesis 2:7
Hosea 11:3
2 Corinthians 4:7
2 Corinthians 5:17
2 Corinthians 10:5
Revelation 22:13
Isaiah 40:28
Isaiah 43:1
Isaiah 54:5
Matthew 3:11
Matthew 6:19
Matthew 6:34
Matthew 25:40
Exodus 16:4
Luke 1:26
1 John 4:18
Romans 8:28
Luke 4:4
Luke 4:18
1 Timothy 2:3
Hosea 4:6
Romans 6:23
Romans 10:14-17

John 1:3
John 3:30
Matthew 12:28
Jeremiah 32:38
Luke 5:58
Mark 11:23
Deuteronomy 30:19

Second Beatitude

John 10:4
Song of Songs 8:6, 14
Genesis 2:7
1 Corinthians 15:10
Isaiah 50:4
Psalm 19:13-14
Psalm 139:14
Matthew 18:6
Mark 1:15
1 Peter 4:8
Luke 15:11
Song of Songs 2:10-11
Romans 3:23
John 8:12
Mark 16:18
1 Corinthians 3:16
Luke 23:34
John 14:18
John 19:26-27
Genesis 1:27
Genesis 3:1-6
Jeremiah 29:11-12
Isaiah 55:11
Philippians 2:9
Isaiah 59:20
Luke 1:78
Genesis 2:23
Galatians 3:13
Luke 18:19
Mark 12:28

2 Samuel 24:14
Jeremiah 30:17
Matthew 18:10
Psalm 19:13
1 John 5:14

Third Beatitude

Mark 12:15
Revelation 21:1
Luke 2:52
Matthew 20:29
Psalm 91:4
Psalm 91:12
Psalm 90:17
Luke 6:12
Luke 18:22
Luke 23:34
Matthew 18:10
Genesis 1:27
1 Corinthians 6:19-20
Romans 8:31
2 Corinthians 5:17
Luke 12:7
Isaiah 49:16
Matthew 12:21
John 14:18
Matthew 11:29
Philippians 4:19
John 14:1
Matthew 5:39
Proverbs 23:7

Fourth Beatitude

Matthew 13:18
Matthew 6:33
Matthew 5:48
Romans 6:23
Romans 10:14

Psalm 34:8
Psalm 37:4
Psalm 23:5
Isaiah 43:1
Deuteronomy 5:6
Hosea 6:1
Hosea 11:1-9
Matthew 25:40
Matthew 25:46
Luke 15:8
Luke 15:11
Matthew 13:46
Colossians 3:11
Psalm 42:2
Psalm 27:5
Psalm 91:4
Matthew 10:16
Matthew 28:18
Ephesians 1:14
1 Corinthians 14:12
Genesis 1:3
John 1:12
Luke 18:35
Hebrews 4:12
John 14:18
Acts 3:15
1 Corinthians 2:9
James 5:16
Revelation 3:5
Genesis 1:27
Deuteronomy 5:7
Luke 18:19
Galatians 5:22
John 14:16-17
Matthew 16:17
Matthew 10:2
Psalm 63:2
John 8:32
Genesis 3:15

Genesis 1:26
Luke 11:9
Matthew 19:14
Luke 18:19
Mark 12:30-31
Mark 16:15
1 Corinthians 2:16
Hebrews 4:16
Isaiah 45:5
Romans 3:23
Romans 2:11
2 Corinthians 5:17
2 Corinthians 12:9
Exodus 16:4
Matthew 17:18
Luke 8:17
2 Samuel 6:14
Mark 11:23
Mark 13:32
Joel 2:12-13
2 Timothy 1:6

Fifth Beatitude

Genesis 3:16
Genesis 1:27
Isaiah 40:28
Isaiah 49:15
1 Kings 21
Psalm 23:6
Psalm 51:3-21
Matthew 25:31
Matthew 24:16
Psalm 34:16
Genesis 1:26
Matthew 24:16
Matthew 25:31
Philippians 4:4
Jeremiah 16:19
Hebrews 12:6

1 Corinthians 3:16
1 Timothy 2:6
Revelation 22:13
Matthew 12:31
John 3:17
Matthew 11:28
John 14:6
John 14:18
John 3:16
John 15:2
Genesis 1:26
Jeremiah 29:11
Isaiah 45:5
John13:13
Luke 9:23
Luke 15:18
Luke 23:34
Isaiah 4:6
Isaiah 46:9-10
Ephesians 4:6
Ephesians 6:9
John 14:16-17

Sixth Beatitude

Galatians 5:19
Luke 2:11
Luke 4:1
Psalm 46:10
Psalm 34:9
Psalm 139:14
1 Corinthians 10:5
Luke 2:51
Luke 22:20
John 17:21
Matthew 11:28
Matthew 16:19
Matthew 27:30

1 Corinthians 2:16
2 Corinthians 5:17
1 Corinthians 15:55-57
Luke 1:46-47
Luke 9:23
Hebrews 4:13
Hebrews 13:5
Revelation 21:1
Revelation 12:7
Joshua 1:15
Joshua 24:15
Romans 6:10
Romans 6:23
Isaiah 45:5
Ezekiel 20:34
Isaiah 55:11
Isaiah 55:6
Jeremiah 29:11
Galatians 5:22
Matthew 11:28
Psalm 91:11
1 Timothy 1:1
Matthew 13:10
Exodus 33:14
Job 37:16
Deuteronomy 30:15-20
Deuteronomy 5:6-21
Deuteronomy 6:4-9
Deuteronomy 7:12-26

Seventh Beatitude

Luke 11:9-13
Psalm 55:22-23
2 Corinthians 5:18
Mark 11:24
Luke 2:4, 11

Luke 21:28
Luke 18:8
Luke 21:29
John 20:19
Isaiah 53:7
Matthew 27:29
Luke 2:14
Matthew 5:13
John 14:3
John 14:26
John 14:27
Psalm 51:12
Mark 16:14
Isaiah 9:5
Isaiah 61:1
Colossians 1:20
1 John 2:2
Hebrews 2:14
Ephesians 2:10
Exodus 13:21
Matthew 2:2
John 3:16
Mark 1:29-31
Leviticus 1:10
Luke 19:41
Luke 24:36
Deuteronomy 9:13
Deuteronomy 5:1
Joshua 1:2-3
James 4:7

Eighth Beatitude

Matthew 5:44
Matthew 10:30
John 1:1-3
Matthew 21:3
Matthew 20:28
Matthew 26:70
John 10:11

Matthew 16:18
Matthew 17:20
2 Corinthians 12:9
Romans 14:12
Romans 6:10
Romans 2:11
Luke 19:41-42
Mark 3:14-19
Psalm 23:4
Psalm 139:13
Psalm 146:10
1 Corinthians 10:13
1 Corinthians 13:7
John 10:14
John 15:7
John 19:2
Isaiah 25:4
Isaiah 53:5
Isaiah 59:20
Hosea 11:4
Deuteronomy 30:15-20
Deuteronomy 7:12-26
Hebrews 13:6
James 3:6
1 John 5:14
Acts 1:9-11
Romans 8:35
Romans 8:38-39
Exodus 3:1
Psalm 56:9
Luke 12:7
Mark:36
John 1:12
John 14:9
Genesis 2:2
Genesis 3:11
Genesis 3:13
Matthew 27:22
Matthew 28:18

Luke 1:76
Ephesians 6:10-17
Revelation 22:17
Luke 12:31
Philippians 2:9
Hebrews 7:27
2 Timothy 1:10
Luke 10:18

Ninth Beatitude

Genesis 9:11
1 Kings 10:14
Jeremiah 17:10
Jeremiah 31:3
Matthew 5:14
Mark 15:18
John 12:47
Isaiah 55:11
Luke 13:18
Isaiah 25:6
Isaiah 61:10
Isaiah 6:3
Isaiah 65:24
1 Corinthians 13:13
Isaiah 35:4
1 Corinthians 13:4
Genesis 1:1-2:4
Genesis 1:27
Genesis 2:21-22
Ezekiel 37:1
Matthew 18:20
John 14:20
Matthew 17:20
Matthew 7:9
Genesis 2:17
John 14:1
John 14:26
John 14:27
John 14:18

John 17:21
Romans 10:9
Ephesians 1:3
Ephesians 1:7
1 Corinthians 13:1
John 15:14
Psalm 139:13
Hosea 11:4
Jeremiah 31:3
Psalm 139:14
Matthew 11:30
Deuteronomy 17:1
Matthew 12:14
Revelation 1:8
Revelation 12:1
Revelation 22:13
Luke 6:27
Hebrews 13:6
1 Corinthians 15:28
1 Corinthians 15:57
2 Corinthians 5:10
2 Corinthians 5:17
1 Peter 4:8

Tenth Beatitude

John 14:1-2
John 14:6
Ephesians 1:3
Psalm 18:14-20
1 Corinthians 15:24-27
Matthew 2:6
John 15:2
Philippians 2:15
Acts 16:31
Revelation 3:5
Exodus 24:14
Genesis 7:11
Matthew 20:28
John 1:12

John 14:18
Like 9:23
1 Corinthians 12:4-6
Matthew 25:15
Revelation 12:7
Luke 2:8
2 Corinthians 4:7

Genesis 14:18
Isaiah 40:28
1 Corinthians 1:24
Psalm 3:3

Made in the USA
San Bernardino, CA
22 August 2019